OXFORD LIBRARY OF AFRICAN LITERATURE

General Editors

E. E. EVANS-PRITCHARD
G. LIENHARDT
W. WHITELEY

Oxford Library of African Literature

A SELECTION OF AFRICAN PROSE
I. Traditional Oral Texts   II. Written Prose
Compiled by W. H. WHITELEY
(*Two volumes*)

THE HEROIC RECITATIONS OF THE BAHIMA OF ANKOLE
H. F. MORRIS

SOMALI POETRY
An Introduction
B. W. ANDRZEJEWSKI *and* I. M. LEWIS

PRAISE-POEMS OF TSWANA CHIEFS
I. SCHAPERA

THE GLORIOUS VICTORIES OF ʿĀMDA ṢEYON KING OF ETHIOPIA
G. W. B. HUNTINGFORD

A SELECTION OF HAUSA STORIES
H. A. S. JOHNSTON

THE CONTENT AND FORM OF YORUBA IJALA
S. A. BABALỌLA

AKAMBA STORIES
JOHN MBITI

LIMBA STORIES AND STORYTELLING
RUTH FINNEGAN

THE ZANDE TRICKSTER
E. E. EVANS-PRITCHARD

IZI BONGO
Zulu Praise Poems
TREVOR COPE

The Trārza *īggīw*, Aḥmad wuld al-Maydāḥ

S̲H̲INQĪṬĪ FOLK LITERATURE AND SONG

H. T. NORRIS

OXFORD
AT THE CLARENDON PRESS
1968

Oxford University Press, Ely House, London W. 1

GLASGOW NEW YORK TORONTO MELBOURNE WELLINGTON
CAPE TOWN SALISBURY IBADAN NAIROBI LUSAKA ADDIS ABABA
BOMBAY CALCUTTA MADRAS KARACHI LAHORE DACCA
KUALA LUMPUR HONG KONG TOKYO

PRINTED IN GREAT BRITAIN
AT THE UNIVERSITY PRESS, OXFORD
BY VIVIAN RIDLER
PRINTER TO THE UNIVERSITY

To my friend
Mukhtār wuld Ḥāmidun al- Daymānī

ديمان فى الناس تبر * وغيرهم كالفخار.
فيومهم يوم عيد * وليلهم كالنهار.

PREFACE

I HAVE called this book *Shinqīṭī Folk Literature and Song* for two reasons. I found it impossible to confine myself entirely to colloquial poetry in the Ḥassānīya dialect, since this would exclude a large quantity of material, both poetry and prose, in Classical Arabic, and a little in Znāga, which portray the customs and thoughts of the Moors with equal authenticity. Furthermore, the music of the region combines both Arabic traditions in the folk-songs sung by the musician class. Secondly, I have deliberately used the name Shinqīṭ in this book, at times, in preference to Mauritania. The existing boundaries of the Islamic Republic of Mauritania contain the majority, but by no means all, of the Ḥassānīya speakers in North Africa. I did not wish to exclude the Sāqiya al-ḥamrā' from my study, yet at the same time I did not wish to include the folk literature of the black peoples of Mauritania, namely the Toucouleurs and Sarakollé, settled along the Senegal river. Shinqīṭ (Shinjīṭ), then, is used in a cultural and geographical sense within the boundaries described by the author of the *Kitāb al-Wasīṭ*, to date the only major Arabic work about his country published by a Moor.

My experience of this region has been limited to three visits, two short and one long, including a very short stay in the Spanish Sahara, and a period of six months with a Mauritanian informant in London. On each occasion I was financially aided by the School of Oriental and African Studies. It would be folly for me to pretend that I have the intimate knowledge of the people of the region possessed by certain French scholars, notably Professor Vincent Monteil of Dakar University and Professor Théodore Monod, the former Director of the Institut Français d'Afrique Noire. Both have shown an interest and advised and helped me to carry out various studies, but for a number of reasons I have found it impossible in the circumstances to submit this text for their comments, and I have been unable to benefit from their knowledge and their experience. I am the poorer for it, and it is my only hope that the results do not fall too far short of expectations which the title may arouse. The detailed translations of the texts, whether oral or written, the vocalization of texts, and in fact the whole approach to the study have been under the constant eye of Mukhtār wuld Ḥāmidun, Mauritania's leading scholar, to whom I dedicate this book. The translations have followed his commentaries, and the vocalization of the texts has, as far as possible, been based on his own, even if at times this has led to some irregularities. Where he left texts unvocalized, I have kept to his text. I have also been helped by the younger scholar Muḥammad wuld Dāddāh, who gave me permission to photograph the manuscripts on music in Chapter 11. This help has ensured that, in the main, the text reflects what the Moors would wish to say themselves.

I have also to thank many others for their help, including Professor J. Segal, Dr. R. B. Serjeant, Dr. T. Johnstone, Mr. D. Hall, Dr. J. Bynon, who has advised me on the Znāga poems, and Mr. J. Abū Ḥaydar; Professor G. Colin, M. R. Mauny, and a number of Mauritanians, including M. Bulla wuld al-Shaybānī, M. ʿĪsā Ṣārr, M. Muḥammad al-Amīn, and, in particular, M. Muḥammad wuld Sīdī Ibrāhīm and M. Isalmu wuld Bāba wuld Ḥamma of Radio Mauritanie, both of whom are experts in the music of their country. The latter has years of experience as an *īggīw* behind him. I owe a special debt of gratitude to members of the Government of the Islamic Republic of Mauritania for their hospitality to both my wife and myself, and in particular to His Excellency President Mukhtār wuld Dāddāh who, throughout, has shown himself interested in various fields of research in Mauritanian culture and history.

If the English-speaking public should gain an impression from this book that the society described seems remote from the life and civilization of the modern Islamic world, it is in part due to the fact that much of the poetry and prose portrays a nomad society which, over large areas of the Sahara and the Savannah, still lives as it always has done, little concerned with the outside world, its tragedy as well as its progress. But the Islamic Republic of Mauritania is also a new country, helped by France and other nations to gain its independence in 1960, and certain features of the old tribal society, such as tribute, slaves, or a leisured aristocracy in vast camps, are no longer a common feature of the people described. There is every reason to hope that the secularized twentieth-century outlook, the iron ore, the new capital, Nouakchott, and the roads, towns, and industries of the future will not totally disrupt and destroy the folk culture of this fascinating people. On the contrary, it may well stimulate new ideas, to be expressed by the musicians and poets in song, in poetry, and in prose.

It may be asked what is meant by 'folk literature' among the pastoral nomads and the oasis dwellers in the Western Sahara and the adjoining Savannah. The Moors of Shinqīṭ, like other lettered Arabic-speaking communities, express their ideas in two different forms of Arabic. On the one hand, there is a corpus of Classical Arabic literature, both poetry and prose, which is concerned with jurisprudence, theology, history, and praise of famous men. On the other hand, their colloquial Arabic dialect—Ḥassānīya—has its own poetry and prosody and choice of subject-matter and its own artistic interpreters who are closely associated with Mauritanian musicians and the troubadour class in Shinqīṭī society. It is tempting but misleading to divorce the dialect from the Classical Arabic, to describe as 'folkish' the poetry in the vernacular and to class the literature in Classical Arabic as part of a sophisticated Islamic school of literature extending from Morocco to Māli.

The folk literature of the Western Sahara is a matter of 'feel' rather than definition. Certain prose works, certain poems, and certain popular tales seem to mirror the soul of the people and to portray vividly the Moors and their environment. It is not difficult to identify the country and the people in the style of the poem or its vocabulary, in the character of the story or in the moral of the fable. This mark of identity may not be shown in the use of colloquial speech, although, inevitably, an expression in Ḥassānīya or Znāga Berber has usually greater authenticity and vividness.

Shinqīṭī folk literature includes the following:

1. Poetry and prose in Ḥassānīya or in Classical Arabic in which Ḥassānīya words and expressions are introduced.
2. Poetry and prose in Znāga Berber or in Classical Arabic in which Znāga words and expressions are introduced.
3. Folk-tales of every description, both oral and written.
4. The lives of saints which portray the Mauritanian concept of sanctity and which reflect the unique status of the scholar class in the society of the Western Sahara and its borders. These biographies are usually written in Classical Arabic since they are used to illustrate some feature of sainthood in Islam or in a specific mystic order.

5. Ḥassānīya and Znāga proverbs.
6. Medical texts which employ a Ḥassānīya vocabulary in order to facilitate comprehension.
7. Texts which specifically describe Mauritanian music and prosody, and where examples of Ḥassānīya verse are introduced in order to illustrate the text.
8. Local legal rulings (*fatwas*) in Ḥassānīya or in Classical Arabic.

By this definition a large amount of poetry and prose may be deemed to represent faithfully the 'folk literature' of Shinqīṭī society in Mauritania and the Spanish Sahara. At the same time a great deal of literature of merit—particularly abridgements of legal texts—will be omitted. Classical Arabic poems which could have been composed in any Arabic-speaking community, and which have only geographical expressions or local proper names to identify them as Mauritanian, are likewise omitted.[1] No selection is an arbitrary selection if it can be shown to reveal more authentically the true mind and soul of the society as conditioned by its customs and its environment. Thomas Hardy's words, describing another stretch of desolate terrain as 'singularly colossal and mysterious in its swarthy monotony', sum up the kind of habitat which has conditioned the mental outlook, past and present, of the Mauritanians.

[1] Mauritanian Classical Arabic poems of all kinds are collected together in *Shuʿarāʾ Mūrītāniyā* (*al-qudamāʾ wal-muḥdathūn*) by Muḥammad Yūsuf Muqlid, published in Casablanca and Beirut, 1962.

CONTENTS

NOTES ON TRANSCRIPTION

Table

’	(hamza)—the glottal stop.
b	
t	
th (ṯ)	as in ‘think’.
j	in Ḥassānīya approximates to a French j (ẕ).
ḥ	a voiceless pharyngal fricative.
kh (ḵ)	as in Scottish ‘loch’.
d	
dh (ḏ)	as in ‘this’.
r	
z	
s	
sh (š)	English sh in ‘fish’.
ṣ	emphatic s.
ḍ (ḍ)	the emphatic correlate of d (see notes).
ṭ	emphatic t.
ẓ	
‘	a voiced pharyngal fricative.
gh (ġ)	the French r grasseyé.
f	see notes.
q	a voiceless uvular plosive.
g	
k	
l	
m	
n	
ñ	see notes.
h	
w	
y	
č	see notes.
ǰ	

System followed

1. My transcription is a broad phonological one. Where the Ḥassānīya poems are transcribed, and not given in the local variation of Arabic orthography, it is based on the native speakers’ concepts of phonemic structure, rather than on the phonemic theory evolved for North African dialect studies. In practice, certain poems have been transcribed in order to illustrate syllabic patterns, or to reduce the quantity of Arabic text.

Ancient poems, or those composed to be read rather than recited, have been presented in Arabic orthography.

2. Classical Arabic is transliterated in a conventional system as shown, unbracketed, above. Tribal, geographical, and personal names, names of social classes, established names of musical instruments, and Znāga words are transliterated, in the main, in the same system, but the system here has not been followed in representing vowels and certain consonants, for example g or ẓ, where this might distort forms established by convention or local pronunciation.

3. Technical terms of music and poetry which are peculiar to Ḥassānīya are transcribed as ordinary dialect words.

The following symbols of transcription need further explanation:

ḍ: a voiced emphatic interdental fricative. In some forms borrowed from Classical Arabic ḍ is realized as a voiced emphatic dental plosive. This latter, minor, variant is not distinguished in the transcription (cf. D. Cohen, *Le Dialecte arabe ḥassānīya de Mauritanie*, pp. 10–12).

f: a voiced labio-dental fricative v̱. It is voiceless (f) in the following phonetic contexts:

(1) (by assimilation) in association with a following, and less regularly a preceding, voiceless consonant;
(2) when it occurs as a geminate or doubled consonant—ff; and
(3) in final position.

This phoneme has emphatic and non-emphatic reflexes. Other phonemes also (for example, b, m, n, r, l, etc.) have emphatic reflexes. These are not distinguished in the transcription, since they appear to most native speakers to be non-phonemic.

ñ [ny] occurs only in words of Sūdānic origin.

č [ch چ] and its voiced correlate ǰ occur only in a few words, more particularly those of Znāga origin, or those associated with tribes of the south-west Trārza who were, or still are, Znāga speakers.

q > g (qāf maʿqūda ڨ / ڴ), cf. p. 194.

The vocalic phonemes:

Short: i, u, a, e. The last is the neutral (obscure) vowel which occurs in English in the first syllable of words like ‘Macaulay’, ‘parade’, etc.
Long: ī (ii), ū (uu), ā (aa) representing both a in ‘father’, and ai in ‘fairy’.
Diphthongs: ay (e^y) as in ‘train’, aw (o^u) as in ‘flow’.

PART I

THE ORAL LITERATURE AND SONGS OF THE PEOPLE OF THE WESTERN SAHARA

1

SHINQĪṬ, THE HOMELAND OF THE MOORS

THE Moors are the inhabitants of a vast region of the Western Sahara adjoining the Atlantic Ocean. To the south their homeland is bordered by the Senegal river. To the east the frontier is the River Niger where it bends northwards in the region of Timbuctoo. To the north-east their marches are approximately along a straight line in the Sahara as far as the pebbly wilderness known as the Ḥamāda, south of Tāfīlālt, in Morocco. The northern and north-western boundary of their territory is a line running due west, ending on the Atlantic shore, approximately at the mouth of the Sāqiya al-ḥamrā'.

The Moors, who number in all nearly a million people, call this whole region Shinqīṭ (Shinjīṭ). It is the name of the small, decaying, but once prosperous, caravan town of Shinqīṭī (Shinjīṭī) in the northern Mauritanian province of the Adrār. It has an ancient history, and is said to have been founded in the year A.D. 777 at the palm-grove of Abb^{w}ayr. The town was resited in the year 1261 on the spot where it now stands. Over many centuries it became a centre for scholars and pilgrims, who regularly left it for the holy cities of Arabia. This caravan of pilgrims passed through the Maghrib, Egypt, the Sūdān, and the Ḥijāz, and their individual dress and manner of speech distinguished them from other pilgrims. Those who saw them called them Shanāqiṭa, and the renown of many of their number in Classical Arabic grammar and in jurisprudence and Ḥadīth conferred on their fellow countrymen an honourable name and a national identity, irrespective of their profession or whether they aspired to scholastic attainments. So the Moors, who call themselves *biḍān*—the 'whites', as opposed to the *sūdān*—their 'black African' neighbours along the Senegal and Niger rivers to the south of them, were named and came to be known after one small town of their homeland. It has given its name to almost the whole of the Western Sahara.

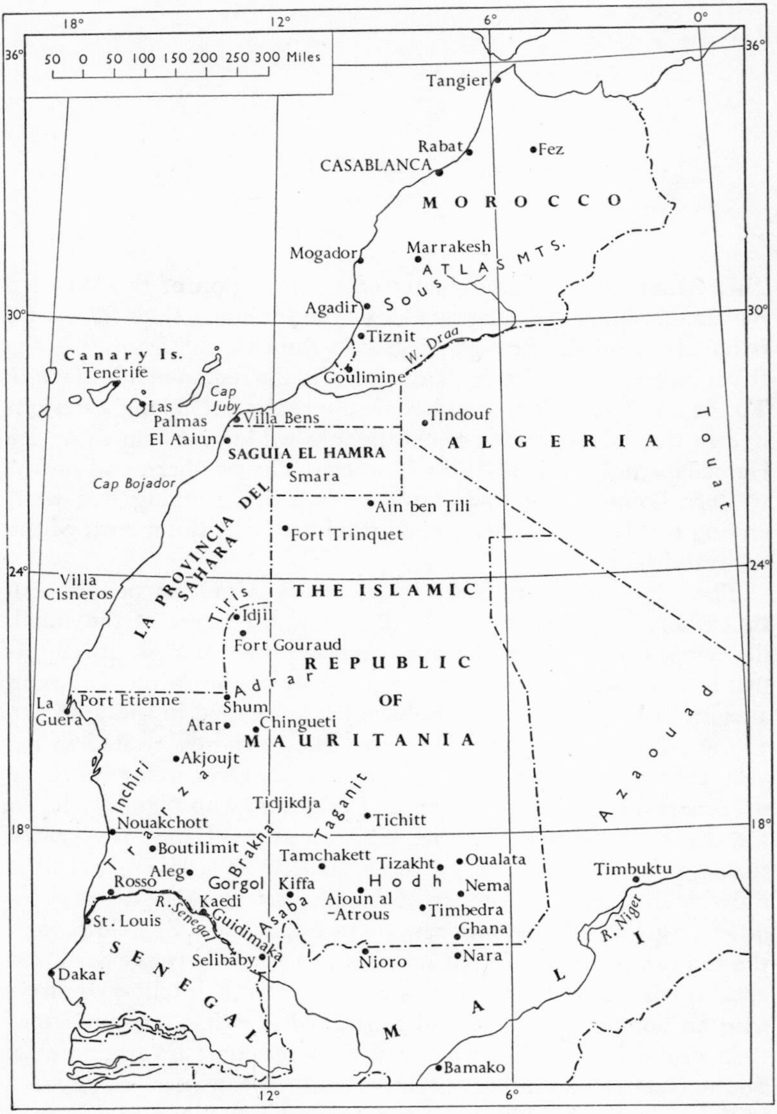

Royal Geographical Society.

Nowadays this cultural frontier has been redrawn with political boundaries that do not coincide with its limits. By far the greater portion of S͟hinqīṭ is now the Islamic Republic of Mauritania, which is the modern heir to the learning of S͟hinqīṭī, Walāta, Tīs͟hīt, and other ancient Saharan caravan towns, and expresses the aspirations of the Ḥassānīya-speaking tribes and peoples. But by no means all the inhabitants of Mauritania are Moors. If the estimated population is in the region of 800,000, about 650,000 of them are Moors, 70,000 Toucouleurs, 30,000 Sarakollé, 30,000 Fulani, and 1,500 Bambára; and an overwhelming majority of the minorities live in the valley of the Senegal river, in villages bordered by irrigated land where they cultivate their millet and their maize. Many of the Moors migrate seasonally and occupy centres beyond the present-day boundaries of Mauritania. There are tribes in Māli, to the north of Timbuctoo, in the district known as Azawād. One tribe in particular, the Kunta, has kindred who are settled or migrate far into what is today the Algerian Sahara. The Spanish Sahara, although sparsely inhabited, is the home of a mainly Ḥassānīya-speaking population. The great camel-breeding tribe of the Rgībāt has clans not only in the Sāqiya al-ḥamrā', but also at Tīndūf in Algeria. Lastly, the whole province of Ṭarfāya in Morocco, to the south of the Wād Nūn, should also be included, since its tribes, the Tekna, for example, are Ḥassānīya-speaking, share the habits and customs, and have close links with the inhabitants of the Adrār of Mauritania. Over hundreds of thousands of miles of desert, mountainous terrain, river-delta, oasis, and savannah the Moors have wandered, settled, raided, traded, and established tribal and political units and religious fraternities. They have diffused the Classical Arabic tongue and imposed their customs, their dress, and their social system as far as the Senegal river; and their dialect, Ḥassānīya, is a national language, which links the Mag͟hrib to Africa south of the Sahara.

Viewed from an aeroplane this region seems nothing but a barren and uninhabited waste, and so it is described in general terms by a Moorish scholar, S͟hayk͟h Muḥammad al-Imām wuld al-S͟hayk͟h Mā' al-'Aynayn. 'There is no doubt', he writes, 'that this country embraces a vast territory and famous towns and many oases and untrodden tracts of barren plain and desert in which no sand grouse has found its way. By and large it most closely resembles the Ḥijāz and Najd, not only as a country but also in its livestock and its plants and its crops, to the extent that a traveller in one could imagine himself to be in the other, so marked is the resemblance, and this is even true of the peoples themselves in their personality, their temperament, and their morals.'

Mauritania is the geographical and cultural heart of Shinqīṭ. It is divided into three main geographical regions, each of which has many features not to be found in the others. The first of them is the Sāḥel, which extends south of a line passing through the towns of Nouakchott (Anwākshūṭ), the capital, Moudjeria (Mujrīya), Tamchakett (Tamshakkaṭ), Aioun el-Atrouss ('Ayūn al-'Atrūs), and Néma (al-Ni'ma). It is a region composed of 'dead' dunes and of plains, out of which emerge, often like scenes from a 'wild-west' *décor*, the low massifs of the 'Aṣāba and the Afulla. Following the rains, which annually exceed 100 millimetres, this whole area is covered with a vegetation of gum-trees and of herbaceous shrubs that provide a good pasturage for herds of cattle and sheep. To the south of this region are the banks of the Senegal river, the Shamāma, which is flooded annually by the rising river and permits the cultivation of millet on a wide scale.

The second region is that of the true Sahara. It is to the north of the Sāḥel and it is formed of 'live' dunes or of rocky plains dominated by the uplands of the Adrār (1,500 ft.), in which is to be found the iron-ore mountain at Fort Gouraud (Afdayrak). The rainfall is very sparse. Yet there is enough vegetation to feed herds of camels, sheep, and goats. Between November and March there are extreme variations in temperature between day and night, and during the rest of the year the maximum daily temperatures can reach 48° C.

The third region is the coast, a sandy strip, with extensive sand banks, and buffeted by high winds. There are shallow and treacherous waters, and only the Baie du Lévrier is extensive and deep. Of the three regions it has the least rainfall—only six days of rain, giving an average rainfall of 24 millimetres per annum—so that a modern port, such as Port Étienne (Anwādhību), is compelled to have a sea-water distilling-plant in order to survive. The Spanish Government also has to face the same problem further to the north.

The Moors have their own geographical regions, and these are based on their own points of the compass. They are not the cardinal points as known in Europe but correspond to 'sectors of orientation' which are embraced by four words: *tall* (approximately the direction of Southern Morocco), varying between north and east; *gebla* (the direction of Senegal), varying between south and west; *sāḥel* (the ocean), varying between west and north; and *sharg* (the east), which varies between east and south. The people of the south-western regions of Mauritania differ from those in the east as to the interpretation they give to these terms. To the people of the west, the directions more closely correspond with the first of the cardinal points mentioned above; to the people of the east, the directions more closely correspond with the second.

Within these regions there is great variety of climate. If, in the main, it can be classed as hot and dry, much depends on the latitude and the proximity of the sea or the river. The climate of the north is healthy and bracing, whether it is hot or cold; the climate of the south is often unhealthy, and this has left its mark on the inhabitants. The Trārza tribes which do not migrate seasonally over a great distance are less numerous, and less healthy, and do not live as long as those tribes that have their habitat in the northern regions or nomadize in certain areas of it. Malaria is particularly prevalent along the river region of Shamāma, which is also notorious for its bad water.

Certain regions and towns of the Western Sahara have a special significance for the Moors. In the far north the Sāqiya al-ḥamrā', the 'red river-valley', has a reputation for sanctity. It is the resting-place of several of the greatest Saharan saints. Not only does it shelter the tomb of Sīdī Aḥmad al-Rgībī, a *sharīf* from whom the Rgībāt tribe claims descent, but towards the east is the ruined scholastic and political centre of Ṣmāra, founded by the warrior-scholar Shaykh Mā' al-'Aynayn al-Qalqamī, at the beginning of the present century. The Kunta tribe identify this region with the haunt of their ancestor Saint Sīdī Muḥammad al-Kuntī, and the birthplace of his son Sīdī Aḥmad al-Bakkā'ī.

Tīris, the south-east region of the Río de Oro, to the north-west of the ancient salt deposits of Sabkhat Ijil, is noted, on the one hand, for its scholars and, on the other, for its lack of water. It is also renowned for camels, for the intense pride of its tribes, and the longings they feel for the region when they are absent from it. There are many legends about it, in particular that of the year called Adhrayr. It is said that long ago Tīris was very fertile. Rains fell repeatedly there for a number of years, and during this period it was the scene of extraordinary events. A weaned camel was ridden before it was a year old, and the she-camels gave birth every year. It is said that the Ahl Bārakallāh, the biggest tribe in Tīris, and responsible for most of its wells, dwelt there for forty years without seeing a funeral. Then one year God deemed that the tribes there should fight each other. They were jealous of each other's prosperity. And so a fearful drought and famine prevailed, and the people fled to the south-west, and forsook their offspring.

The Adrār is an impressive sandstone massif, circular in shape. When the rain falls it descends the slopes into the valleys and waters the numerous palm-groves to be found there. There are perhaps 400,000 date-palms, and no less than 3,000 out of 10,000 tons of dates are consumed each July by Moors who come from all parts of the Sahara for the festival of date-picking, the *gayṭna*. The surplus is stored or exported to other African states. Hundreds of tons of wheat and barley are grown annually. It is the yield of the seed sown in April in the oasis plots. The region is also one of vegetables and fruit, such as melons. Mint is grown, and this is a precious commodity for the Moors, who infuse it into their richly brewed tea, the hall-mark of their hospitality.

The Adrār is divided into the *ḍhar* and the *bāṭin*. The former, the 'back', is the upland plateau region in which are to be found the caravan towns of Shinqīṭī and Wādān, the former almost engulfed by sand, the latter equally ruined but rising upwards on the slopes of a rock outcrop to a fort-like minaret. It had a reputation for learning and choice dates, and it was a commercial rival of its neighbour. The *bāṭin*, the lowland of the Adrār, is in the valleys to the south-west of Shinqīṭī. There is Āṭār, the capital of the region. A few miles distant is a small oasis called Āzūgi, a legendary 'city of the dogs'. It is a village of huts and tents in the ruins of an Almoravid citadel. Nearby is the tomb of the Imām al-Ḥaḍramī, a companion of the Almoravid leader Abū Bakr b. 'Umar ('Āmir), whose own tomb is in the valley which bears his name at Al-Bayba, about thirty miles to the south of Tijikja, the capital of Tagānit. Authentic or not, his epitaph is a heap of stones on which are incised the words 'May God have mercy on Sīdī Abū Bakr b. 'Āmir'.

Tagānit, like the Adrār, is stony and mountainous, and also rich in dates. Unlike the Adrār it is within the region of the Sāḥel. When the former is dried up and roasted by the sun, Tagānit is green, speckled here and there by black sandstone and orange sand. The atmosphere and character of a prairie become more and more marked further to the south. There are flowers, trees, and birds of coloured hue. Al-Rashīd is noted for its magnificent palm-groves. It is claimed that the excellent quality of its dates is due to two mountains which enclose the valley and protect it from the winds. Springs and natural water pools (*gelta*) abound. Five days from Tijikja towards the Ḥawḍ, the far eastern province of Mauritania, is the largely ruined caravan centre of Tīshīt. It is a town similar to Shinqīṭī, with a reputation for scholarship, and the dry-stone architecture of its ruined buildings has a peculiar excellence of finish and design which makes it one of the finest architecturally, if not the finest, of the ancient towns of the Western Sahara.

The Ḥawḍ, 'the basin', the south-eastern province, is a region of savannah, of great herds of cattle and African game—lions, wart-hogs, and sometimes elephants. It faces Māli and the interior of Africa. The landscape is often a monotonous plain of prickly scrub and the twisted trunks of baobab trees, but sometimes there are red and brown ranges of rocky terrain, weird in shape and eroded by the wind. There are ruined cities, the sites of Awdaghust (Tegdaūst), Ghāna (Kumbi Ṣāliḥ), and Tīzakht, all major centres of the Middle Ages and relics of a Sūdānic or Berber society which characterized the region before the entry of the Banū Ḥassān.

Walāta remains the sole representative town of the civilizations of the Ḥawḍ of former times. It is both Moorish and Sūdānic. It was once famous for its houses, which were painted and decorated with geometric designs and furnished in a manner sumptuous by the standards of the Western Sahara. Here and there they survive, but the niches in the pillars have no flickering lamps, the studded doors are closed or sealed, and there is no merchant within. There are raised benches built up against the outside walls of the houses where men once sat to discuss business or scholarship in the winding lanes sheltered from the sun.

In the Trārza, the Mauritanian province in the south-west, the last of the Znāga-speaking Moors survive, encamped amidst the dunes and forests of acacia and gum trees. Among these tribes the Awlād (Banū) Daymān are noted for the great number of their historians, jurists, and those skilled in medicine. In the interior of the Trārza is the Islamic centre of Boutilimit (Būtīlimīt). It is associated with a leading scholastic family among the Moors in recent times, that of Shaykh Sīdyā (Sīdīya) and his descendants. Shaykh Sīdyā the Great (1780–1869), chief of the Awlād (Banū) Abyayrī, founded the *zāwiya* at Boutilimit, and his work was continued and expanded by his son Sīdyā Bāba, who entered into friendly relations with the French. At first the *zāwiya* was a camp of tents or hutments where the Arabic studies of the pupils were conducted by a number of tutors who supervised their courses. The *zāwiya* at Boutilimit is now a modern educational institution, housed in a permanent building, with opportunities for students from other African states to come and study there.

Between the Trārza, Tagānit, and the coastal region of Inshīrī is a desert region known as Awkār. It is this region which has inspired one of the most characteristic descriptions of the country by a Mauritanian poet.[1] Part of his poem is specifically concerned with this district, yet at the same time it seems to embrace much of the entire Mauritanian landscape. In its archaic adoption of ancient Arabian form and style, it avoids a feeling of artificiality, since two similar landscapes, Arabia and the Sahara, have evoked a similar response. The poet is Sīdī Muḥammad wuld al-Shaykh Sīdyā, and his poem was composed during a journey he made to the Awlād (Banū) Dalīm, a tribe inhabiting large areas of the Spanish Sahara.

My stay is prolonged in the spring encampments. Would that I knew what benefit has a settled life for one like me!
My stay is prolonged only by the choice of the Almighty, not my own.
I had no intention of coming there but the hand of God's predestinations cast me there.
The heart has grown weary of their cold and their dampness and its moist tender herbage in the early mornings,
And stones which are like whetted knives, and tree trunks like dagger blades.
I wish I knew! The slave is one conditioned to compulsion although he appears in the form of one who has free option.
Will the recompense of a return to Awkār ever be granted to me?
Where familiar landmarks appear to you shining in a blaze.
Their beauty delights the eyes of those who see them,

[1] Aḥmad b. al-Amīn al-Shinqīṭī. *Kitāb al-Wasīṭ fī tarājim udabā' Shinqīṭ*, Cairo, 1958 (2nd printing), p. 265.

If the hand of rain adorns them with tender herbs which blend the beauty of their whiteness with verdure.

That is my land, which I love and long for. It is, indeed, the habitation of free men.

Its water is sweet and only the finest vegetation grows there.

The *sarḥ*[1] tree, the mimosas, and the *arṭā*[1] send forth shoots, like one who imitates the virgin's tattoo marks in the sand dunes.

It is not a land the waters of which are brackish, shooting forth plants to feed the inhabitants of Hell.

A tumult has dwelt there, anarchy persists. It has made no distinction between its night time and the day.

Cares afflict you, like clouds which come by night. What a host you are to their spectre!

A host, hastening like an excellent she-camel, does not entertain the harbinger of cares.

My companions hastened (to leave), nothing remained to be done, except to tighten the saddles on the sleek and sturdy riding beasts.

They brought them near, fully grown with their humps towering above them like the summits of a conspicuous landmark.

Their lofty humps guarantee for those who ride them proximity to a goal which had been distant.

Their herders have let them go their own way for a time, grazing as long as they liked from rich plants;

For a while on chamomile and *ḥamḍ*,[1] then on *qarqad*[1] and *jidār*.[1]

They passed the month of Jumādā in the spring herbage making for the spots where rain had fallen.

[1] sarḥ—*Cadaba farinosa.*
arṭā—*Calligonum comosum.*
ḥamḍ—*Salicornia furticosa.*
qarqad—gharqad (large boxthorn) or qarqadān (*A. miticum* or *A. bidentatum*)?
jidār—*Rhus tripartitum*; cf. *Kitāb al-Wasīṭ*, p. 436.

2

WEST SAHARAN SOCIETY

THE Moors who inhabit the Western Sahara are usually described as a mixture of Berber and Arab peoples. Over a period of many centuries they have intermarried and, owing to the desert environment, to certain marked cultural traits, to the presence of 'black Africa' to the south, and to certain historical events, they have bred a distinctive physical type, and evolved a distinctive culture and social structure.

As is to be expected, this society shares many features with its Saharan neighbours, and in fact with pastoral nomadic societies as far distant as the Persian Gulf. Such similar societies in such similar terrain are bound to appear alike, and it is very easy to assume some cultural or ethnic connexion. The Moors themselves, for their own motives, have always been ready to stress or assert by genealogies these far-distant connexions. Such claims are generally questioned by those who have studied nomadic societies of this type, namely arabized African societies in which there has been every incentive to make such assertions. But in fact it matters little whether they are true or false, or even whether it is possible to prove their authenticity. As a social fact the connexions are real, they exist, they are believed in. The Moors themselves will stubbornly defend their claims, and the assumption of their authenticity determines the attitude they will adopt towards their neighbour, what obligations they have towards him, and what privilege they may expect from him in return. In short, his lineage delineates a Moor's social and historical horizon, the frontiers of his time and space. Within it is his life, and to it he owes his primary allegiance.

Every clan (*qabīla*, pl. *qabā'il*) is made up of supposed descendants of a common ancestor. The different sections (*fakhdh*, pl. *afkhādh*) of the clan claim descent from his various sons. The clan is in theory patriarchal, and in times of need, in war for instance, succour is sought from paternal kinsmen. But there are also aspects of tribal life which show a secondary allegiance and the strengthening of ties with the maternal side of the family. A pregnant wife, for example, often goes to live temporarily with her mother. When a woman of the Rgībāt marries a man of another tribe, the couple frequently set up a home with the bride's family group. The latter adopts the bridegroom into the clan. Examples such as these are typical of the social importance accorded to women among the Moors. Polygamy is allowed in theory, but the monogamous family unit is much more characteristic of them. Certain genealogies, particularly those of the fundamentally Berber Zwāya tribes of the Trārza, contain the names of female forebears. The most noted example of this is in the *Kitāb al-ansāb* (the book of genealogies), a work written by the eighteenth-century Trārza scholar, Wālid wuld Khāluna, which opens rather surprisingly with the statement that 'the mother of al-Mukhtār b. Muḥammad Saʿīd al-Yadālī is Ahānīlla bint al-Muṣṭafā b. ʿUthmān b. Amr Agda Faẓmah, al-Dījakī by residence, Agda Yamjaj by lineage, and her mother was Fāṭimah bint Muḥunḍ Agdhagshūdhya from the tribe of Ṣalāḥ which was in the south'. The Berber character of this lineage is obvious from the names of persons and tribes referred to in it.

The actual status of the Moorish woman and the authority she possesses vary considerably, however, according to her social position and the extent to which she has slaves to carry out her manual tasks. In general her authority will extend at least to her own household. A portion of the tent is her domain, wherein she keeps her clothes, her saddle, water skins, mortar, and cooking utensils. If her lot is not a privileged one she will grind the corn, milk the ewes or the cows, make butter and cheese, bake the bread, and prepare meals for guests who are always numerous and likely to turn up at any time. She washes, cards, and spins wool. She stretches and weaves material to be used for clothes or for tents, the latter being made of goat's hair mixed with camel's hair or wool. She also prepares and decorates skin cushions, tea-bags, and saddle-bags, and twines various types of rope. While it is her primary task to bring up her family, this does not prevent her in many cases from enjoying a share of Arabic learning and even contributing to it. In medieval times her accomplishments in this respect often received greater notice and praise than were accorded to her spouse.

Each Moorish tribe is composed of clans whose ancestors are

held to be related or closely associated, and the tribe is usually known by the name of its paramount clan. The Rgībāt, for example, claim descent from a single common ancestor, Sīdī Aḥmad al-Rgībī, who because he was a *sharīf* entitles all Rgībāt to the title of *shurafā'*. But in fact no tribe, even if its claim to a certain ancestor be authentic, consists of members who are such by virtue of consanguinity alone. This is because of the institution of *'aṣaba*, whereby the determining factors which govern affiliation to a certain group may be extended, reinterpreted, or modified. Clans may be brought into a tribe as tributary vassals by conquest, or an individual or group may form a brotherhood with another individual or group, for the payment of blood debts, the settlement of injuries, or for many other kinds of obligations. In theory the pact keeps both parties on an equal footing and does not demand a specific sacrifice or tribute. But in certain parts of the Western Sahara, more particularly in the Spanish Sahara, a ritual is carried out to seal ties of obligation between the parties concerned, whether it be on an equal footing or under some kind of vassalage. This is the custom of the *dhabīḥa*, totally unknown among tribes north of the Wād Nūn and the Jabal Banī on the southern borders of Morocco. It involves both the sacrifice of a sheep or goat, and a contract of protection, which ties a social group to a stranger who sojourns on its territory, or who crosses it. In fact, this protection is assured not by the entire group but by one of its notables, who over a period has received the honour or homage of the tribe and who has come to dominate it. Because of his wealth this notable has won over the nomads of the neighbourhood and can count on their armed support. It is a common way for oasis chiefs to assert their authority. Further south in Mauritania it is a *ḥurma* or *gharāma*, a form of collective tribute, which ensures the protection of a vassal tribe by its overlord. To what extent this is imposed will depend on the social status of the tribe concerned. The *im^{w}rāgen* fishermen, for example, who have a subordinate status and who fish along the Mauritanian coast, paid, or pay, tribute to their warrior masters. It is imposed only on fishermen actively engaged in their profession, and is proportional to the number of times that each fisherman casts his nets, as well as to the amount of fish he catches. Where a representative of a warrior tribe can supervise, the *ḥurma* is one-tenth of the fish caught; elsewhere, when supervision is from a distance, the value is fixed at a certain quantity of dried fish, fish oil, and fish roes. If, on the other hand, the group concerned is of superior status, as, for example, certain of the Zwāya clans—those known as Zwāya 'l-ḍ(ẓ)ill (of the shade) —the group retains certain privileges not accorded to others.

Within the social structure of the Western Sahara those who variously call themselves 'ʿArab', 'Maghāfira', or 'Ḥassān' are regarded as paramount. There are historical factors which have brought this about, but it is doubtful whether history can adequately explain the presence of certain tribes in the group. Strictly speaking, the term 'ʿArab' should be applied only to the aristocracy claiming descent from the Banū Maʿqil. The term 'ʿArab' is to be distinguished from the term Banū (Awlād) Ḥassān. The latter indicates all classes of the Maʿqil group, both the aristocracy and those of lower status. The name of the ancestor, Ḥassān b. Maʿqil, has come to be associated with the dialect of Ḥassānīya. 'ʿArab', however, has a different significance for whichever social group may happen to use the term. To the lower classes of the Banū Ḥassān 'our Arabs' is synonomous with 'our Lords', to whom they owe their allegiance. To the scholastic, non-*ḥurma*-paying Zwāya,[1] who are largely of Berber descent—known as Zwāya 'l-shams (of the sun)—'our Arabs' means those privileged Ḥassān who happen to be in a state of mutual or subordinate relationship with them. The term does not imply overlordship, since the title of 'Zwāya' implies their own sufficient status and honour as free men. Certain tribes of Mauritania are regarded as 'ʿArab' or Ḥassān, but the lettered Moors who are aware of Saharan genealogy dispute this status. Among such tribes are the Īdaw ʿĪsh, originally descendants of the Lamtūna, the Berber Almoravids who were in the Sahara long before the Banū Ḥassān. The Mashḍūf of the Ḥawḍ are also Berbers. The Awlād Bū Sbāʿ and the Rgībāt both claim

[1] The term Zwāya, also spelt Zawāyah, and Zawāyā, indicates one of the major social classes in Mauritanian society. It is applied to tribes whose special role in society is the direction of the spiritual life of the community, teaching, the extension of cultivation by well-digging, and the organization of caravan trade; *Kitāb al-Wasīṭ fī tarājim udabāʾ Shinqīṭ*, 1958 edition, pp. 475–9, 'Notes sur les classes sociales et sur quelques tribus de Mauritanie', by A. Leriche, *Bull. I.F.A.N.*, 1955, série B, nos. 1–2, pp. 173–4 and 197–9, and 'Shiyam al-Zawāyā' by Muḥammad b. Saʿīd al-Yadālī (d. 1166/1753) in *Chroniques de la Mauritanie sénégalaise*, Paris, 1911 (ed. by Ismael Hamet), pp. 14, 219–42, and Arabic text, p. 51. Zwāya 'of the shade' are those tribes which have need of protection. This expression dates from the time of the war of Sharr Bubba (1644–74) when the power of the Banū Ḥassān was established in southern Mauritania. Zwāya tribes which need no protection are known as Zwāya 'of the sun'.

to be *shurafā'*, descendants of the Prophet; in fact, they were originally Zwāya. There is no historically fixed status or position for a clan or a tribe: but the social significance of a class distinction which at one time may have had an ethnic origin and have been based on at least an element of historical fact survives. It may originally have been brought about by a total independence achieved by the tribe, by the domination it asserted over its neighbours, by the particular social pattern of the tribe, or by the particular activity it subsequently adopted. There are also Zwāya tribes, such as the Awlād Abyayrī and the Īdaygub, who in theory claim descent from the Banū Ḥassān, even though their name, their kindred, or their history, indisputably reveals their Berber origins.

The Arab historians and genealogists are in dispute as to the descent of the Banū Maʿqil (or ʿAqīl), from whose son Ḥassān the Arabs of Mauritania claim their descent. According to Ibn Khaldūn, the Maʿqil are in origin a tribe of the Banū Qaḥṭān of the Yemen, and are descendants of Quḍāʿa b. Mālik b. Ḥimyar. Yet another genealogy, which is claimed by many Saharan tribes, makes them descendants of Jaʿfar al-Ṭayyār b. Abū Ṭālib. Whether either of these claims has any authenticity whatsoever need not detain us here. But there is certainly sufficient historical evidence to show that the Banū Maʿqil, and their branch the Banū Ḥassān, were established as an Arab tribe in Southern Morocco in the fourteenth century. By the sixteenth century the accounts of Leo Africanus and Marmol Carvajal confirm the presence of the Banū Ḥassān as a group of Arab clans claiming a common descent, and expanding southwards from the region of the Wādī Darʿa. The names of these Arab clans are the same as those of existing tribes in the Western Sahara. Thus Duleim is the eponym of the Awlād Dalīm, Burbus that of the Barābīsh, Vodei that of the Awlād Ūday from whom descend the existing tribes of the Trārza and the Brākna, through Maghfar wuld Ūday. Other Arab tribes, famous in Mauritanian history, are less fortunate in having outside evidence to testify to their existence in the Northern Sahara at so early a date. It is clear that since the migration of these tribes southwards, these Arab lineages, particularly in view of the system of vassalage and other forms of assimilation, have now reached such a degree of intermixture that little value can be attached to them, except in so far as they have become associated with certain geographical localities. One group known as the Awlād Yaḥyā wuld ʿUthmān has established itself in the Adrār. A second group established itself and was to play an important historical role in the south-west, in the Trārza. A third group is that of the Brākna, centred further to the east. The Īdaw ʿĪsh of Tagānit are regarded as Ḥassān, but have no sound claim of any kind to a lineal descent from Ḥassān b. Maʿqil. The leadership amongst them is invested in the descendants of Bakkār wuld Swayd Aḥmad. On the other hand, two tribes now resident in the Ḥawḍ have far greater claim to authentic Arab descent. The first of these, the Awlād Mubārak, formerly held sway over great areas of Mauritania. The second tribe, the Awlād al-Nāṣir, claims descent from Maghfar wuld Ūday. The Mashḍūf of the Ḥawḍ, Massūfa-Berbers, also call themselves Arabs, by virtue of the fact that after they conquered the Ḥawḍ in the nineteenth century they attained paramount status, and subsequently integrated the remnants of the Awlād Mubārak into their tribe. The Barābīsh are one of the most ancient clans of the Banū Ḥassān, and have established themselves much further to the east, in that region of the Sahara of Māli known as Azawād. The Awlād Dalīm are similarly of ancient stock. They occupy the area of the Spanish Sahara adjoining the Atlantic Ocean, each *fakhdh* having its own chief. Lastly, certain tribes of the Wād Nūn area of Southern Morocco claim Arab descent, notably the Tekna, who are divided into two groups, the Ait al-Jamal and the Ait ʿAthmān.

Two qualities distinguish the tribes called Ḥassān. The first of these is the bearing of arms to fight the enemy, and the second has already been mentioned, the privilege to levy a *gharāma* or *ḥurma* on those they conquered. The latter may often be a simple protection fee: in return the warrior tribe offers protection against armed attack, and will also in time of famine and drought offer aid, either in the form of food or of the loan of livestock. The tribute is not normally paid collectively. It is a matter of the family headman of the tributary group paying a predetermined annual fee to a specific family headman of the protecting tribe. It is the privilege of a warrior when he travels to use the camps of his tributaries for his accommodation, and the vassal headman is under obligation to satisfy his guest's demands. This system has been greatly abused, and the history of the Moors is full of local revolts by certain Zwāya clans or tribes against their protectors.

Clan and tribal government among the Moors does not differ fundamentally from that found in the Sahara among other Arab tribal groups. Any nomad family can submit its elder as a candidate for election to the office of chief, on condition that he is not already chief of the family. In selecting a chief full account is taken of certain qualities he may possess, especially courage, generosity, piety, eloquence, culture, and wealth. The assembly, the *jmāʿa*, of a tribe, is the council of the chiefs who represent each fraction or subdivision of the tribe. This assembly chooses the most esteemed and wisest of its members to be its leader. But as chief of the tribe his powers are very limited, and he cannot take decisions without submitting them to the assembly, in whose hands both legislative and executive powers are concentrated. Normally the chief is chosen to preside over everyday meetings. In certain circumstances, however, and invariably when the discussion touches on legal matters, a member of the Zwāya is asked to preside over the meeting. Each tribe has its own law code, which is interpreted and modified when necessary by the tribal council. Besides his intimate knowledge of the *sharīʿa*,[1] the member of the Zwāya fraternity among the nomads will know the *ʿurf*, the orally transmitted customary law of the Saharan nomads. In Mauritania parts of this customary law were discussed in detail and evaluated by Shaykh Muḥammad al-Māmī in the nineteenth century in his masterpiece, *Kitāb al-bādiya*, 'The Book of the Customs of the Nomads'. In the Spanish Sahara the law was written down by Shaykh Māʾ al-ʿAynayn and his descendants early in the twentieth century. The Rgībāt have written *qawānīn*, criminal laws by which members of the tribe can be judged. The *ait-arbaʿīn*, the council of twenty for each of the two paramount shaykhs of the two territorial divisions of the Rgībāt, enforce the law. In practice among the Moors, the more remote the community and the more nomadic it is, the more likely that the *ʿurf* will predominate in the actual running of the tribe's affairs. Where the Moors are settled in oasis towns, or where there are Zwāya in large numbers, the *sharīʿa* will be followed. At least this will be so in theory, although among the tribes of the Zwāya, and especially those which preserve quaint Berber customs or ancient traditions, there are likely to be many legal rulings (*fatwa*s) that do not in fact strictly conform to the *sharīʿa*.

[1] *Sharīʿa*. The canon law of Islam.

In the Spanish Sahara, where the Zwāya are far fewer in number than they are, for example, in the Trārza, and where the communities are widely scattered, the *ʿurf* is preferred to the *sharīʿa*, particularly in the law of succession and in penal law, where the code of retaliation is still in force. In general blood-money can be paid, but there are some circumstances, such as the case of the murder of a father or mother or husband, when it cannot be accepted and capital punishment is enforced without any possibility of appeal. Death is also the penalty for homicide when the victim's family is unwilling to accept blood-money. If the homicide is unpremeditated, the price of 100 camels and 500 pesetas must be paid for a man victim, half for a woman. The loss of an ear is compensated by the gift of a woman slave, and less serious wounds or injuries by that of a varying number of camels. Theft is punished by compulsory restitution of the stolen object and payment of four times its value; or, as among the Rgībāt, by the strict application of the *sharīʿa*, i.e. by the amputation of the thief's hand. In the case of adultery a man has the right to flog his unfaithful spouse, to shut her up for three days, and to refuse to live with her. A woman taken in open adultery can be publicly stoned by her tribe. Among certain tribes reciprocal adultery is held to be a capital crime, and in some cases the *jmāʿa* has been compelled to pronounce a verdict of death for the convicted pair.

All charges are made before the *jmāʿa*, and the *jmāʿa* passes sentence. In intertribal disputes the issue will be settled by the two tribal councils at a combined session. If it turns out that no agreement is possible then the issue is referred to a saintly Zwāya family, whose authority can transcend that of the *jmāʿa* in certain matters, such a family as that of Shaykh Mā' al-ʿAynayn.

Marriage is almost always within the clan, and usually within the joint family. In general, the marriage prohibitions of the *Qur'ān* are strictly observed. Consecutive polygamy, where a man has several wives in succession but never more than one at a time, is very common, although it is not unusual for a Moor, particularly among the Zwāya, to remain attached to his first wife throughout his life. The wife has the right to ask for separation when she desires it, and if divorced she can contract a new marriage three months after her separation. If there are children it is the duty of the father to maintain them.

Moorish society is classified very broadly into those who are 'free' (*aḥrār*) and those who are 'slaves' (*'abīd*). Apart from the warriors, the Arab aristocracy, and their tribal groups and vassals, the Zwāya form the dominant element and of late have come to the fore as the majority of the leaders in the new Mauritanian State. It is customary to call them Berbers, or descendants of the religious leaders of the Ṣanhāja, those Muslims whom the Almoravid leaders sent as missionaries to preach and propagate their military movement in the Sahara in the eleventh century. But the Zwāya themselves have taken great pains in their sundry genealogies to establish Arabian connexions, either by claiming descent from Arab units which, it is said, participated in the Almoravid movement, or by presenting themselves as former Banū Ḥassān who joined the Zwāya, having forsworn the use of arms, as an act of repentance or religious devotion. Yet others, on devious or threadbare evidence, assert a blood relationship with descendants of the Prophet or with the Quraysh or Anṣār or various of the Prophet's companions. The Īdaw 'Alī, for example, claim descent from 'Alī b. Abū Ṭālib, through his son Muḥammad b. al-Ḥanafīya; the Midlish assert their Umayyad ancestry; while the Kunta, a tribe scattered over large areas of the western and parts of the central Sahara, claim descent from the Arab conqueror of the Maghrib, 'Uqba b. Nāfi'.

The Arabs who have become Zwāya are an unusual group. Known as *tyāb*, there are some who were 'converted' at an early period, while others are more recent converts. To the Zwāya, the term 'conversion' means not only that the Arab concerned has forsaken his arms, his most prized possession, and adopted the Zwāya calling, but that he has taken upon himself all the obligations of Islam and has dissociated himself completely from unjust and unlawful acts.

There are two types of tributary. The first are those referred to as *znāga*, 'white tributaries', and also known as *laḥma*. In theory, they are the descendants of the Ṣanhāja, other than the Zwāya, upon whom the Banū Ḥassān imposed a *gharāma*. According to the Moors, the Ṣanhāja in their own class structure assigned to the *laḥma* certain manual activities, such as agriculture and herding, and some commercial undertakings. They have been compared with the weft of a woven fabric. It was their duty to provide aid and to pay the *zakāh*, obligatory alms, to those engaged in the *jihād* or in religious instruction. The *Zwāya* likened their ideal

Islamic society to a woven fabric of which the warp, of the finest quality wool, was their own community and the Ṣanhāja warriors, the *mujāhidūn*,[1] while the gifts paid by the *laḥma* were the weft of this fabric.

The *ḥrāṭīn*—the coloured tributaries—are manumitted slaves or their descendants. They are sedentary, live in separate tribal groups, and have their own chiefs, but they remain protected by their former masters, and their property reverts to them if they have no offspring. The master, at the time of granting them their liberty, gives them a kind of 'dowry'—a dwelling, a cow, a sheep or a goat, and an implement. The services rendered by the *ḥarṭānī* to his former master and the tribute he pays him may be regarded as a reimbursement of this 'dowry' or the interest on it, as well as payment for the protection afforded him. In general, the *ḥrātīn* are landless negroid folk, of varied origin, working as share-croppers in the plantations of landlords, who furnish the land and the water and who normally receive half of the crop produced. It is curious that there is no general rule as to how these two types of tributaries are to be treated. In the Trārza, for example, the *gharāma* is imposed on all those who are of Ṣanhāja origin, without distinction. The Trārza tribes show more regard for the *ḥrāṭīn*, and entrust them with confidential tasks in order to humiliate the *laḥma*. In the Brākna it is the latter who are held in higher esteem; certain of their tribes are rich, while their cousins in the Trārza are despised.

Servants or slaves are fewer among the Moors than among some other Saharan communities, and they are of differing status. The *nānma* are descendants of slaves captured in the days of the Almoravids. They are the most numerous, and many of them have become *ḥrāṭīn*. They cannot be sold, and in most respects are treated like members of the family. Their name is derived from a Znāga word which indicates integration into, or adoption into, a family. In certain tribes of the Zwāya, for example the Ahl Bārakallāh, both *ḥrāṭīn* and slaves are of great value, and the Zwāya children are told never to sell their slaves, their books, or their

[1] *Mujāhidūn.* According to the Moors the ancient Berber community of the Western Sahara was organized by the Almoravids in the eleventh century into three classes:

1. al-Mujāhidūn, who were warriors of Islam and who fought unbelievers.
2. al-Zwāya who were religious teachers and jurists.
3. al-Laḥma who were herders, cultivators, and traders.

lands. A slave can be used as a shepherd, a tiller, or a gum-collector, and at times he is given a certain liberty of work, provided he regularly renders what is due to his master. The second category of slaves, *tarbiya*, indicates those who have been recently acquired. They are despised as men of no status, even if they are treated in more or less the same way as their colleagues.

There are two particular social groups in Moorish society which are universally despised. They consist of free men, yet in many ways they seem to stand apart from all other social groups. The first of these is a people known as the Nmādi, who live to the north of Walāta on the eastern marches of Mauritania. They are divided into four nomadic groups and they are now very few in number. Each Nmādi has a personal patron among the Moors, who will lend him a camel for the annual hunt and victuals for the winter. In return his patron is provided with the skins of dead antelopes or dried meat or leather thongs. The Nmādi keep away from the camps and towns, and they have no slaves or vassals. They live behind wind-breaks, and their household equipment is of the most primitive kind. Each Nmādi hunter has three or four dogs, which he has bought from the Moors, for the Nmādi do not themselves breed dogs. A Nmādi hunting party may last a fortnight. On the night before their departure the men perform ritual dances, which usually portray a successful hunt. During their march the hunters move on foot, with little or no break during the day (at times they march during the night). Several animals are regularly hunted, principally the addax, but also the oryx, ostrich, bustard, and an occasional eagle. Antelopes are run down by the dogs, and then hamstrung by the hunters. When the herd is alarmed and flees, the wounded animals are killed by spear-thrusts. The meat is then cut into strips and dried in the sun. The next day's hunt is not mentioned during the course of the evening meal or discourse. The Nmādi fear that evil spirits may hear of their plans and spoil their hunt the next day. In all probability the Nmādi are of Berber origin, even if they speak their own peculiar brand of Ḥassānīya.

The artisans, referred to as *ṣunnāʿ* or *mʿāllemīn*, are another debased, although indispensable, social class in Moorish society. In a short chapter on the tribe of the Liḥrākāt who, it is said, are descended from blacksmiths, the author of the *Kitāb al-Wasīṭ* draws attention to the peculiarity of the people of the Sahara in this respect, when compared with the urban population of Morocco or the Near East. There a skilled man is treated with respect rather than with contempt, and there are examples from the early period of Islam to show that a blacksmith found that his occupation in no way detracted from his social standing. The author is at a loss to explain how this contempt for the artisan could have arisen, and suggests a satire composed by the Arab poet Jarīr against al-Farazdaq, in which he taunts him by saying that his grandfather was a blacksmith. However, in several other parts of the Muslim world smiths are despised and feared because of their powers of magic and sorcery, and it seems likely that they enjoyed a higher regard and status in the region before the entry and conquest of the Banū Ḥassān.

In Mauritania this contempt for the artisan is expressed in a number of local sayings—'the slave and the artisan, there is only a tray of ash between them', or 'there is no good in the blacksmith though he be learned'. The latter is a pun on the words *m'ällem* and *'ālim*, and the poet Muḥammad wuld Haddār, himself of the Liḥrākāt, has introduced it into a poem:

By God it is a virtue to dispense with women, and he who follows his passions will repent of it.
I loved Ḥaddādīya[1] for a long time, and she knew that I had become mad with love of her.
Not once did I see the benefit of that; 'there is no good in the blacksmith though he be learned'.

There are sayings current in Mauritania that the artisans broke a tooth of the Prophet, so he cursed them, and that their ancestor was one born from the dung of an ass or a wolf. As in certain other Saharan societies, these smiths are also held to be descended from Jews or Negroes or to be of mixed descent.

The traditional attitude of the Moors to the Negro is neatly expressed in the following poem:

The resemblance of the 'blacks' to the ant is quite remarkable, except that the ant is not a merchant.
They are like the ant in blackness and in number, and like it in carrying and in the way they walk.

Many artisans cannot be distinguished from other Moors by their appearance, and it seems clear that Mukhtār wuld Ḥāmidun is right when he says that they are descendants of Wolof from

[1] *ḥaddādīya* means a woman blacksmith.

Senegal and of certain Berber and Arab tribes. It would seem that their lot is more pleasant among the Zwāya, but even here there is often an innate prejudice. Certain of the Zwāya, for example, will not allow a blacksmith, a carpenter, or a goldsmith to act as an *Imām*.[1]

The artisans are organized into clans which pay tribute like other vassals, and they are both nomadic and sedentary. Their skill can be seen in all kinds of tools and implements, in jewellery, locks, sugar-hammers, vessels for preparing food, saddles, and camel equipment. The wives of the artisans limit their work to the making of skins into saddle-bags, hold-alls, cushions, and fur blankets, and the fashioning of receptacles for holding water or butter. The artisans gain their living by their daily work, and in former days there were fixed payments for each object they made or repaired—in the form of meat, live animals, or cereals.

Nomadic pastoralism, trade, agriculture, and raiding were the main features of the economic life of the Western Sahara. Those Moors who today are nomads migrate annually, with a tendency to move towards the sea coast in spring and autumn, the north in the summer, and the south in winter. Those of them who own garden plots and palm-groves in the oasis centres of the Adrār and Tagānit return there at the time of the date harvest in July or August. The Moors attach great nutritive and medicinal value to the *balaḥ*, the unripe date; and the harvest, the *gayṭna*, is a time when large numbers of Moors with their families congregate in the date-groves in order to eat them.

In the palm oases the agricultural year of the *ḥrāṭīn* follows a regular pattern. In June the date-palms, laden with fruit, are watered, and in the following two months the dates are collected. In September the fields are sown with melons, and tended by the women and children, who at the same time pasture the animals, while in the date-groves millet known as *mutri* is sown. In November the *ḥarṭānī* will sow more millet or beans, watch over the progress of his fields of melons, and water the millet in the palm-groves. In December he and his companions will go and collect the millet from the palm-groves, or prepare the ground and sow barley and other cereals. In January the women and children

[1] *Imām*. The leader in prayer. The prohibition of artisans from filling this office is characteristic of certain of the Zwāya tribes in the Trārza.

will look after the fields, and continue to gather in beans and melons, while the men irrigate the cereals and the date-palms. In March the corn and beans are harvested and gathered, while the men carry out the artificial fertilization of the palms. Throughout April and May the millet is harvested by the women and children, and the upkeep of the date-grove is the principal occupation of the men. The cereals, and some of the dates and melons, are sold for the purchase of clothes, or of tea and sugar, or exchanged with the nomads for milk and meat.

The nomads themselves sometimes practise a form of agriculture. After a heavy fall of rain, when there is a good pasturage around the rock pools, they plant barley, millet, and water-melons.

The Moors are great traders, not only within the Sahara and its border areas, but also in regions much further afield in West Africa. In Dakar, for example, there is a large Moorish community, and many of them are shopkeepers. In the local markets, in centres such as Goulimine, Āṭār, and Tijikja, the nomads bring their camels and goats to exchange or sell, in return for the yield of the oasis plots and commodities and foodstuffs imported from Senegal, Māli, and elsewhere—particularly for such luxuries as tea, sugar loaves, mint, and articles made by the artisans.

Commerce has been one of the principal activities of the Zwāya, and the development and decline of such towns as Walāta, Wādān, and Shinqīṭī have been determined by the fluctuating fortunes of their leading citizens, by periods of security and insecurity, and most importantly by the change of certain caravan routes during the course of the centuries. Representatives of the nomad tribes remain permanently at these centres in order to act as brokers, butchers, bakers, and interpreters. Throughout the Western Sahara the discovery of some region rich in deposits, or yielding some product in great demand, has always been likely to affect the general direction of the caravan routes, although some of them may have been used continuously since prehistoric times. There are numerous routes from the areas rich in gum in the Trārza, which converge on the River Senegal, and the returning caravans bring with them various extra-Saharan commodities and cereals. There are other important routes from the main salt deposits in the Trārza, again direct to the river, or from Sabkhat Ijil in the north, via the towns of the Adrār and Tagānit, along which slaves, received in exchange for bars of salt, ground-nuts, cotton materials, and Sudanese handicrafts, are brought back. There is a continuous sale of herds of cattle in the region of the river, and of camels in the markets of Southern Morocco. The coastal area was also a terminus for the fluctuating caravan routes of traders bringing gold, gum, feathers, and slaves, in exchange for horses and weapons. The Portuguese, Spaniards, Dutch, English, and finally the French, all had trading-posts there between the fifteenth and the eighteenth centuries.

The wild behaviour of the Trārza Moors while selling gum to Europeans on the banks of the Senegal river and the anarchy in their community at that time are recorded in descriptions in European works written between the seventeenth and nineteenth centuries. La Courbe wrote that 'All these Moors have no king at all, but each canton recognizes as its master someone from a rich and important family amongst them. They often make war, the one against the other, without declaring it, the strongest making a sudden intrusion into the territory of the weakest in order to pillage and carry off all that it comes across. After this it retires until the other finds a suitable occasion to take its revenge. Nevertheless they respect the 'marabouts' or clerics of their faith, and they leave them in peace because they fear their amulets and their charms.'[1] But feelings against Europeans were sometimes bitter. The following Classical Arabic poem by the Mauritanian Zwāya poet al-Hādī wuld Muḥammad al-ʻAlawī is a sermon in which he mentions three European gum merchants who were famous for their wealth.[2] One of them was called Jijam, another Gazbār (Gaspari?), and the third Wīt or White (an Englishman?)

Strive after God. Pursue not trade nor pleasure.
He who enjoys this world's wealth must repent.
Nothing endures except the heaven's Creator
So let men race and strive to reach their Lord,
The Living, the Almighty, the Eternal.
This world is vanity, it does not last,
Nor has it existed since the dawn of time.
Jijam has died—how profitless are my words!
He purchased every caravan he could.
In hell he mends his ways, eternally.

[1] La Courbe, *Premier voyage du Sieur de la Courbe fait à la Coste d'Afrique en 1685*, Paris, 1913, p. 146.
[2] *Kitāb al-Wasiṭ*, pp. 76–78.

He bought gum from the tribe of the Aghlāl.[1]
Now he is chained and manacled in irons.[1]
He left the honey-pots in neat array.
His thirst—may God my refuge be—is unassuaged.
His rotting flesh torments his mighty bones.
He failed, only to stay and roast in hellish flames,
He did not merit the mercy of the Merciful,
Woe to him, Christian's guile availed him nought.
His is the fate of Wabār,[2] and Gazbār is a follower in his steps.
Wabār vanished before them both. Nations once lived in splendour and have perished.
Their raiment was dust, their blood was unavenged.
Their dwellings fell in ruins, uninhabited.
No ship, nor fort, nor horse protected Wīt.
While still alive he was as good as dead.
No chick nor dove[3] preserved him from his fate.
Amazed, he saw swine stunned by cudgel blows,
Slain by vile shepherds—and yet he was a giant!
Jujube and tragacanth trees were close at hand,
But then it was he died of foul disease.
Woe to the boon-companion of the Franks,
Who shake the dice and while the time with chess.
He has no wealth with God, save flowing tears.
He passed his days in pleasure, pomp and show.

He who observes things finds them to be void
Of substance, like a mirage to mislead.
The covetor of this world, by Zamzam's Lord,
Covets that thing of which he has no need.

The independent attitude of the Moors is largely a result of their mobility. The tent life of so many of them has made it comparatively easy to escape their foes by disappearing into the often inaccessible interior of their sandy domain. Notwithstanding the stony mansions of the oasis *qṣar*, or the straw and palm-leaf

[1] A pun on the word *aghlāl*, 'manacles or fetters' and the tribe of Aghlāl.

[2] Wabār was a tribe from the most ancient times in the south of Arabia. God destroyed this tribe and settled *jinn* in their place.

[3] The reference to these birds is obscure unless the poet has in mind a local belief, found in Moorish medical lore, that 'if the victim of small-pox is together with doves and pigeons, his soul will be preserved if it is God's will, since their proximity is a protection from small-pox, paralysis, and apoplexy.

shade of the *ḥawsh* or the *tīkkīt*, the *khayma*, the tent, remains the symbol of Moorish society, a microcosm of all its owner's social relationships.

The Moorish tent will always be one in a group. If the camp is small—a *frīq*—it may have up to fifteen tents; if it is a *maḥṣar* it will have well over fifty. A number above this is nowadays a rare occurrence, but it was once common during tribal wars. A *ḥalla* was the camp of a great chief, comparable to a moving court or town.

Paul Dubié[1] has left a detailed description of the *maḥṣar* of the Amīr of the Trārza. At the centre of the camp stood the Amīr's tent, large in size and orientated south-east north-west. Before its entrance, to the west, was an unoccupied space, where important travellers halted their camels, and where the evening entertainment was held. Not far distant was the *lemsīd*, the open area demarcated for prayer. Further to the west was the tent of the personal troubadour of the Amīr, and beyond it enclosures, one for cows and calves and another for camels, next to a shepherd's tent. Immediately behind the Amīr's tent was a group of four or five tents owned by his servants. It was their task to serve him and his family, to cook, fetch water, look after the children, and guard his herds. Tents in other directions were occupied by his relatives. To the north-east and to the south-west, behind the Amīr's tent and that of his eldest brother, were Zwāya tents, each occupied by a *ṭāleb*, whose occupation was to look after religious ceremonies of various kinds and to perform clerical and legal duties. At the limits of this inner section of the *maḥṣar* were the tents of three or four families of artisans.

Further away still, some two hundred yards distant to the north-east, were two parallel rows of tents, fifteen in all, belonging to the *ḥrāṭīn*. They constituted the personal guard of the Amīr, following him to war and carrying out various menial tasks. At about the same distance north were twelve tents belonging to a group of courtesans, and to the south-east twelve tents of noble sections of the princely family, of the Awlād Aḥmad wuld Dāmān. They played the chief role in choosing the princes. They followed them to war, together with their own partisans and tributaries.

In a period of crisis or danger each section sent a contingent of warriors to the *maḥṣar*. Attendance there was obligatory in any

[1] Paul Dubié, 'La vie matérielle des Maures', *Mem. I.F.A.N.*, no. 33, Dakar, 1953, pp. 110–252.

case, for the permission of the Amīr was needed in order to travel or to erect a tent elsewhere. To act without such authority was gross insubordination. At certain times of the year the *maḥṣar* was moved near a well with abundant water, and where the slaves could be sent to collect gum from nearby forests.

The Amīr of the Trārza, by virtue of his office and his wearing of the order of the 'white pantaloons' (bestowed on the Amīr, ʿAlī Shanḍūra, by the Sultan of Morocco, Mawlay Ismāʿīl),[1] possessed a number of rights and was entitled to certain dues: wrecks on the coast, hospitality, and transport were among the rights; while dues included the tax on salt deposits and the customs exacted from European commerce. Foreign tribes which crossed the Trārza paid a *ghafara*, protection money. In his turn the Amīr guaranteed the security of their goods. Another *ghafara* was paid by the Moors of the Trārza who left the country, for longer or shorter periods. Sometimes it entailed the annual payment of a certain number of animals, at other times a fixed amount of conveyed merchandise. On certain occasions the Amīr would be paid *maʿūna*, a gift which each warrior chief received from his subjects on special occasions, for example at a marriage, or upon departing for a war, a long journey, or an important reception. In time of war the Amīr made life easier for his subjects, and in order to rally full support to himself distributed captives and herds to his warriors. The Amīr received a half of the *diya*, the blood-money paid to every family of the tribe in case of murder or grave injury. But at the same time he contributed a half of the payment of the *diya* paid by his own subjects.

Another right which he shared with other chiefs of the Arab aristocracy was the right to a third of the well water. It was one of the conditions imposed by the Arabs on the Ṣanhāja, after the war of Sharr Bubba (1644–74), that the latter should give one bucketful of water in three to any warrior who presented himself at a well. This right was particularly resented by the Zwāya, as was also

[1] In 1703 ʿAlī Shanḍūra, the third son of Haddi, the Ḥassānī prince of the Trārza, visited Mawlay Ismāʿīl, the Sultan of Morocco, in order to obtain his military support against his rivals and to enhance his own status in southern Mauritania. The Sultan was flattered by the homage shown to him. He had observed that all the Mauritanians who came to his court wore black pantaloons, so he conferred on ʿAlī Shanḍūra the sole right to wear a pair of white pantaloons, a mark of his nobility. ʿAlī Shanḍūra died in 1726/7, but the right to wear white pantaloons was continued by his successors.

the fact that they were obliged to offer hospitality for three days to any warrior who asked for it.

The Amīr was responsible for the upkeep of all his family, and in reality he was responsible for the maintenance of almost the whole of the *maḥṣar*. The power he enjoyed, however, was very limited. He was at the mercy of his supporters, whose loyalty was always suspect. In principle the succeeding Amīr was chosen by the *jmāʿa* of the warriors from members of the ruling Amīr's family and preference was usually given to the eldest person eligible. The Amīr would designate as his successor his son, his brother, or some other relative, but this would not prevent a bitter struggle for power after his death. The most warlike competitor with the most powerful supporters would succeed in the end.

The Moors were to know many struggles for power of this kind, not only within one particular princely house, but between houses; and never in their history, or at least never since the Almoravids, was their entire territory to be integrated under the control of one central authority until the nationalist movement of our own times, and even now the process is far from complete.

In general their culture has been preserved, and has flourished at times, through the maintenance of the *status quo* of their tribal life and its system of mutual obligations and impositions, and through a perennial equilibrium between their society and the environment of the Sahara and the Sūdānic borderlands. To the Moors the upsetting of the *status quo* has seemed one of the most terrible calamities that has befallen them. In the words of a Ḥassānīya poet:

This world is topsy-turvy but the world to come is sure.
Lineage is mixed, and this [present state of things] is something between, neither one thing nor the other.
Oh be more bountiful to us!
The Zwāya *ṭāleb*, and the warrior, are both of them poor in this world's wealth;
While the meagre tributary now is fat and filled, and the *ḥarṭānī*—have no doubt—is proud and groomed.
The slave is owner of two flowing shifts, while the slave girl keeps her weight through drinking milk.
He who is learned in the faith has since forsaken it. Thus it remains, confused and in a tumult.
This world is topsy-turvy but the world to come is sure.

3

LANGUAGES AND DIALECTS OF THE WESTERN SAHARA

MAURITANIA has two non-Arabic languages. The first of these is Sūdānic, and called Azayr. It is very ancient, and perhaps represents an autochthonous African language spoken widely in parts of the Western Sahara when its southern regions were subject to Ghāna, Māli, and Takrūr. There are innumerable stories of the existence of non-Berber, non-Arab peoples in certain localities who were enslaved by the Almoravids. Sometimes they are described as Negroes, other sources refer to them as Berbers or 'Christians'. Some local scholars confuse Berber and Azayr.

Azayr is to all intents and purposes extinct, and only one or two speakers of it can be found today in the towns of Wādān and Tīshīt. It survives, however, in certain place-names; Shinqīṭī, for example, is derived from an Azayr word, *shi-n-gede*, meaning 'the horses' springs'. It may also survive in certain loan words and in proper names which have the nasal prepalatal *ñ*. But it plays no part in the folk poetry of Mauritania, and those words in the songs which have a prepalatal *ñ* have come into the country from the people south of the Senegal river.

The other pre-Arabic language, Znāga, is still spoken, albeit to a lesser and lesser extent, by certain tribes in the south-west of Mauritania. It is a variety of Berber which the author of the *Kitāb al-Wasīṭ* likens to the Shluḥ Berber dialect of Morocco, and it has a morphology and syntax akin to those of other Berber dialects. Many of the commonest place-names in Mauritania are related to one Berber dialect or another. Āṭār is Aḍaṛ in Shluḥ—'the foot of a mountain'. Adrār in Berber means 'mountain', and Tagānit in Shluḥ means 'forest'. The Trārza is particularly rich in Berber place-names.

The coexistence of Berber and Arabic personal names side by side is very widespread in Mauritania, especially in the Trārza. Furthermore, many of the Arabic names are themselves so distorted by local usage as to be very difficult to recognize, for example ʿAbdaḍḍa for ʿAbdallāh, and Muḥunḍ and Muḥamma for Muḥammad.

The existing Znāga-speaking community is now located in the Trārza, although not so long ago Znāga-speakers were to be found widely scattered in Mauritania. There is evidence from rock engravings in the Spanish Sahara, the Ḥawḍ, and elsewhere that Ṣanhāja tribes who used the Tuareg *tifinagh* script, or one similar to it, were once present in parts of the Western Sahara where now only Ḥassānīya is known.

Today there are probably fewer than 13,000 Znāga speakers in the whole of the Trārza, some 5,000 among the Īdab al-Ḥasan, 3,000 Tandag͟ha, and 4,600 among the tribes which know themselves as the Tas͟hums͟ha. At the period of the Zwāya's bitterest resistance to Ḥassānī supremacy the Znāga tongue was a symbol of their independence. Whoever spoke their tongue was regarded as an ardent Muslim. Many of them knew Classical Arabic as well. They believed themselves to be superior to the Ḥassānīya-speaking Arabs. The latter knew their dialect but they were indifferent to Classical Arabic and they were sometimes lukewarm in their faith. The Znāga-speaking Zwāya were so proud of their tongue that less than a century ago it was possible to find some of them who were quite ignorant of Ḥassānīya. Among families of the Īdab al-Ḥasan, Znāga was employed to the exclusion of Ḥassānīya, and young men heard speaking the latter were reprimanded by their elders. In the mosque Znāga was looked on without disfavour. The elders encouraged the children to remember it. Znāga was described as a noble language in which a blessing could be found. In the reading of the Qur'ān, Znāga was sometimes used in order to explain words to pupils. The women cherished the tongue as much as, if not more than, the men. But some scholars tended to frown upon it in academic circles, fearing that the correct pronunciation of Arabic was impeded by it. Eventually the younger generation succumbed to Ḥassānīya, and Znāga itself has evolved under the influence of Ḥassānīya and Classical Arabic. Like most other Berber dialects, it has no script, and it has adopted Arabic via Ḥassānīya to make a permanent record of its literature.

Ḥassānīya is the lingua franca of the Western Sahara. Notwithstanding regional variations in pronunciation, morphology, and vocabulary, it has become a language capable of producing its own folk literature, and it helps to bring together Saharans of widely differing ethnic and social groups. Although those who speak it claim, proudly and with some justification, that it is 'purer' and closer to Classical Arabic than the dialects of several of their North African neighbours, it retains some highly individual features. These give some indication of its ancestry and establish its particular affinity with other Beduin dialects.[1]

[1] See Appendix, p. 194.

4

THE HISTORICAL DEVELOPMENT OF ḤASSĀNĪYA POETRY

WHEN the tribes of the Banū Maʿqil, the sons of Ūday, Dalīm, Barbū<u>sh</u>, Raḥmūn, and others moved south from the Darʿa region of Morocco in the fifteenth century, they came into contact with the remnants of a superficially arabized Berber and Soninké society, which had been welded into some form of unity under the Almoravids in the eleventh century, and later under the hegemony of Māli. These tribes were not Arabic-speaking. In the thirteenth century Ibn Saʿīd al-Ma<u>gh</u>ribī records the inability of the Gudāla Ṣanhāja of the Atlantic coast to understand Arabic, and adds that an interpreter was needed for mutual comprehension. The Portuguese and other travellers who visited the region in the later Middle Ages made the same discovery.

The Maʿqil, from whom the Banū Ḥassān are an offshoot, settled in the Moroccan Sūs in the thirteenth century, and it is not unreasonable to conjecture that they came into contact with Andalusian poetic forms. But it is also possible that this poetry was not unknown to the lettered Ṣanhāja Almoravids settled in remoter regions of the Sahara. An Andalusian Arabic influence in the Sūdānic kingdoms is indisputable. It can be seen in the calligraphy of epitaphs discovered in Gao. The poetry of the Maʿqil must also have been influenced by the changes which took place, early or late, in the poetry of the Ma<u>gh</u>rib as a whole, a poetry which retained classical subject-matter such as eulogy, satire, and love, but which progressively abandoned or modified the classical metres, dispensing with the *iʿrāb*, the fully inflected forms of Classical Arabic, and creating new metres whilst retaining some unity of rhyme. In Morocco a change of this kind took place in the Saʿdian epoch, when the Ḥassānī drive south into Mauritania and towards the Niger was at its peak. If no direct contact ever existed it would seem that a parallel poetic development took place in different regions of the Arabic-speaking Ma<u>gh</u>rib at about the same time. Professor Colin calls the Moroccan poetry *malḥūn* and suggests that it arose under Beduin influence. It represented a popular reaction against the Andalusian tradition. *Malḥūn* ignored the old metric systems and used a special *koine*, but above all, like *zajal* (strophic verse), it made a complete break with the forms of quantitative poetry and based its metres on the number of syllables in each verse or hemistich. It was exclusively syllabic and rhythmic, and it was eminently suited to partner the music for which it was composed.

Mauritanian society, over a period of several centuries, was to lose much of its Berber or Sūdānic character—for example the Tuareg veil and the Berber tongue. It was to be politically dominated and linguistically integrated by the Banū Ḥassān. But in their turn the Arabs were to modify their own social customs, to favour monogamy, and to adopt a Saharan class structure which pre-dated their arrival.

The literary and artistic expression of this new society was the prerogative of three classes. The prestige and wealth of the Ḥassānī aristocracy, like that of the rulers of Māli and the Ṣanhāja princes before them, demanded the permanent presence of a court poet to praise, to lampoon, or to act as family archivist. The Ḥassānī chiefs held poetry in the highest esteem, but it was left to the Zwāya scholastic fraternity to systematize the new metrical forms that the poetry needed and to link them with the Classical Arabic poetry which was their monopoly. Lastly, it was the musicians themselves, the *īggāwen*, who were to wed the music and the poetry. They were to be the poets laureate of the Banū Ḥassān, whose princes ruled and fought in the Western Sahara up to quite recent times.

Mauritanian scholars, while obviously not precluding the antiquity of some musical culture in the region, agree that the specifically Moorish music we now know arose in the sixteenth century and was the invention of an unknown group of musicians known as 'the men of Awlīl', a locality on the south-west coast of Mauritania near the Senegal river. There is no evidence to support this claim. It is almost certain that a musician class, Soninké influenced, existed in Mauritania prior to the Ḥassānī invasion. The word *īggīw* (pl. *īggāwen*) is derived from Sūdānic languages, but it also bears a Znāga Berber stamp. As a musician class is endemic in Sūdānic societies, and is absent from other Saharan communities, it is reasonable to assume that these people were an element in Southern Mauritania (Takrūr), and perhaps in the Ḥawḍ. Both districts were at times subject to the Māli and Songhai monarchies.

Whatever form of music may have existed before the Ḥassānī settlement, the experts are at least agreed that it was about the year 1700 that *leġna*[1] came into being as an art form among the Ḥassānī and Znāga-speaking communities. Three outstanding *iggāwen* brought this about: ʿAlī wuld Mānu of the Trārza, and G͟harḍ (ẓ) wuld Balg͟hām and Saddūm wuld Nǰartu, both of the Awlad Mubārak. Of these three troubadours Saddūm is probably the most famous. (He is not to be confused with another poet, Saddūm wuld Āgmattār.) Before Saddūm wuld Nǰartu poetry composed in honour of Ḥassānī chiefs was either in rhymed prose or else in the form of an extended ode or *qaṣīda* with very little variation in rhyme or rhythm. The accompanying music, it is said, was wholly Arabic or Berber in type. Saddūm introduced a number of changes. He joined the *qaṣīda* form to a new musical style divided into two aspects (*jaamba*), one 'white' and the other 'black', the former Arabic in character, the latter inspired and influenced by Negro music from the east and from across the Senegal river. He also invented a new form of poem called a *rasm*. At least one *rasm* has survived. It is in honour of the uncle of Bakkār wuld Aʿmar (d. mid-eighteenth century), chief of the Īdaw ʿĪs͟h, amongst whom Saddūm settled after first living among the Awlād Mubārak (see Chapter 9, poem 1).

The reputation of Saddūm aroused the envy of the poets, and the following incomplete poem of his, if it is authentic, shows that he was confident of the superiority of his talents:

> G͟harḍ and ʿAlī (are worthy poets) but Ibn al-Mayyāḥ is more important than both of them.
> I am never one to shame them,
> Worthy poets, but I am their victor in my verse.

Bakkār wuld Aʿmar, Amīr of the Īdaw ʿĪs͟h, tempted him to go to the province of Tagānit. He awarded him a regular payment on all the caravans, an offer which no *iggīw* could resist. As he grew in status and renown, so he received further gifts and, it is said, each warrior and Znāga tribal group annually gave him one sheep per head of the adult population. After the death of Bakkār wuld

[1] See p. 40.

Aʿmar, Saddūm acted as poet laureate for his son Muḥammad Shayn, who died in 1810. Saddūm lived until about 1800, and one of his *qaṣīda*s shows that it was composed after the events of Ḥanīkat Baghdād (about 1778) where his former patrons, the Awlād Mubārak, were decisively defeated. The event is echoed in his poem.

ʿAlī wuld Mānu, the ancestor of an existing family of *īggāwen* who bear his name, was the personal troubadour of the Trārza prince ʿAlī Shanḍūra, whom he accompanied on his expeditions. A short poem of his in honour of Aʿmar, the eldest son of ʿAlī Shanḍūra, survives.

It was either ʿAlī wuld Mānu or Gharḍ wuld Balghām or perhaps a little-known poet, ʿAlīya wuld Bačīča, who inspired the composition of a non-Ḥassānīya ode, one of the most famous in the Western Sahara, by the saint and scholar Muḥammad al-Yadālī. The ode is Classical Arabic poetry in its vocabulary, but its metre is so closely modelled on a Ḥassānīya prototype, and is so widely sung by the *īggāwen*, that it deserves special mention. The *qaṣīda* is in praise of the Prophet and begins:

> The blessing and peace of God be upon my beloved the best of mankind.
> Translucence made manifest, at hand is his sustenance, beneficent in mercy, a heroic lion.

The rhyme scheme is a b a b, then c c c b, d d d b. The poem has forty-seven verses of strung epithets, each pair of words having five syllables. The persistent rhythm produces a monotonous, hypnotic effect. In his choice of words the poet reveals his knowledge of Ṣūfism, and he shows his skill in the employment of word patterns and puns of every kind. But the endless repetition detracts from the aesthetic value of the poem, and its form is not remarkable. The internal rhyme scheme and the short hemistichs have an Andalusian pedigree, a feature first pointed out by Professor Massignon,[1] but the interest the poem arouses in the Sahara bears little relation to its literary merit.

There is some doubt as to the original motive for its composition. In one place in his commentary al-Yadālī states that on setting out on a journey he passed a troop of musicians who were making

[1] L. Massignon: 'Un poète saharien: la qasida d'al Yedali', *Revue du Monde Musulman*, vol. viii, 1909, pp. 199–205.

merry to the sound of stringed instruments. 'They were playing a melodious air, most agreeable to listen to, upon which they were singing a very beautiful song in *malḥūn*. I was enchanted by this popular song and decided on the spot to compose a poem in the same metre, in praise of the Prophet.' Elsewhere a Ḥassānīya poem is given as the source of inspiration. Each hemistich is dominated by a five-syllable rhythm.

According to al-Yadālī he once heard an *īggīw*, either Gharḍ wuld Balghām or 'Alī wuld Mānu, praising the Amīr of the Brākna, Aḥmad wuld Hayba, who died in Rajab in 1762, in an ode which begins with the words:

> My question will cause no surprise. I am seeking a reward.
> Who is a young Arab gallant except Ibn Hayba?

The author of the *Kitāb al-Wasīṭ* quotes another verse from this Ḥassānīya poem; as it does not appear in the poet's commentary it may not be authentic, but it more closely resembles the pattern of the ode:

> An air which I am playing, I shall perform earnestly.
> I shall find its utility on the day of judgement.[1]

The subsequent history of his *qaṣīda* is best told in the poet's own words:

> When I recited this ode, imitating the Ḥassānīya poem, one of the chiefs of the Banū Maghfar was wroth against me on account of that imitation, because the poem was in praise of him. In their view that is the most telling way of angering one of them. If a poet composes a *kerza* (a Ḥassānīya ode) in praise of a man, then distorts part of it or imitates it with another, in measure and in rhyme, and with it praises another man, then he is exposed to his anger. Men say such and such a person has robbed the *kerza* of so and so, and has given it to someone else. In their view it is as though he has all but slain him. I continued to hear that he was angry with me on account of that, until he heard one night of my arrival at one of the tribes. When he encountered me, his face betrayed his anger, and he said to me, 'Why have you stolen my *kerza* and treated me thus?' I said to him, 'Yes, I have taken it, and I have given it to one who is superior to both of us.' All he did was to lower his gaze, pensively, for a while, then he raised his head and said, 'You have spoken the truth.' At that time he gave me a number of clothes, then he made that gift a charge on his part.

[1] *Kitāb al-Wasīṭ*, pp. 223–6.

Another account says that the prince gave him a camel and made it an obligation both on himself and on his offspring. In fact, he seems to have treated al-Yadālī as though he were a *iggīw*, whose tongue was to be feared and whose services were profitable, and al-Yadālī later composed a very famous ode in honour of this prince.

It is significant that most of the greatest poets in Ḥassānīya lived during the second half of the eighteenth century and during the nineteenth century, the same period as the great poets and writers in Classical Arabic whose works are discussed in the *Kitāb al-Wasīṭ*. In the early twentieth century, notwithstanding noted exceptions, all forms of artistic expression were to suffer from the continued insecurity which prevailed in the region. But if the quality of the poems declined, there was no lack of poets to compose them, and in future years, helped by the recent revival of Moorish national feeling, the radio, and the superb artistry of certain musicians, there is every prospect that this art will continue to have its supporters among all classes of Mauritanian society.

5

THE FORM OF ḤASSĀNĪYA POETRY

Leġna is the Mauritanian name for the syllabic folk poetry, both recited and sung, in the Western Sahara. It is the local manifestation of a type of poetry, popular throughout North Africa, which may have originated in the *zajal* of Arabic Spain. The poetry has a common basis and draws upon a common inheritance. Its originality lies in the way the Saharan Moors have fashioned it to suit their own artistic needs, closely related to their music; new metre patterns and rhyme schemes have been systematically introduced.

The basis of all Ḥassānīya poetry is the *batt* (pl. *btuut*). This word, which must, it seems, be derived from a verb in Arabic meaning 'to cut', is the metre of the hemistichs in all forms of the poetry. It is the equivalent of musical notation. The Moors compare it with the word *baḥr* in Classical Arabic poetry, but this comparison is open to objections, since the two forms of poetry differ fundamentally in scansion, stress, and the form of words permissible both in hemistich and in verse. Ḥassānīya prosody is based on the number of syllables in each hemistich, each *taafelwiit* (pl. *tifilwaaten*), as it is called. As the author of the *Kitāb al-Wasīṭ* remarks, 'That which is taken into consideration amongst them is the number of vocalized letters. They pay no heed to the unvocalized letters, whether they be few or many.'[1] The Moors have symbols in their prosody to represent the *batt*. A dot represents a vocalized letter (*mutaḥarrik*); a vertical line an unvocalized one (*sākin*). A long vowel, provided that it is immediately followed by a consonant, is also represented by a vertical line. It is known as *sukuun mayyet*. In short, an open syllable is represented by a dot, a closed syllable by a dot followed by a vertical line.

It can easily be seen that such a system of notation and metre has very limited possibilities, because a poet can only lengthen or shorten the number of syllables he employs in each hemistich.

[1] *Kitāb al-Wasīṭ*, p. 73.

In certain lengthy poems of praise an extended hemistich may seem apt for the occasion, but in the long run it is bound to lead to monotony. Twelve syllables seems to be the maximum the *iggīw* is prepared to tolerate, or to sing, in any one hemistich.

The Moors have therefore adopted another method of introducing variety into their poetry. Although no attention is paid to single unvocalized letters, the positioning of two immediately adjoining unvocalized letters in a single hemistich (unless they happen to be at the very end of that hemistich) is sufficient to vary the metre in their system. The juxtaposition of two unvocalized letters occurs in the following circumstances:

1. Where a long vowel is immediately followed by an unvocalized consonant, for example *daar* = ·||.
2. Two unvocalized adjoining consonants, for example *bayt* = ·||.
3. A doubled consonant which is unvocalized, for example *batt* = ·||.

There are, of course, variations. It is permissible in certain metres to reduce the two unvocalized letters to a single quiescent in one hemistich of the verse and not in the others. The hemistich is then called *mamluuḵa*, a passive participle derived from an Arabic verb meaning 'to dislocate'.

This, very briefly, is how the different Ḥassānīya metres are scanned. The metre determines the rhythm of the poem and the way in which it is sung, and so it affects also the subject-matter of the poem which must be appropriate to the music. Experts in *leġna* divide the metres into two groups. The first group is collectively known as *lebtayt* (the little *batt*). Metres in this category have no unvocalized pairs, except at the very end of the hemistich. The shortest is *batt waaḥed*, where the hemistich is a single syllable, the longest *lebtayt et-taamm*, where the hemistich has eight syllables. In the second group the hemistich varies in length from five to seven syllables, and the unvocalized pair is introduced in different positions in the hemistich in order to vary the metre. There is also a third category known as *thaydiina*. This is confined to the *iggāwen*. Within it are associated several metres, some of which have a pair of quiescents. They are more fully discussed in Chapter 11. According to the Moors it is these metres which approach most closely an original so-called 'Hilālī' form of prosody, or perhaps a rhymed prose which once was popular. The names of the metres are Ḥassānīya or Znāga.

Lebtayt

1. *batt waaḥed*

This metre, where each hemistich is a single syllable, is rare and did not gain a footing until the turn of the century. Some experts do not deem it worthy of inclusion with the others, for in their view its aesthetic value is slight, and its possibilities so limited that it can be no more than a device to exhibit wit. The following poem was composed by Mḥammadh Bāba wuld Aḥmad Yūra in praise of Umm al-Manīn (al-Mu'minīn), the daughter of the Amīr of the Trārza, 'Amar (d. *circa* 1893), the son of Muḥammad al-Ḥabīb.

fumm	umm	The mouth of Umm al-Manīn (Manayn)
lum	nayn	is a pretty mouth.
fumm	zayn	

Between the third and fourth hemistich there is a *caesura*. This poem is called a *ṭal'a* (c c c b c b).

tam	ra	Red date.
ḥam	ra	

This poem is called a *gaaf* (a b a b).

bag	ra	Brown cow.
šag	ra	

This poem is also a *gaaf* (a b a b).

kell	zayn	All beauty is in the eye of the beholder.
fil	'ayn	

This poem is also a *gaaf* (a b a b).

2. *batt aṯnayn*

In this metre each hemistich is disyllabic. It is, strictly speaking, the simplest form of *lebtayt*. The following written poem was composed by the Spanish Saharan poet Sīdi Sālim. It is addressed to Shaykh Mā' al-'Aynayn.

1. emnayn	1. When,
2. baydiin	2. with two hands

3. zayniin	3. which are lovely,
4. eṭlabt	4. you asked for
5. leḥniin	5. compassion (rain),
6. waqsatt	6. you sought
7. assḥaab	7. the rain cloud,
8. nezlet	8. it fell,
9. wattraab	9. and the earth
10. nabtat	10. brought forth plants.

This poem is a *ṭalʿa* (c c c b c b), concluded by a *gaaf* (a b a b).

ḥadd ef	luʿgal	A man in a shallow well (is tied to it)
baʿd ef	liʿgal	like a camel's tether.

This poem is a *gaaf* (a b a b).

3. *batt aṯlaaṯa*

In this metre each hemistich is trisyllabic.

eš-šawr biih	etzakriif
haa mayjiih	etlafliif

This musical air on account of its grace needs no embellishment, shortening, and abridging.

This poem is a *gaaf* (a b a b). The first hemistich breaks the rule of *lebtayt* by introducing two adjoining unvocalized letters.

4. *ḥwaywiiṣ*

This metre of four syllables is no longer in fashion. Nowadays it is identical with the succeeding metre, *batt kamsa*. However, examples of it in its original metre are not unknown, and the following is an example:

kent efla ʿyaad :	maaši lawwaad :	bel menhen gaadd :
enjiih enjiih :	maryam ḏa zaad :	gaalet ši fiih :
gaalet li ʿan :	ḏaak enkalliih :	wel gaalet lan- :
waasi-h waasiih :		

Once I chased fair ladies, and those I had a chance to visit, I did so. Maryam has also had something to say. She told me to stop that. I'll do what she says, yes, I'll do it.

The poem is a *ṭalʿa* (c c c b c b), concluded by a *gaaf* (a b a b).

5. *batt ḵamsa* (*ḥwaywiiṣ*)

This metre of five syllables is one of the older metres. The following is an example from the *Kitāb al-Wasīṭ*:

maḏa men waḵši : fiina yatmašša : maahu-mḵalla ši :
(u) laahu-mḵalla ša.

What a base sponger walks in our midst. He leaves nothing, not even a ewe.

The poem is a *gaaf* (a b a b).

6. *lebtayṯ en-naageṣ*

This metre has six syllables. It means 'the incomplete little *batt*'. It is one of the most common metres in Ḥassānīya poetry.

The following example is a poem by Muḥammad wuld Sīdī Ibrāhīm, a well-known enthusiast and artist in *leġna*, who is employed by Radio Mauritanie, Nouakchott. In it he satirizes himself, holding his lineage (*nasab*) up to ridicule, and echoing popular scepticism on this important issue.

muḥammadin laḵḍar : lawnu men ahl andar :
ešriif u gaṭṭ aḵṭar : buuh aʿla leḥraakaat :
maftuuḥ af kell eḍhar : weḍaḥḥak laʿlaayaat :
maḏkuur aʿla dakaar : aḵṭar fil-layl u baat :
ʿand eḥraaṭiin afdaar : emʿa ḥarṭaaniyyaat :

Muḥammad wuld Sīdī Ibrāhīm is dusky-skinned and comes from the people of Saint Louis. He's a descendant of the Prophet. His father once paid a visit to the musician tribe, the Liḥrākāt. He's eloquent in every 'mode' of music, and he makes the ladies laugh. It is said that he went to Dakar and that he spent the night in a house amongst the freed and dark-skinned slaves of the gentle sex.

The poem is a *ṭalʿa* (c c c b c b), concluded by a *gaaf* (a b a b).

7. *tayduum*

This metre has seven syllables. It means 'the baobab tree'. It is among the less common metres, since those that have seven syllables are usually not *lebtayt*, and contain pairs of unvocalized letters. The following is an example:

haaḏu huuma ḥagg aḏnuub : li gellat ban eḥdiida :
(e)ngaal alyaana ḏatnuub : maanak gaayes min(t) diida :

Indeed these are misfortunes, due to the breakdown of an iron tip-up lorry. I am told on an occasion such as this—you are not going to (meet) Dīd's daughter.

The poem is a *gaaf* (a b a b).

8. *lebtayt et-taamm*

This metre has eight syllables. It means 'the complete little *batt*'. It is one of the most, if not the most, common of metres in modern Ḥassānīya poetry. The following is an example:

ḏan-naṣṣ enduur en-naṣṣu lak :
fin-naaṯi wenta naṣṣu lii :
elli rayt ana naṣṣu lak :
welli rayt enta naṣṣu lii :

When we select our lady friends, this rule must mutual be:
The one I find will half be yours, I'll share the one you see.

The poem is a *gaaf* (a b a b).

Metres which in origin introduce pairs of unvocalized consonants

1. *haṯw-jjraad*

This metre is named after the scattering of dust by the locusts. It is similar to *batt ḵamsa*, and some experts regard it as identical, including it within *lebtayt*. Others disagree, however, on the ground that nowadays a pair of unvocalized consonants is sometimes found centrally placed in the hemistich.

The following is an example. It is indistinguishable from *batt ḵamsa*.

naʿraf dahr aʿyiit : enji yalmaqiit :
leḵyaam efḥaašiit : ḏaak al-ʿalb aḏriik :
efzarr efaršiit : umm er-reġwa ḏiik :
biihem muʿtanya : ruuḥi yal-maliik :
murri yad-denya : magall etwaaliik :

I recall a time, O God, when, sometimes, I used to frequent the tents on the fringe of that dune yonder, in the neighbourhood of Afarshīt, which bears the name of Umm al-Raghwa. My soul yearns for them, O God. Woe to you world, how unstable you are!

The poem is a *ṭalʿa* (c c c b c b), concluded by a *gaaf* (a b a b).

2. *el-ʿaṭša*

This metre means 'thirst'. It appears to be one which compresses the preceding metre, so that two hemistichs of *haṯw-jjraad* combine to form one hemistich of *el-ʿaṭša*. Caro Baroja does not refer to it as a poetic metre at all, but as a musical form in which the praises of the Prophet are sung. As a metre it is very rare.

3. *sġayyer* (*tigaadriin*)

This metre means 'very small', and it is linked both to metre no. 5, below, *tigaadriin*, and to preceding metres, in that its hemistichs alternate between seven and five syllables, the former with a pair of unvocalized letters before the last two vocalized letters. The metre is also very rare, and the most famous example of it is the definition of it by al-Walī wuld al-Shaykh Saʿd Būh:

(e)sġayyer maa fiih ṭamʿa : mustagsi ḏannayt :
mennu taafelwiit sabʿa : ḵamsa taafelwiit :

sġayyer is not to be coveted, I reckoned it to be very difficult. It has a hemistich of seven (syllables), and (another) of five.

The poem is a *gaaf* (a b a b).

4. *lubbʷayr*

This metre means 'the little well'. It is a very common Ḥassānīya metre of seven syllables, and is found in two forms. The pair of unvocalized letters immediately precedes the final vocalized letter. If this occurs in all four hemistichs of a *gaaf* it is known as *entaaṭraart* (*Psorta plicata*). If it occurs in only the first and the third hemistichs it is known as *agiilaal* ('that which has the tail cut').

The following is an example of *entaaṭraart*, selected from the manuscript of Chapter 11:

ʿannak baʿd ila kaan ḵuuk :
emniḏamb alli ṭaalʿu :
šakaa-lak wajjah biih buuk :
fekkuuh emnalli ḵaalʿu :

If your brother complains to you about a sin which he has committed before God, you should obtain for him the favour of your father, and free him from that which makes him afraid.

The poem is a *gaaf* (a b a b).

The following is an example of *agiilaal*:

gaymat lubbʷayr emgaddʿa : ʿaks el-lak̲ra masruuma :
kiif enguulu lemraggʿa : (u) kiif enguulu masuuma :

The first hemistich of *lubbʷayr* is knotted, in contrast to the second which is free. Thus is pronounced (the tribe) Lemraggʿa, and thus (the tribe) Masūma.

The poem is a *gaaf* (a b a b).

5. *tigaadriin*

In this metre of seven syllables the pair of unvocalized letters immediately precedes the two final vocalized letters, although at times their position can be altered by placing one of the unvocalized letters in a different position in the hemistich.

The following is an example taken from the manuscript of Chapter 11:

aʿd̲arni yas-siid femjiik : af gellet laadaab wayyaak :
hammi fiik ekbiir waʿliik : ḥemlu mennu fiiḥ yarʿaak :

Pardon me, O Lord, for coming to you in so unseemly a way. I have great need of you, but to you the bearing of my need is a light thing, as a wind. May God watch over you.

The poem is a *gaaf* (a b a b).

6. *bu ʿumraan*

This seven-syllable metre is reckoned to be one of the most ancient, and it is named after its inventor. But nowadays its popularity has waned, and other metres have taken its place. The pair of unvocalized letters immediately follows the first vocalized letter. The following is an example:

yar-rabb el-buʿd emni hiir : diirni beglayb enzidaan :
bayn yalla saani wel-biir : wadmaar u ḥufrat wadaan :

O Lord, Oh, to be remote from Hīr, put me in Glayb Anzidān. O God, between Sāni and al-Bīr, between Admār and Ḥufrat Wadān.

The poem is a *gaaf* (a b a b).

7. *mraymiida*

In this metre of seven syllables the pair of unvocalized letters immediately follows the first two vocalized consonants. This is a very popular metre. The following is an example:

ebgayt fid-daar enguugi : wejruuḥt el-ḵadd ibaanu :
wemšaat walfi yeyuugi : fislaamt allaah umaanu :

I remained in the camp to weep, and the grooves of my cheeks bear witness to it. My beloved, my dear one has departed, in God's peace and his safe keeping.

This *gaaf* is a famous one by the slave poet, ʿAbd Masūma. He fell in love with his master's wife, and to punish him his master tied him to a stake in the sun and left him to perish while the tribe left to seek new pasturage.

Apart from its original prosody, Ḥassānīya poetry is characterized by an individual poetic form and rhyming pattern. The simplest form of poem is the *gaaf*, which is of four hemistichs. These are either of uniform rhyme or, far more frequently, the odd and even hemistichs terminate in the same rhyming letter. This type of verse is found not only in Ḥassānīya poetry but also in Znāga verse. (Little of the latter has survived, and it is reckoned to be influenced by, and thus to post-date, Ḥassānīya poetry.) If the *gaaf* has three verses of two hemistichs, it is called *gaaf emsattat*, and if it is of uniform rhyme, *gaaf aḥmar* (red *gaaf*). If the *gaaf* is extended throughout the poem it becomes a *kerza* ('dishevelled hair'), an ode.

The other typical Ḥassānīya poetic verse form is the *ṭalʿa*. It has been defined as a poem which must contain at least six hemistichs. The first, second, third, fifth, seventh, ninth, etc. have the same rhyme, while others are alternated, the number of verses always being even. A typical pattern of a *ṭalʿa* is c c c b c b c b. The first three hemistichs are called *ḥumr aṭ-ṭalʿa* (the reds), while the fourth is called *kasra*, because it breaks the uniformity of the rhyme.

A *ṭalʿa* (pl. *aṭlaʿ*), if it is complete, must always begin or end with a *gaaf*. The second and fourth hemistichs of the *gaaf* rhyme with the rhyming letter of the *ṭalʿa*. Sometimes the term *ṭalʿa* is loosely used to mean a poem which has both *gaaf* and *ṭalʿa*, or a whole poem which in fact may have several *aṭlaʿ*. In the latter a single *gaaf* suffices, joined to the first or the last *ṭalʿa*. If the poet wishes to stress the unity of the idea in the poem, or to give additional pleasure to his audience, he makes the poem 'bite its tail', *'aaḍḍ esbiibu*, whereby the sense expressed in the last verses relates back to the opening verse or *maṭla'* of the poem. Although the *kerza*, whether extended *gaaf* (*kerdaadya*) or *rasm*, is by no means unpopular with the *iggāwen*, they prefer the poem to be short.

If the *gaaf* is found in both Ḥassānīya and Znāga poetry, what of the *ṭal'a*, apparently rare in the Znāga poetry of Mauritania? The scholar Mukhtār wuld Ḥāmidun maintains that 'the form of Ḥassānīya poetry is derived from *zajal* and *muwashshaḥāt*.[1] Andalusian influences came into the country through cultural and commercial connexions, and especially the invasion of the Banū Ḥassān from the Maghrib, where they had remained for many centuries and were influenced by the environment; likewise through the Almoravids, although no example of theirs survives locally; and from Timbuctoo and the Sa'dian rulers who opened up direct communications between inner Africa and Morocco.' This Spanish influence is confirmed, quite independently, by the author of the *Kitāb al-Wasīṭ*, who quotes a Classical Arabic poem composed by the Tīris poet, Limjaydrī wuld Ḥabīballāh.[2] The vocabulary is Classical Arabic but the structure of the poem is Ḥassānīya. It is a *gaaf* of three verses, and three *aṭla'*, each of three verses. The author describes it as an example of *tawshīḥ*, adding that it is known to the people of the Sahara as *al-ghinā'* (*leġna*). Ibn Khaldūn mentions a form of poem very similar to the *ṭal'a* in vogue in the fourteenth century. 'The Arabs have another kind of poetry,' he writes, 'which is widely in use among them. It employs four lines (*ajzā'*) of which the fourth has a rhyme different from the first three. The fourth rhyme is then continued in each verse through the whole poem.'[3]

In addition to the *gaaf* and the *ṭal'a*, there are other forms of

[1] Muwashshaḥ and zajal were strophic forms of poetry which had become popular in Arabic Spain by the beginning of the eleventh century. Both forms were based on a refrain, and they were sung. Zajal was improvised until Abū Bakr Ibn Quzmān (d. 1160) made it a literary form. Muwashshaḥ developed in Spain, whence it spread into North Africa and the East. Zajal and muwashshaḥ inspired the Castilian popular verse form of villancico which was used for hymns and Christmas carols. A typical scheme of a muwashshaḥ is aa bbbaa cccaa dddaa, etc. For a detailed study of the relation between these two forms see S. M. Stern, 'Studies on Ibn Quzmān', *El Andalus*, vol. xvi (1951), pp. 380–4.

[2] *Kitāb al-Wasīṭ*, p. 216.

[3] Ibn Khaldūn, *Muqaddima* (tr. F. Rosenthal), New York, 1958, vol. iii, p. 414.

poem where the rhyme scheme is uniform in a series of hemistichs. Reference has already been made to the *rasm*, where the number is four. Another kind of poem known as *mzaareg* ('that which rushes') has a uniform rhyme scheme of three hemistichs, in the pattern a a b, a a b, a a b, etc. Lastly, mention should be made of the *tebraaʿ*, a poem of the Mauritanian women. In this category are to be found songs which they improvise about a lover or a husband, where the rhyme is uniform and the metre is regarded as separate from those already discussed.

Ḥassānīya poetry is a form of *zajal* suited to the peculiarities of the dialect, closely linked to the music of the region. It has evolved its own prosody, perhaps its most original feature, in order to systematize its syllabic forms. Its inspiration came first from the north; it established itself in the southern Sahara, then once more returned to the north, the Ḥassānīya-speaking tribes beyond the Jabal Banī of southern Morocco again adopting and adapting the prosody and style of this southern poetry. In the course of its evolution it has incorporated Saharan Berber elements and the music, both primitive and complex, of the neighbouring Sūdānic cultures of Māli and Senegal.

6

MUSICIANS AND POETS

In a reference to the poetry and music of his fellow countrymen the author of the *Kitāb al-Wasīṭ* has this to say about those who make it their profession. He is addressing an Arabic-speaking reader in the Near East, and he wishes to point out certain individual characteristics of the arts of the Saharans. 'This *zajal*', he writes, 'is called *ghinā*', and he who performs it is called a *mughannī* (singer) whether he be learned or ignorant, noble or lowly. He is not the same as the singer known in the Orient because the latter is a person who sings to the people for hire. Such is not the case in Shinqīṭ, since the term is only applied to a caste known as the *īggāwen*. He who sings and is not of this caste is called a *nashshād*.'[1]

Here the author makes a very clear distinction between the *īggīw* and the *nashshād*, and the reason is not merely one of class distinction but also of moral standing. The *īggāwen* occupy an ambivalent position in the eyes of their fellows. It is as though Moorish society has been forced to accept them as fulfilling a useful if not essential role in their community. Yet at the same time they are despised, partly because their profession in no way reflects the higher goals which the Islamic tradition enjoins. There is a local saying that 'the *murābiṭ* cannot be a friend of the *īggīw*'. They are also disliked because they scatter their praise and their flattery on all and sundry for pecuniary reward. To the more puritanical Zwāya, their greed and their ability to threaten a foe or hold a friend to ransom have branded them as immoral, corrupt, and as base in nature as they are low in social status. 'Suspect the *īggīw*,' say the Zwāya, 'his tongue is hidden beneath his beard like the viper in the grass.' Their detractors have gone further; traditions have even been invented to damn them, and the greatest figures of early Islam have been enlisted in the cause. It is said that the first *īggāwen* came one day to the mosque to ask the Prophet Muḥammad for something good to eat. The latter having

[1] *Kitāb al-Wasīṭ*, p. 75.

nothing to give them at the time, and weary of their importunity, offered them a few blessed hairs from his beard. Instead of keeping them they sold them for a paltry sum. It was then that ʿAlī said to them, 'If you had kept them you would have gained all you could have wished for, but since you have sold them you will be neither rich nor poor.' It is for this reason that the *īggāwen* are always so needy.

Yet even among the Zwāya there were always voices raised in their defence, arguing that music and song were far from being worldly occupations, were indeed spiritually most rewarding, as many sayings of the Prophet testified. Moreover, the author of a master work of Arabic literature, the *Kitāb al-aghānī*, had nothing but praise for this art, which above all others harmonized the soul with the divine, and was a source of great joy in an otherwise harsh and monotonous environment. The warriors had no such ethical qualms, because although the troubadours were expensive they were essential in the intertribal combats which raged among the Mauritanians. In battle the *īggāwen* excited and sustained the ardour of the combatants; they played the lute, the *tidīnīt*, and chanted in the style known as *faaġu*. They tended to keep away from the fighting and only approached the battlefield when the battle was over. Even so acts of bravery by them were not unknown.

To the average Moor of modern times, now that the tribal wars are over and the former class distinctions have less impact, the *īggīw* of outstanding merit is no longer subject to moral or social discrimination. The *īggīw* and the *tīggiwīt*, men or women, are appreciated for their intrinsic musical accomplishments. A singer's 'fans' will dispute the respective merits of a player, or the quality of his or her voice may arouse the intense affection or aversion of rival partisans. In Mauritania everybody is fascinated by the artist's skill, and by the emotional impact and response this music and the accompanying poetry produce. A contemporary *īggīw* such as Sīdāti wuld Abba has become identified with national culture and national aspirations since Mauritanian independence.

The difference outlined in the *Kitāb al-Wasīṭ* between the Mauritanian and the Oriental singer is not as striking as the fact that the Moors differ entirely from the Tuaregs in this respect. It would seem natural to find a close parallel between the two societies, in view of a common social and historical heritage. But among the Tuaregs there is no class specifically concerned with music and its performance. The Tuareg women, for example, rarely sing before the men, yet among the Moors a visit to a *tīggiwīt* to hear a performance on the *ardīn*, the Moorish harp, is a regular, if expensive, entertainment. Many women musicians are famous and rich, and their opulence is often matched by their obesity. Such a performer as Yāqūta mint ʿAlī Warakān, now resident in the old town of Nouakchott, is able to support a comfortable, well furnished house; and, like so many of the *īggāwen*, she jealously guards her songs and recitals, in these days when there is extensive tape-recording for nation-wide broadcasting, and rivalry and competition amongst the *īggāwen* themselves. She has unlimited pride in her own talents, as the following improvised poem of hers reveals:

From what ruby, O Lord of the throne, is Yāqūta?
From the source of pearl and ruby she is fashioned.
In the form of a dark-eyed ḥūrī He has shaped her,
As He wished, and the people love Yāqūta.
Yāqūta, her renown is supreme, and any youth
Who says the name Yāqūta, then her name is his sustenance.
There is no lady like her in Mauritania,
Nor in Senegal, nor Gambia, nor Fūta.
She is the full moon, but without a blemish in it, and
Her spouse is a sea, but without a great fish in it.

Īggīw is a word borrowed from communities across the river. It is *gêwel* in Wolof and *gawlo* in Toucouleur. The Mauritanian form of the word has a Znāga stamp, as is shown by its feminine form, *tīggiwīt* (plural *tīggāwāten*). The Sūdānic character of the name of the musician class in Mauritania, and the fact that this class is absent in the central Sahara, support the supposition that in this respect Moorish society, at least in the Trārza and the Ḥawḍ, has been greatly influenced by the culture of Māli and its neighbours. Ibn Baṭṭūṭa, in describing the entourage of Mansa Sulaymān, mentions the court singers and their gold and silver *gambri*s, and adds that the Sultan's special bard played on an instrument of reeds and gourds while singing poetry in praise of the Sultan and his deeds, accompanied by female musicians.

The Sarakollé of Guidimakha, Soninké tribes settled in the river regions of southern Mauritania, also have a musician class, the *diarou*, who have a special status beneath the warrior nobles and the *murābiṭūn*. Each noble family has its own family *diarou*, with a special role to play. They accompany the men in battle, praise their victories, and in our days recount and sing the story of the family and their genealogy. Each *diaré* who succeeds his father adds something of his own invention. The *diarou*, like their Moorish counterparts, had a right to say what they liked. Certain of the bards in the Sūdānic communities achieved an even higher status. They were the kings' counsellors, they memorized the constitution, tutored the young princes, and were the archivists of their masters' family traditions.

It is reasonable to assume that this type of society was once typical of Mauritania, as of its neighbours, since culturally far more of the country was then Sūdānic than is now the case. Nevertheless, there was also a type of musician akin to those of other Saharan nomads, who was typical of the kind of bard found in other Arab lands, a descendant of the great poets of pre-Islamic Arabia. Many of the existing musician families in Mauritania are of ancient stock, and as these families never marry outside their class they have maintained their family traditions from generation to generation without a break. In the Trārza, for example, can be found the Ahl Mānu, the Ahl al-Būbbāna, the Ahl ʿAlī Warakān, and the Ahl Ingdhay; while among the Awlād Mubārak, there are the Ahl Nǰartu and the Ahl Gharḍ. It is to Saddūm wuld Nǰartu, Gharḍ wuld Balghām, and ʿAlī wuld Mānu that the Moors owe fundamental changes and innovations in their music and their poetry, but how much of this is fact, and how much tradition, embellished by tribal pride, will probably never be known. At least throughout the nineteenth century the *īggāwen* played an important part in Mauritanian history, and their customs, their arts, and their social standing acquired a definite form. Within it they blended in an ingenious way the arts of the musicians of the Sūdān, those of the Arab and Berber-speaking Saharan tribes, and musical traditions of the Maghrib of a far higher and more sophisticated order.

Perhaps the most famous of all families of *īggāwen* in Mauritania is that of ʿAli Khaja wuld al-Dandān, who was born in the Ḥawḍ, among the tribes near to the Māli border, during the late seventeenth century. His lute, his *tidīnīt*, called 'Umm laʿbāra', which was of gigantic size, soon gained him a reputation amongst the tribes whom he inspired to fight in time of battle, and all the chiefs competed for his favours. He left a son called Njartu, who was able to recite his poetry, and to play an instrument well, before he came of age. As he grew up he too acquired a reputation, particularly among the tribes in eastern Mauritania. He encouraged the warriors in battle, like his father, but he never took part in a battle because he was of too low a status to be killed. It was a great disgrace at the time that an *īggīw* should die in this way, and if a tribe was bereft of, or lacked, *īggāwen*, then it was a sure indication that it lacked standing or honour in the community. Njartu had a son called Saddūm. He was more renowned than his father and his grandfather. He grew up amongst the Kunta tribe at Qaṣr al-Barka, until his renown spread far and wide. It was said that his voice was louder than the sound of any musical instrument. He continued to perfect his art and to improve the form of the musical instruments he played; he systematically arranged the music of his time into separate scales, entries, rhythms, and moods; and he modified poetic forms to suit the music. Before his time the odes composed in praise of the chiefs were improvised according to no special pattern, and the accompanying music was Arab in type. Not only did Saddūm systematize poetic metre and rhyme, but he also introduced Sūdānic forms of singing into the music and established the principle of two distinct kinds of music, the 'white' and the 'black', each indicating its respective source of inspiration. His example was followed by other musicians and poets, and the people flocked to hear him. When war broke out between the Kunta and the Īdaw 'Īsh, Saddūm went to the tribes of the Brākna and then to the Awlād Mubārak. But the tradition of each Mauritanian tribe tries to associate Saddūm in some way with its victories and achievements. It is said that he went from one tribe to another, praising every Amīr and staying with him for a short time, then moving to the court of another. On one occasion when war took place between the Awlād Mubārak and other Ḥassānī tribes, Saddūm returned to the Kunta. The story of the family then became linked to the Īdaw 'Īsh, where the great Amīr, Bakkār wuld A'mar (d. 1761/2), persuaded Saddūm to stay in Tagānit, and granted him a regular duty on the caravans. When a split occurred among the Īdaw 'Īsh, Jaysh, the elder son of Saddūm, followed the chief of the Abakāk and the younger, Muḥammad (Maḥmādu), followed the Shrātīt. According to Mauritanian tradition, Muḥammad married Mint al-Zamal, and had a number of sons, two of the most noted being Abba Fāl and ʿAlī. As for Jaysh, there is a tradition that he ended his days among the Kunta. According to one tradition his son Abba had three sons, all noted *īggāwen*, Saddūm, Alfa, and Ubbād. Alfa dwelt in the camp of the chief of the Awlād Sayyid al-Wāfī, and married Garmi, the daughter of Mint al-Zamal; from her he had three sons, Sīdāti wuld Abba, al-Shaykh wuld Abba, and Saddūm wuld Abba, and three daughters, al-Lūla, Mulla, and al-Zuwayn.

'Saddūm, the second son, dwelt in the camp of the Awlād Sayyid Bū Bakr, but he did not marry amongst them. He composed a very famous *kerza* in *thaydiina*, called *anna*, in which the genealogy of all the Kunta tribe is extolled, and he is credited with the following line in Ḥassānīya:

> O God, if you slay me, then do not slay me save amongst the Kunta.

Of all the family of Saddūm wuld Njartu he is held to be the most like him in his poetry and his singing, but not in his taste in music. His extensive repertoire, however, gave him the widest reputation. Eventually he left Tagānit and went to the Adrār, where the Amīr Aḥmad wuld Aḥmad wuld ʿAydda received him and made him his *īggīw*. He stayed in the Adrār for the rest of his life. He had no offspring save a daughter Layta, whose mother was a slave girl, and a blind son called Jaysh.

Ubbād, the third son, is noted for his tall stature, and his very large *tidīnīt*. He does not sing, nor does he put poetry to music, and the reason for his lack of tuition in all the arts and accomplishments of the *īggāwen* is that his mother was a slave girl, and that he grew up with his mother; but he is a noted player of the *tidīnīt*. He has one son, Saddūm, who was brought up by his uncle Saddūm wuld Abba, and he is as competent a musician as his father in Āṭār, the Adrār capital, where they live.'[1]

All of the *īggāwen* have poetic talent, but by no means all of the great Mauritanian poets in Ḥassānīya are *īggāwen* or are capable of playing an instrument with skill. There are as many outstanding poets in this art as there are musicians. Names such as Muḥammad wuld Haddār, ʿAbd Masūma, and Muḥammad wuld Aḥmad Yūra are continually being quoted as the composers of poems suitable for singing both in Classical Arabic and in Ḥassānīya.

[1] *sic* M. Bulla wuld al-Shaybānī al-Kuntī.

According to the author of the *Kitāb al-Wasīṭ*, Muḥammad wuld Haddār was renowned for his singing. He was a member of the tribe of Liḥrākāt, one which had a reputation for skill in composing in Ḥassānīya, and he was a master of short witty verses on local subjects. But some of his poems are of far greater length and substance, in particular one addressed to the Amīr of the Trārza, Sīdī wuld Muḥammad al-Ḥabīb (d. 1871). The latter had given Muḥammad wuld Haddār the task of copying the great commentary on Khalīl, *al-Muyassar al-kabīr*, by the scholar Maḥanḍ Bābā (d. 1860). When he had finished his task the poet wished to keep the paper he had not used for his copy—hence a reference in his poem to the surplus being the right of the artisan. As the Amīr demanded the paper back, the poet wished to compose a satire against him. However, when he realized that he risked having his tongue cut out as a punishment, he composed this poem, which both enhanced his reputation and brought him financial reward (Chapter 9, poem no. 5).

The names of ʿAbd Masūma and Muḥammad wuld Haddār are linked in a folk story which centres on the grievous fate of the former, when his master, convinced of the slave's love of his wife, tied him to a stake to perish. The source of the story is Muṣṭafā wuld Ačfagha ʿAmar of the Ahl Haddār.

Muḥammad wuld Haddār was once madly in love. One day he composed two hemistichs of a poem in honour of his mistress, but he found himself unable to finish it, and like many other poets he went away to seek out a colleague who would complete it for him in the same rhyme and with the right meaning. It was then that Muḥammad wuld Haddār, after days of wandering, arrived at the site of a camp where he found ʿAbd Masūma tied to a stake in the sun. Muḥammad greeted him and then asked him why he was in such a plight, but the slave poet did not reply. Muḥammad then approached to loosen him, but the other indicated that he had no wish to be freed. Then Muḥammad realized that he too was in love. In order to confirm his suspicions he began to recite a poem in front of the slave, beginning 'Oh my eye, you have dispersed your tears'. In reply ʿAbd Masūma began to recite his famous verses, 'I remained in the camp to weep, and the grooves of my cheeks are a witness to it'.

Muḥammad realized that this poor slave was not only in love but that he was also a poet, none other than the one he was looking for. He asked him to complete his poem, in metre *lubb^{w}ayr*. The slave replied, 'If it is connected with love, yes, if not, then I am unable to do so.' Muḥammad recited his two hemistichs:

baali bilmawsam yenkwa : warmaag ed-damʿa kaaṣu :

'My heart is branded by the fire, and my eye-lids blinded by tears',

and immediately the slave poet completed the *gaaf* with two other hemistichs:

kiif el-ʿuud alli yenšwa : raaṣu u neznez raaṣu :

'Just like the stick which is roasted at one end, and water flows from it at the other.'

This poem is an echo of a poem by another Moor, Muʿāwiya wuld al-Sadd al-Tandag͟hī, in Classical Arabic:

My eye and heart hurt and watered after your departure. Two slaves are a branch in the green Egyptian willow. Water flows on one side of it, when a fire, kindled on its other side, blazes.

The *Kitāb al-Wasīṭ* mentions a poet of the Īdaw ʿAlī, al-Hādī wuld Muḥammad, who was a jurist and a reciter of poetry, pious and austere. He was extremely witty and had a knowledge of how to hold the attention of assemblies. He was a master in both Classical Arabic and Ḥassānīya poetry, and the people differed in their verdict as to whether one was more successful than the other. His greatest foes were the warriors of Ḥassān, who feared his tongue, for he was for ever mentioning their bad habits in his colloquial verses. The common people could remember these, and were influenced far more than if the verses had been composed in Classical Arabic verse.

Amongst more recent poets in the vernacular, equally talented in Classical Arabic and Znāga, was the Trārza scholar, Muḥammad wuld Aḥmad Yūra al-Daymānī, who was born in 1855 and died in 1922. He entertained the assembly, was swift at repartee, and was keen-witted, alert, and skilled in the literary arts. His poetry is noted for its simplicity and its conciseness, and, in his Classical Arabic verse, for the introduction of Ḥassānīya expressions or sayings current amongst the Mauritanians. He was a scholar, with an encyclopedic knowledge of the history and the topography of the Trārza, where he was semi-permanently encamped. His poetry of all kinds follows both the mood and the form of Moorish *leġna*, and apart from vocabulary and metre there is little difference in character to distinguish them. The following are examples in Classical Arabic:

Al-Abaytar yonder has appeared and al-Buḥbūḥ will appear shortly after. May not the heavy downpour which goes at morn and at even to those haunts be intermittent!

O Lord of Moses who called him in the valley, grant us blessing in the tent of Ibn ʿAyyād, a tent the lord of which rejoices at the guests' coming, amidst tea-glass, kettle, and silver teapot.

O thou because of whom my heart is infatuated and well-nigh crazed. Slay not my heart, my heart is captivated. You slew it once in time, and it said 'nine' just as Gābūn said 'nine'.[1]

Muḥammad wuld Aḥmad Yūra was equally a master in Ḥassānīya, and one of his most delightful poems is addressed to a camel. It is a *ṭalʿa* in metre *lebtayt en-naageṣ*.[2]

The poet is addressing a difficult camel which had been given to him by his in-laws. It was a custom in Mauritania that, when a man married, his wife-to-be bought him a camel, a cow or two, or a small flock. His wife presented Muḥammad wuld Aḥmad Yūra with a decrepit camel. He said to the latter:

O al-Wag͟hra—look at that well yonder, the cause of my misfortune (because my beloved is there). I know, may God watch over you, that you are weary and the midday heat is great, and that you are old in years, and that the water which you have drunk has made you heavier and weaker. But in spite of all, oh al-Wag͟hra, journey on a little—you are not despised (?).

[1] The poet here refers to the local story of a hyena who challenged a lion to a buffeting contest. The hyena smote the other ten times without any effect. The lion in his turn struck once, whereupon the hyena cried, 'Nine, spare me the tenth'.

[2] René Basset provides a version of the text in his *Mission au Sénégal*, Paris, 1909, pp. 618–19.

7

MAURITANIAN MUSICAL INSTRUMENTS, RECITALS, AND DANCES

THE Moors would agree with the saying of a medieval troubadour that 'verse without song is like a mill without water', but in order to sustain a song, to give it weight, colour, and excitement the singer needs the accompaniment of a musical instrument, whether he plays it by himself or whether he is a participant in a small orchestra.

In this respect the Moors, considering their nomadic life and their poor resources, are remarkably accomplished and talented. They have adopted a range of musical instruments suited to their needs. Some of the instruments are akin to, if not identical with, those of their Sūdānic neighbours, while others are so individual as to distinguish the sound of their music from that of any other kind of Arab or Berber music in north-west Africa.

The simpler instruments are those to be expected in any African community. The typical drum, *ṭbal*, is a half calabash with a skin stretched over it to form a resonator. It is tied to a stake driven into the ground. The drum is now the instrument of *ḥrāṭīn*, but in older days it was used to transmit messages, and it summoned the warriors to battle. Another kind of percussion instrument is the *daghamma*. It is a very elongated gourd which has been dried and emptied of its contents. It is wider at one end than the other. Both ends of it are open. The left hand manipulates the wider end of the instrument, which rests against the soft inner parts of the thigh or the calf, while the right palm opens and closes the upper narrower opening according to a determined rhythm. The sound is dull and heavy, but it is enhanced by the noise of the rings or the bracelets on the hands and arms of those who perform with this instrument. Another percussion instrument is known as a *gaḥgāḥ*. It is pear-shaped and has a single opening at the top. It is held in both hands and beaten rhythmically on a rug laid on the ground in front of the performer. The *kuṣel* is a much smaller gourd, filled with small stones and shaken while certain dances are being performed.

Mauritanian wind instruments are of an equally simple kind, even if great skill is demanded from the player. The *naffāra* (pl. *anfafīr*) is a small flute peculiar to the region of Tagānit. A more widespread instrument is the *zawzāya* (pl. *zawzāyāt*) played by the herders and *ḥrāṭīn*, and cut from the root of the tree called *ṭalḥ* (*Acacia tortilis*).

Stringed instruments, however, are the true accompaniment to poetry in Mauritania, and the way they are made and played is a testimony to the ingenuity and musical talent of the *īggāwen*, who throughout the course of their history have created a vast repertoire and a variety of styles and manners of playing them. Among the children and the *ḥrāṭīn* the musical bow is popular (*zagʿārī*, pl. *zgāʿīr*). It is made from a piece of curved wood, with a cord of either plaited string, leather, or palm-fibre. In between the string and the wood, which is placed on the ground, the performer rests a half calabash held in position by his left knee. This calabash acts as a resonator. The player holds the bow with his left hand and strikes the cord with his right, somewhere between the bow and the dome of the inverted calabash.

The rebec (*rbāb* or *gambra*) is an instrument of the *ḥrāṭīn*. It is a kind of lute with a single string. It is a very ancient instrument in the Sahara and is not unlike the Tuareg *amzad* or monocord violin, which the women play with a bow.

The two chief instruments in Mauritanian music are the lute, *tidīnīt* (pl. *tidānaten*), and the harp, *ardīn* (pl. *irdīwen*). Both these instruments have unusual features which suggest extra-Saharan connexions, either in their form or in the way they are played and used. The *tidīnīt*, for example, is not untypical of West Africa. But the fact that it has four strings distinguishes it from some other instruments from neighbouring regions beyond the Senegal river. The traveller Cadamosto, writing in the fifteenth century, notes that in the kingdom of Senegal 'They have no musical instruments of any kind, save two, the one is a large Moorish "tanbuchi" which we style a big drum; the other is after the fashion of a viol; but it has, however, two strings only, and is played with the fingers, so that it is a simple rough affair and of no account.'[1] Yet

[1] *The Voyages of Cadamosto*, translated by G. R. Crone, Hakluyt Society, no. lxxx, London, 1937, p. 51.

by the time René Caillié travelled in West Africa the Moorish lute had five strings, which have since been reduced to four, each string representing, so certain scholars say, a humour or temperament.[1] This idea is reflected in the type of music to be played on the instrument and the type of verse to be sung to the sound of it. In Mauritania again, unlike certain other regions, the lute is not usually plucked with the nails, but with a bone blade mounted on a leather ring (*ḍfar īggīw*) worn on the index finger of the player's right hand. It seems clear, however, from earlier accounts, such as that of Father Labat, which describes the Moorish nomads when they were in the process of settling in western areas of the Sahara, that their poetry was accompanied by musical instruments that resembled guitars.

The *tidīnīt* is an instrument played only by men. It is made from *ādres* wood (*Commifora africana*). This tree has a smooth bark used for a variety of purposes, to tan skins used for carrying water, and to make sandals and various kinds of milking receptacles. It is used in the fabric of tents, for friction lighting, and for small mortars. The resonator (*tāzuwwa*) (1, see fig. opposite) is oval-shaped with a slightly pinched waist. A piece of skin is stretched over it. There is a circular opening in the skin for the firm attachment of the lower part of the handle to the body of the instrument. Often the rim of the resonator has percussion rings attached at fixed intervals. The instrument has a long copper or wooden handle, which is sometimes richly decorated with inlaid silver. At the extremity of the handle is a flat piece of iron (*ḥarba*) (2) edged with a row of silver or copper rings (*k͟hurṣ*, pl. *ak͟hrāṣ*) (3). The instrument has four strings made from horse-hair. The *īggāwen* like the hairs to be fine. They are more sensitive to the touch, and it is easier for the player to combine the two ways of the 'black' and the 'white'. The two central strings are known as *al-muhrayn* (s. *muhr*) (4), while the two outer have a Znāga name (*tās͟hubbaṭ*, pl. *tīs͟hubbṭen*) (5). The latter are shorter than the former. The strings are fixed to the upper part of the handle by leather rolls at spaced intervals. A string which is nearer to the instrumentalist when he plays is called *taḥtāni* (lower), and the one which is further away is called *fawgāni* (upper). The strings are stretched above the skin of the resonator and attached to the bifurcated base of the handle (*tāmunānt*—canoe) (6), which is fixed centrally in the resonator. The strings are raised well above the

[1] René Caillié, *Journal d'un voyage à Tembuctou*, Paris, 1824–8, p. 94.

level of the stretched skin cover, by means of a four-notched bridge (*ṣaydāḥ*—female camel) made from a piece of calabash. It is attached to the fork of the handle. The seated player supports the instrument on the right side of his chest and holds it horizontally. He places the handle of the *tidīnīt* between the thumb and the four fingers of his left hand, with his fingers resting on the strings. With his right hand relaxed the player strikes the strings with the extremity of his nails or with the bone blade fixed to his index finger. A very skilled player will use only three of the strings.

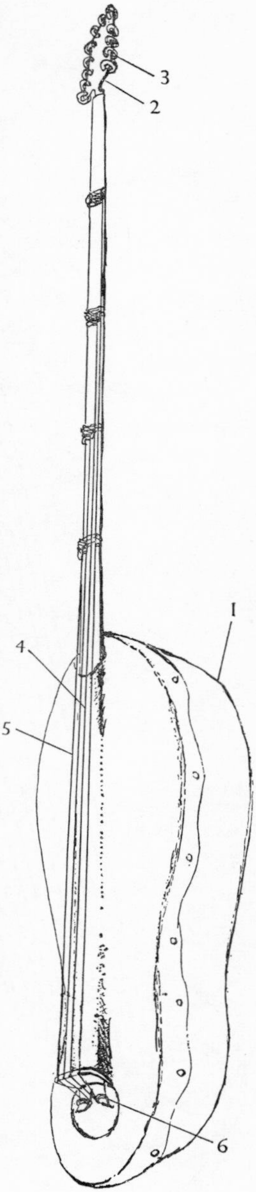

The *ardīn* (fig. on p. 64), a harp played only by women, has a resonator made from a half calabash, the lower part of which is known as *laghshāsha*. The top of it is covered by a stretched skin sewn at the edges. Two engraved metal plaques (*ḥarba*) (1), edged with silver or copper rings (*khurṣ*, pl. *akhrāṣ*) (2), rest on the skin and act as a percussion instrument. The player of the instrument may have partners on either side of her who will either tap the skin with their palms or beat it with their fingers. In either case the plaques will vibrate. The interior surface of the skin is sometimes decorated with talismans and magical inscriptions, while the outer, visible, face is not infrequently decorated and painted geometrically with designs typical of Mauritanian leather-work. The rest of the frame of the instrument consists of a handle and a transverse arm. The long wooden handle (*ʿamūd*) (3) is fixed at an oblique angle to the skin stretched over the calabash, and its base often rests on a shell at the bottom of the calabash.

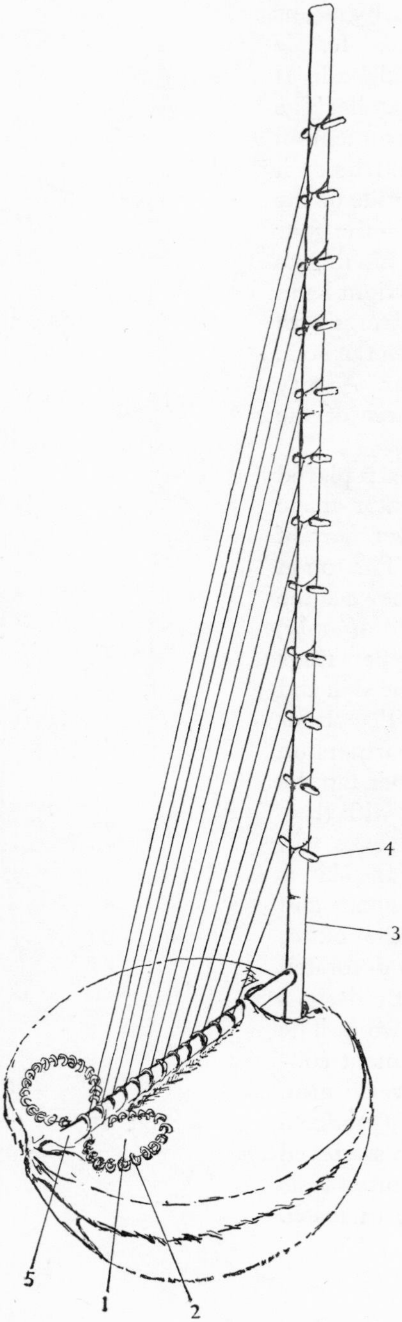

The earliest description of a Mauritanian instrumentalist I have so far discovered is the portrait of an *ardīn* player by the French traveller Sieur de la Courbe, who first journeyed in this region in 1685:

'Ensuitte, elles firent chanter leur guiriote; elle tenoit une espece de harpe dont le corps fait d'une calbace couvert de cuir avoit dix ou douze cordes qu'elle touchoit assez agreablement; elle commença donc a entonner une chanson arabe assez melodieuse, mais fort languissante, a peu pres a la maniere des Espagnols ou Portugais, l'accompagnant de sa harpe avec beaucoup de mesure, mais ce qu'il y avoit de plus agreable c'est qu'elle se passionnoit extremement et faisoit quantité de petites façons et de mouvements de teste, faisant remuer a mesure tous les gris gris et pendeloques, montrant les plus belles dents du monde; tout ce que je trouvay a redire, c'est que ses mots parroissoient extremement rudes et comme tirez du gosier.'

Premier voyage du Sieur de la Courbe fait à la Coste d'Afrique en 1685, published by P. Cultru, Paris, 1913; page 172.

There are ten to thirteen holes for pegs (*debbūs*) (4) in the handle. The sheepgut strings (*laʿṣab*) are fixed with loops to these pegs. At the bottom these same strings are wound at intervals on the shorter transverse arm (*tāmunānt*), (5) which bisects the skin top immediately above the *ḥarba*. The extremity of this arm is held in position by a raised portion of the skin. The performer places the harp on the ground against her right leg which is folded close to her body. Her left hand, the back of it resting on her knee, grasps the handle, which is supported by her shoulder. The handle is placed between her thumb and fingers. She strikes the strings with the nails of her right hand.

The art of playing both these instruments requires years of training and instruction, and it is not uncommon to find miniature models of both instruments in the houses and tents of the *īggāwen*. Their sole purpose is to instruct children in the technique of the instruments they are learning to play.

The musicians are either visited, or are asked to perform by a family or a camp on a special occasion, in a private gathering or at a public feast. Thus the *īggāwen* are always on the move, although the further north the tribe is located, the fewer are the visits paid by the *īggāwen*, and those in regions of the Spanish Sahara have usually come from the Trārza or elsewhere in Mauritania. When an *īggīw* performs, it is usual for the singer to face his musical accompaniment, two, three, or four musicians, and for his audience to be in a semicircle. Poems are sometimes composed impromptu and the singer is asked to interpret them. The audience joins in the performance at suitable points by rhythmic clapping or exclamations of praise, although this is deemed to be unseemly if songs in *baygi*, the mood of sorrow and of nostalgia, are being sung, or if musical compositions in this style are being played. Sometimes the musicians will form a line, with, for example, two players of the *tidīnīt*, a singer, and a player of the *ardīn*. The Moors have no objections to men and women participating in the same musical performance. As the author of the *Kitāb al-Wasīṭ* remarks, 'he who loves to listen, goes to them (i.e. to the *īggāwen*) in their homes, and they sing to him, both their male and their female, their youth and their elder, and not one of them has any feelings of embarrassment in front of the other.'[1] Before a musician begins, he needs a short period of preparation in order to clear his voice or tune his

[1] *Kitāb al-Wasīṭ*, p. 75.

instrument; then, satisfied that he is ready to begin, he enters on the particular scale demanded by the nature of the poem he is singing. The skill of the *īggāwen* in this respect has impressed every listener who has been entertained by them. 'They have "strings"' (instruments), quotes the *Kitāb al-Wasīṭ*, 'which they strike and which have strings of gut. If one of them strikes his string, he who is expert among those who are present knows in what "mode" he is playing, and the latter corresponds to the poetic metre from which he has recited a verse, be it *al-ṭawīl* or *al-basīṭ*.'[1]

To Western ears the singing of the *īggāwen* is often harsh, although a singer like Yāqūta mint ʿAlī Warakān has a very sweet-toned voice, gentle and rather sad. The men singers have great power and extreme range in their voices, and at the climax of their singing they drape their blue or black turbans over the lower part of their faces in order to accentuate the sound of their singing. If they know that they are going to tax their voices, the *īggāwen* drink a potion (*girigṭa*) to counteract fatigue. This drink, which must be swallowed lukewarm, is made from fat, salt, sugar, pepper, and onions cut up into small morsels and then mixed in water.

A concert of Mauritanian music can be of long duration, and it is natural that the singers should prefer short poems or verses which introduce a variety of rhymes or rhythms in their structure. Hence the need for a refrain, to knit an ode together and to break the tendency to monotony.

Moorish folk-dancing, and similar forms of display and entertainment, may not have the colour and splendour of those in Morocco, among the Berbers of the Atlas for instance, or of those of 'black Africa', but they are a vital part of local cultural activities. Dancing is a custom, for example, among the Mauritanian women when participating in a social gathering among themselves, and it is sometimes quite impromptu, revealing a talent for mimicking the movements of birds, animals, and human types.

Further north, in the Spanish Sahara, where musicians are less common, dances of various kinds are performed both in the camps and publicly in centres such as ʿAyūn al-sāqiya (El-Aaiun). Señor Angel Morales, in describing the Río de Oro, has noted that festivals and dances there are invariably accompanied by singing and the rhythmic beat of a tamtam. At weddings, and during circumcision ceremonies, the *īggīw* sits cross-legged to the sound of

[1] *Kitāb al-Wasīṭ*, p. 75.

drumming and then moves the upper part of his body in an effeminate way to the rhythm of the song, while singing in a melodious voice. After acclamation by his audience, he rests, then clasps his hands and changes to songs of war and battle. The tamtam beat is accentuated and, while he sings, those who are present, seated in a circle, accompany him with a refrain. All their bodies swing from side to side, and they beat the palms of their hands. The rhythmic beat becomes faster and faster, and it seems as if the head of the performer is detached from his neck. Suddenly there is silence, and the performance ends. Comments are exchanged, and glasses of tea are circulated to the participants.

Among these northern dances, the *gedra* has achieved world-wide fame. It is associated with the 'blue men' of the south Moroccan town of Goulimine, although it is typical of all the Ḥassānīya-speaking Moorish tribes of the Moroccan Sahara and adjacent districts. It is not at all typical of Mauritania, further to the south. A dance similar to it is described by the English traveller Jackson, who visited Morocco at the end of the eighteenth century:

> Amongst the Arabs the girls dance in a very superior style; the Arabian ladies of the Mograffra tribe, as well as those of Walad Abbusebah, eminently excel. I remember passing a night in one of their douars, on the confines of the Sahara, with a large party of Arabs, and instead of going to sleep, the Sheikh of the douar sent for six elegant females, who engaged our admiration till the morning. Judging of the movements of these dancing Arabs with the sentiments of an Englishman, they would be thought somewhat lascivious, but the manners and customs of the country reconciles to propriety these spirited movements. Signor Andrea de Christo, a Venetian merchant, was with me, and declared he had never seen better dancing in Italy.[1]

Nowadays the performance of a *gedra* is invariably included in the folklore festivals held in Morocco. It has been recorded on disc and filmed, on innumerable occasions. It is an extremely profitable and often routine tourist attraction; nevertheless, a well-danced *gedra* can still be an exciting and colourful spectacle. If in the past it has been the erotic nature of certain of the dancers' movements, the sight of their half-naked abandon, and the co-ordinated clapping by their kneeling male accompanists, which have been the chief attraction for the writers and illustrators of travel books,

[1] *The Empire of Marocco*, p. 159.

there are other writers on the Spanish Sahara and elsewhere who have drawn attention to the long hours of preparation these dancers must endure in order to beautify their appearance for the occasion, and the attention which they must pay to their hair, their jewellery, their toilet, and the dyeing of their hands with *ḥinnā*'. This, combined with the subtle gestures and movements of the dancers' arms and hands, and their perfect poise when seated or kneeling, transforms the *gedra* into something far more artistic and elegant than the frenzied drumming in the background suggests: something more akin to artistry of a high order, typical of the great musicians of Mauritania.

8

THE BACKGROUND OF MAURITANIAN MUSIC

THE originality of Ḥassānīya poetry is not as great as the originality of the music to which it is sung. The varied influences which have entered this region from Nearer Asia, and from the Maghrib and the Sūdān, have transmuted the music into an original art which is adaptable enough to provide the accompaniment to poetry in whatever metre, whether it be in Classical Arabic or in Ḥassānīya.

Up to now this music has not been the subject of a detailed study. Those who have described it in general terms or who have recorded examples of its styles have been faced with two formidable obstacles: on the one hand the reticence which the *īggāwen* have shown in discussing or explaining the complexities of their art, and on the other the fact that their whole musical tradition, like the poetical, is an oral tradition; most of the *īggāwen* do not possess the neat, pigeon-hole mentality of the Occident.

One cause of misunderstanding is the use of two different words, *leġna* and *azawaan*. It now seems clear that *leġna* is a popular term, which simply means 'sung folk poetry'. The term *azawaan*, a word derived from the Arabic word *wazn*, meaning 'measure', is applied exclusively to the music. It is the instrumental art of the *īggāwen*, and songs in both Classical Arabic and Ḥassānīya are sung in the various *ḍhuur* into which *azawaan* is divided.

Azawaan is an Arabic type of music. It came from the Near East, has spread and developed in the Maghrib, Spain, and elsewhere, and extended its influence to east, to west, and across the Sahara as the handmaid of Islamic culture. *Azawaan* is a type of music which is fundamentally a series of songs or of instrumental pieces arranged in a certain order, so as to form a kind of suite, where each movement contrasts with its predecessor, and yet at the same time the suite retains an underlying unity of style, idiom, and development which maintains the continuity, and which arouses and then satisfies the emotions of the listener. Such a series of songs arranged and categorized is a feature shared by two differing Arabic arts, the *azawaan* of the Moors of Shinqīṭ and the *nawba* of the learned musicians of the Maghrib, who are the custodians of the music of Arabic Spain.

The music is performed according to a pre-established succession of themes. The texts of the songs are interchangeable, but the musical forms remain without change in their order or their structure. Mauritanian music has been described as a music which has no beginning and no ending. It is like a stream which, if entered by a musician, carries him onwards in the direction in which it is going. He cannot return to the beginning. The nature of the music precludes it.

Each movement in this suite the *īggāwen* call *ḍhar* (pl. *ḍhuur*), a 'back', or rather 'the back of a dune', which acts as a route for a camel or a caravan to follow. In the past this term has been translated by 'mode'. But, apart from the specific meaning the latter has in Western music, in all probability it is not an accurate indication of the intentions of the *īggīw* himself, or the effect he wishes his performance to have on his audience. The individuality of each *ḍhar* primarily relates to the way in which its music is performed. Words like 'style' or 'mood' are more appropriate.

To some Moors the notable feature of the four *ḍhuur* is that they typify humours, elements, and states of the soul. They claim that this is a Saharan version of the neo-Platonic theory, developed by the great Arabian musicians, of a concord between the strings of the lute, rhythms, the signs of the Zodiac, the cosmic forces, the seasons, temperaments, and qualities. All these are expressed through, or within, their quadripartite scheme.

The first *ḍhar*, *kar*—an onomatopoeic word—denotes happiness, satisfaction, well-being, and an outpouring of religious emotion. It is a vehicle of praise both religious and profane. *Kar* leads to *faağu*, perhaps a Bambára word, the *ḍhar* which stimulates the bile. It expresses force, pride, courage, and anger. It is the mood of war songs chanted in battle. *Siññiima*, a Sūdānic word, is the most frequently performed *ḍhar*. It is a mixture of the others. It denotes balanced yet somewhat complex emotions. Lastly, *baygi*, 'the little remnant', is the *ḍhar* of sadness. It is suitable for songs of nostalgia and the heart's suffering. In its religious context it expresses supplication and the torment of the soul. A complete musical performance begins with *kar* and ends with *baygi*, but it is also possible for the *īggīw* to play in only one of them, depending on the circumstances of his performance. These names have been generally accepted throughout the whole of the western Sahara, although it has become common in Tagānit, the Adrār, and elsewhere in Mauritania to substitute *lebtayt* for *baygi*, since the latter is the vehicle for the singing of Ḥassānīya poems in that metre. There is no disagreement amongst any of the *īggāwen* as to this fundamental division of their music, although some stress the strictly musical quality of their art and have little or no interest in any abstract theories.

Within each *ḍhar* there are two distinct ways of singing and performing, the 'black', *lakḥal*, and the 'white', *labyaḍ*, and it is customary to keep to one or other in a performance. The former is claimed to be a Negro way of singing. It is forceful, and unsuitable for expressing finer shades of emotion. With it are associated extreme modulations of the voice, but even more, the tightening of the strings of the *tidīnīt*, when it is played. Many of the *īggāwen* prefer it, and it is also a sure and quick way to arouse the emotions of an audience. The 'white' way of singing is preferred by the sophisticated and those of elegant taste. It is harmonious, without the violent modulations to be found in its opposite, and the strings of the *tidīnīt* are loosened and slack. The Moors claim that it is of Arab-Berber type. It is held to be the more ancient of the two and has developed from the simple music of the nomads. The division of the 'black' and the 'white' has led to regional differences in terminology. It also distinguished the *tidīnīt* from the *ardīn*, since the laws which govern the styles in which the instrument can be played are less strict for the latter instrument.

Within the 'black' and 'white' ways for each of the four *ḍhuur* there are differing forms of execution. They have been described in very general terms as 'major' (*irtifaa*ʿ), 'intermediate' (*tawassuṭ*), and 'minor' (*ḵefaaḍ*). They appear to be ways of establishing transitions from 'black' to 'white' within the consecutive patterns of *ḍhuur*. Some of these are of considerable note, since they are familiar terms to Mauritanians who have only an average knowledge of *azawaan*. One term in particular, *gnaydiiya*, is known universally in Mauritania. It is the diminutive form of a word denoting a shepherd's camp. But descriptions of its exact significance differ widely, and are sometimes contradictory. To the scholar Leriche it is the 'major' form of execution in *labyaḍ* in every *ḍhar*, although he lists many of the names in the 'major' form of the 'black' way. In eastern Mauritania its use seems to have been extended to cover 'major', 'intermediate', and 'minor' as well. Muḥammad wuld Sīdī Ibrāhīm, and *iggāwen* consulted, regard *gnaydiiya* as a mixture between the 'black' and the 'white', or as a form of playing, difficult to execute, which is best regarded as a separate way altogether. It seems that only the expert *iggāwen* are able to explain its function in their music.

Ḥassānīya poetry is linked to these musical categories, on the one hand by its meaning, for example whether it falls within the emotional context of one or other of the four *ḍhuur*, and on the other by the innumerable *eŝwaar* (sing. *ŝawr*), 'airs'. Classical Arabic poetry has its corresponding *neḥya*. Both words indicate 'direction' in Ḥassānīya. The rhythm of the chosen *ŝawr* decides which song is to be sung, since the rhythm of the *ŝawr* and the song must correspond. It is interesting that in Tuareg poetry and music there is a term *anea* meaning both 'poetic rhythm' and 'sung air'. The poems are likewise not sung to an arbitrary air. Certain sung airs correspond to certain poetic rhythms, and one can only sing verses to the airs which correspond to their rhythm.

In this respect, however, a distinction should be made between Ḥassānīya poetry and Classical Arabic poetry. Mauritanian music and Ḥassānīya poetry are now a single art, and the former has given birth to and nurtured the latter. There is a strictly observed limitation on the metres which may be used in a given *ḍhar*. In *faaġu*, for example, an *iggīw* may only sing Ḥassānīya poetry in *bu 'umraan* or *mraymiida*. No such rule applies to Arabic poetry. The *iggīw* selects his poems to suit the mood, primarily by their subject-matter. The metre of the poem is only secondary, although in fact a tradition has grown up that certain metres are most appropriate. In *faaġu*, for example, *al-ramal* and *al-rajaz* are more popular than any other.

The table opposite represents the various *ḍhuur*, in the 'black' and 'white' ways and *gnaydiiya*. They form the musical structure of *azawaan*, as agreed upon by a number of players of the *tidīnīt* and musical experts consulted in Mauritania. Each principal way of singing and playing (called 'intermediate' by Leriche and Balandier and Mercier) has a subsidiary *rediif* (called 'minor' by

ḍhar ظهر	The 'black' way (*jaamba*) الطريق الكحلاء	*gnaydiiya* الكنيديّه	The 'white' way (*jaamba*) الطريق البيضاء
kar كر	[1]*entemaas* انتماس [2]*sayni kar* (*ma yukarraṣ*) سيني كر (ما يخرّص)	*enweffal* انوڤّل	[1]*mekka mūsa* مكّ موس [2]*el-faayez* الفايز
faağu فاغ	[1]*tenaččuuga* تنچّوگه [2]*sayni faağu* سيني فاغ	*ššbaar* الشّبار or *faağu lekbiir* فاغ الكبير	[1]*ssruuzi* (*'arraay essruuza*) السّروزي (عرّاي السّروزه) [2]*et-teḥraar* (*el-ḥurr*) التّحرار (الحرّ)
siññiima سنّيمه	[1]*siññiimat hayba*[3] سنّيمة هيب [2]*meqaččuuga* (Ḥawḍ) مقچّوگه or *lebyaaḍ* لبياظ or *etbaybi* (Trārza) اتبيبي	('black') *el-mawsṭi* الموسطي ('white') *menčalla* منچلّه	[1]*et-teḥzaam*[4] التّحزام [2]*eññaama*[5] انّيامه [2]*rrbaabi*[6] الرّبابي (a) *leggetri*[6] لكّتري (b) *čaynna* چينّه (c) *liyyin* ليّن
baygi or *lebtayt* بيگي	*baygi* بيگي intensive form *a'ḍḍaal* اعضّال	*el-mukaalef* المخالف or *baygi jjraad* بيگي الجّراد or *baygi lekbiir* بيگي الكبير	*el-'itiig* العتيگ

[1] Entry (*dkuul* دخول) brought about through tightening the strings of the *tidīnīt*.

[2] Subsidiary (*rrdiif* الرّديف) brought about through loosening the strings of the *tidīnīt*.

[3] Also called in western Mauritania *zzraag* الزّراگ.

[4] Included in *faağu* by some *īggāwen*.

[5] Not subsidiary to those who include *et-teḥzaam* in *faağu*.

[6] A blending of white and black.

Leriche and Balandier and Mercier).[1] The latter appears to exhibit a tendency to play towards its opposite. A *rediif* in the 'white' way indicates a tendency towards the 'black', and vice versa. *Eññaama*, for example, is 'blacker' than *et-teḥzaam*; *meqaččuuga* is less 'black' than *siññiimat hayba*. Regional differences allow for a certain licence as to which category a certain manner of playing is to be classed in. These divisions are fundamental, but *azawaan* in all its forms is infinitely more complex, since within each *ḍhar* are to be found thousands of *ešwaar* and entries. New forms are continually being added, whilst others are falling into disuse. Themes from European and Egyptian music are being absorbed, often unconsciously. The forms change, but the established *ḍhuur* of *azawaan* remain.

[1] A. Leriche, 'Poésie et musique maure', *Bull. I.F.A.N.*, t. xii, July 1950, pp. 729–50. G. Balandier and P. Mercier, 'Notes sur les théories musicales maures à propos de chants enregistrés', *C.R. IIe Conf. international occident*, Birsau, 1947, Lisbon, 1952, vol. v, pp. 135–92.

PART II

POEMS, FOLK-TALES, AND TEXTS OF SHINQĪṬ

9

ḤASSĀNĪYA AND ZNĀGA POETRY

ḤASSĀNĪYA poetry, according to the French scholar Leriche, is 'the truest and most spontaneous reflection of the Moorish soul'. It is composed and enjoyed by men and women of every class in the community, and every conceivable subject may be represented in it. The poems which arouse most pleasure are of a light and humorous kind, but it would be a mistake to ignore the touch of melancholy in the joy of the Moors and the bite and sarcasm in their humour.

It is also a mistake to regard Classical Arabic as the exclusive language for poems with a serious or deeply religious subject or for those which are complex and abstract in their content. There are many Ḥassānīya poems on religious themes, and many a lengthy *kerza* is in praise of famous men. In short, there is a Ḥassānīya 'literature', which includes poems long and short, slight and serious, sentimental and devotional. If nature had been kinder, lengthy works in prose, ranging in subject-matter from medicine to jurisprudence, might also have survived.

Shaykh Muḥammad al-Māmī, who died in 1865, is known to have composed a number of Ḥassānīya poems on mystical subjects and on an eccentric theory about how to calculate the number of stones on the earth's surface. If we are to believe the Mauritanians, this great scholar is the author of poems in Ḥassānīya on an unprecedented range of subjects, unique perhaps in any known colloquial dialect of the Arabic language. According to the text of the unpublished manuscript of *Dhāt alwāḥ wa dusur*, by Sīd Aḥmad wuld Asmuhu, it was Shaykh Muḥammad al-Māmī who 'put all the sciences into verse, jurisprudence, grammar, belief in the unity of God, logic, rhetoric, the biography of the Prophet and genealogies and astronomy, in poetry both beautiful and flowing and well composed in Ḥassānīya. The ear is never tired by it, notwithstanding its length, rather its beauty is enhanced, when it is recited, to those who listen to it. It is among the greatest wonders. It is a *dīwān* of all the Islamic sciences.'

The claim that there was a wealth of Mauritanian colloquial poetry on all kinds of abstract subjects is by no means fanciful, as is conclusively shown by the survival of two Znāga poems by the scholar Wālid wuld Khālunā. No other known poems in Znāga, at least in recent times, are so long, and the fact that they survive in Arabic script is of particular interest.[1] They are also representative examples of Zwāya scholarship in the colloquial language. There is also little doubt that the famous *rasm* of Saddūm wuld Njartu, dating from the same period, is authentic, as are other poems in praise of famous personalities.

The majority of surviving Ḥassānīya poems can easily be classified under such subjects as panegyric, eulogy, satire, love song, jest, or simple ditty. Many are inspired by Classical Arabic poetry, and in general it is clear that the imagery, the subject-matter, and the style of a very large number of Ḥassānīya poems reflect Jāhilī poetry to a greater or lesser extent. Others echo Umayyad poets, the ʿUdhrī love poets in particular, and ʿUmar b. Abī Rabīʿa, or they are modelled on non-poetic literary forms, an exchange of correspondence, for example. A dialogue frequently occurs. Elsewhere the poet is content with simple description. In a few verses he conveys all he feels or wishes to express by associating his ideas with certain objects, or with animals, for example with a charred branch or a wandering camel. Very often the meaning of the poem is obscure, and some form of commentary is needed. The situation which brought about the composition of such a poem is so local or so temporary that its intention is now open to innumerable interpretations. Of the thousands of Saharan poems only a small number are likely to have survived, but now and then Ḥassānīya, and, it seems, Znāga, have produced a poet of genius, and his masterpieces are applauded and remembered by Zwāya scholar and humble shepherd alike.

CLASSICAL ḤASSĀNĪYA POETRY

The opening verses of the rasm *of Saddūm wuld Njartu*

The famous *rasm* of Saddūm wuld Njartu in praise of Aḥmad, the uncle of Wuld Bakkār wuld Aʿmar (d. 1761/2), is almost forgotten today. Copies of the complete text are rare, and while it is possible to find

[1] See p. 153.

īggāwen who know the poem, they do not always agree on the order of the verses or even that of individual hemistichs within each verse of the *rasm*. There are said to be about thirty-seven verses, and the examples quoted here in the text are the generally-accepted first six verses, together with verse 9 and verse 11. The text has been prepared by Mukhtār wuld Ḥāmidun.

The *rasm* contains six vocalized consonants in the first and the third hemistichs, while the second and the fourth hemistichs have three vocalized consonants. The first three hemistichs share the same rhyme, while the fourth hemistich rhymes in the *rawī* of the *kerza*. All the hemistichs end with two unvocalized consonants, and the first vocalized consonant in the second and the fourth hemistichs is followed by two unvocalized consonants.

Many of the words in the poem are archaic, and it has not always been possible to obtain a close translation. Sometimes the poet may coin words for purposes of rhyme.

I

1. مِيرْ اَعْرَبْ تِنْزِلَاطْ x (اُ) كَيرْ وِرَاطْ x
وَٱنِيزْرِكْ وُالتَّشْمَاطْ x بِالسَّمْعْ شَاعْ

2. اَنْبَطْ نَبْطَتْ ٱلَانْبَاطْ x كُوطْ ٱلَا كْوَاط x
سِلْسِلْتِ التَانَبَاطْ x سِرُّلْ كَاعْ

3. اَحْمَدَّيّ صَلْبَاطْ x جِيلْ ٱلَانْبَاطْ x
بِالسِّتْرَبِيهِمْ حَاطْ x مِيرْ ٱلَارْبَاعْ

4. سَخِي مَاهُ كَنَّاطْ x نَهْرْ اُشْطَاطْ x
لِلزَّهْوْ اَرْهَاطْ اَرْهَاطْ x نَايْرْ اَنْوَاعْ

5. وُاخْنَادِيدْ اَلتَّصْمَاطْ x (اُ) نِظْوْ خَرْوَاطْ x
وَاسَرْ كُوحْ اَهْيَهَاطْ x نَاعْمْ اَرْبَاعْ

6. عَنْدُ كِيفْ اَكُيَاطْ x فَلْطْ اَلاَفْلاَطْ x
اَحْمَدَّيّ صَلْبَاطْ x أعدُوهْ دَفَّاعْ

. . . .

. . . .

. . . .

. . . .

9. فَاهْلُ مَاهُ جَنْجَاطْ x غَيْرْ خَيَّاطْ x
وُاتْجَعْطِيطْ اَلتَّصْلاَطْ x حَاكْثُرْ كَاعْ

. . . .

. . . .

11. عَنْدُ مَدْفَعْ كَطْكَاطْ x لَصّْ تَنْكَاطْ x
جَعْبُ ثَنْتَيْنْ اَحْنَاطْ x بِيهْ صَكَّاعْ

1. The prince of the Arabs of Tinzilāṭ, Gīr, Irāṭ, Inyizrig, and Ta<u>sh</u>māṭ, and of great renown.
2. Chief of the Anbāṭ [Ṣanhāja],[1] of the chiefs of the Īdaw ʿĪ<u>sh</u>, the leader in whom inherited, deeply rooted, noble chieftainship lies.
3. Aḥmad, the caster of the Īdaw ʿĪ<u>sh</u> to the right and to the left, he the prince of the scattered groups has gathered them all together by his valour and his manliness.
4. He is generous, none need despair of his bounty. It is like the flowing river. He is the bestower of every kind of dazzling and precious wealth.

[1] The word *taanabaaṭ*(*it*) indicates leadership among the Īdaw ʿĪ<u>sh</u>, just as *tedaymiin* indicates the leadership of the Banū (Awlād) Daymān.

5. Milch camels, abundant in milk, and the exhausted horse, yet winner in the race, and the great fat four-tooth stallion.
6. For him to give these away is like the paring of the nails. He is the one who lives in luxury and who scatters his opponents headlong.
9. Among his people he is no contender, rather he is the one who repairs that which is unsound. As for the stubbornness of oppression, surely he brings it into his subjection.
11. His is a gun of hard, metallic click. A collector of spoil, it boasts of barrels twain, and he is sure and deadly in his aim.

Ḥassānīya Eulogy

II

1. يَا السَّايِلْ عَنْ اَخْيَارْ لَعْرَبْ : وُازْيَنْهُمْ دِينْ وُانْزَلْهُمْ اَمْلَيْكْ
2. بُو بَكْرْ وُلْدْ هَنُّونْ وُلْدْ اَللَّبّْ : وُلْدْ بُو سَيْفّْ وُلْدْ اُودَيْكْ

1. O you who ask about the best of the Arabs, the most pious in religion and the most angelic bearer of compassion,
2. (he is) Bū Bakr wuld Hannūn wuld al-Labb wuld Bū Sayf wuld Ūdayk.

This *gaaf*, in an irregular metre, is quoted in the manuscript text of *al-Ḥaswa al-baysānīya fil-ansāb al-ḥassānīya* by Shaykh Muḥammad wuld ʿAbd al-Wahhāb wuld Aḥmad wuld al-Ḥājj ʿAbd al-Wahhāb al-Nāṣirī (d. *circa* 1256/1840), one of the most important Saharan historical texts on the tribes of the Banū Maʿqil and their entry into the Ḥawḍ and the Māli border regions.

This Ḥassānīya poem is very early in date. According to the text, 'as for the family of al-Labb b. (wuld) Bū Sayf (pronounced with an emphatic *lām*), they were the first of the kings of the Banū Maghfar among the cattle people and in the land of the "blacks". The first of them was their ancestor al-Labb wuld Bū Sayf wuld Ūdayk wuld Ambayg Bū Garn. Then came his son Hannūn al-Kawrī wuld al-Labb, and he was among the élite of the Banu Maghfar (Awlād Ghwayzī). He was killed by the Awlād Mubārak in the battle of Jagum' (*circa* 1161/1748).

In Praise of a Camel

1. مَا تْلَيْتْ وَحْلَ لِلّخُطَّار : عُدّْتْ نَغْلَبْهُمْ كَانْ اَجْرَيْتْ

2. فَوْكْ لَبْيَظْ جَمْلَ اْلمُخْتَارْ : اُذَاكْ وُل اَجْمَلْ تَاشِدْبِيِتْ

1. I have not remained a wearisome burden on travellers. I now outstrip them when I run,
2. upon al-Abyaḍ, the camel of al-Mukhtār, which is the offspring of a camel of the Tāshidbīt.

This *gaaf*, which is an irregular *bu ʿumraan* in metre, is attributed to ʿAlī wuld Mānu, the first *īggīw* of the Ahl Mānu. It was composed in honour of al-Mukhtār wuld Aʿmar wuld ʿAlī Shanḍūra (d. *circa* 1270/1853/4), who had given the poet a camel.

In Praise of Hamza

1. مَارْتَ انْ حَسْبَكْ عَادْ اِنَهْوَلْ x مَارْتَ انْ مَا كِيفَكْ رِزْكَانِ

2. فِيكْ حُمُّ اُفِيكْ اَمْهَلْهَلْ x اُ فِيكْ بُو هَمَّادْ اُ كَانِ

1. A token that your lineage has been sung, a sign that there is not one of the Awlād Rizg like you, (is)
2. that among your forebears are Ḥummu, Amhalhal (Muhalhil), Bū Hammād and Kāni.

This *gaaf*, in *el-batt lekbiir* metre,[1] was probably composed in praise of Hamza, a prince of the Awlād Rizg (d. *circa* 1274/1857/8), or, less likely, of ʿAlī Wunnās, who died in the eighteenth century.

To Muḥammad al-Ḥabīb

1. The knight of the Agi(u)nni Arabs (Tagānit), al-Munjāʿ (Ḥawḍ), and al-Kirāʿ (Trārza)
2. has taken the surplus from me, and the surplus belongs to the craftsmen.

[1] See p. 165.

3. He has taken the surplus from me, he who tames the stubborn Ḥassān,
4. master of a hundred horsemen, repulser of foe and succourer of a friend.
5. It is he who supports God's children, and the surplus belongs to the craftsmen.
6. He has taken the surplus from me, he who gave me a camel pair,
7. the bestower, without distinction, of his gifts unto those who ask,
8. he, the cistern of comer and goer, and the surplus belongs to the craftsmen.
9. He has kept the surplus of the writing, the one who suffices his friends.
10. In weighty affairs which threaten, he gives safe and plentiful pasture,
11. in the land where terror is constant, and the surplus belongs to the craftsmen.

This famous poem consists of a *gaaf* (verses 1 and 2), followed by a *ṭal'a* (verses 3 to 5), a second *ṭal'a* (verses 6 to 8), and a third *ṭal'a* (verses 9 to 11). Each section of the poem is knit together by a refrain which quotes a Moorish proverb. The metre of the poem is *lebtayt en-naageṣ*. The poet is Muḥammad wuld Haddār (cf. Chapter 6, p. 57). René Basset provides a version of the text in his *Mission au Sénégal*, pp. 383–5, and A. Leriche in *Bull. I.F.A.N.*, t. xii, July 1950, pp. 723–4.

Sīd Aḥmad wuld Awlīl in praise of Sīd Aḥmad wuld Mukhtār wuld Bū Sīd, one of the princes of the Awlād Mubārak (Ambārak) of the Ḥawḍ

This *kerza* is a translation of an imperfect text written down by the *īggīw* Isalmu wuld Bāba wuld Ḥamma wuld Nafar, a descendant of Sīd Aḥmad wuld Awlīl. Awlīl, an *īggīw* of the Awlād Mubārak, was a contemporary of Saddūm wuld Njartu and one of the creators of *azawaan* in Mauritania. The poem is *bu 'umraan*. The epilogue is in the same metre.

1. After the Lord of all creation, no one is worthy of your attention.
2. Be he Arab, or be he non-Arab, his deed cannot compare with, or better, yours.

3. Nor can anyone acquire what you possess. In you, all ways and qualities are combined.
4. In you bounty, goodness, justice, noble character, and sound judgement may be found. May God watch over you.
5. Firm trust, zeal, and joy belong to none but you.
6. The bounty and goodness of all men, near and far, however great they be, your greatness reigns triumphantly over all.
7. If you are enraged, then vain is the one who says that he will block your path.
8. You bring down oppression on the oppressors, and there is pleasure in your justice to your clients.
9. O pillar of Islam, your noble character is true, but hateful also can your countenance be,
10. and if you speak in rage to anyone, the fire of anger flashes in your eyes.
11. The intense heat of the sun, in the season of hot winds, that heat intensifies your zeal.
12. When you ride a horse and loosen the belt, to this is linked your courage in attack.
13. The great mercy which you show to women and men is a gift which God has given you.
14. Yet with regard to (the gift of) wealth and slaves, God has made your bountiful nature pitiless.
15. If you are, by nature, shrewd and understanding, then this is manifest in the path you tread.
16. The words you say are true, they lead to manifestation of your bounty.
17. Your comprehension cannot be fathomed. A mighty torrent from the desert valley has found its course there.
18. You conceal your hatred. You do not reveal it in the words you use.
19. You do not show it to the one who blames you, if he stirs up commotion to outwit you.
20. It is hidden away for the one who merits it, and if he hovers aloft, he is disgraced.
21. You meet him face to face and expect hostility, but he is clement, and he treats you in a courteous way.
22. And when he treats you thus, yet he conceals a ruse, then it is not hidden from you.
23. You quell the mighty explosion—it does not suppress you.

24. And if your army is defeated through adversity (the enemy), then what lion (volcano?) can be compared with you?
25. And if dissension troubles your people, you put this matter to right and bring that matter to nought.
26. You rectify this through skill and by resolve, when it is likely to corrupt.
27. But (you are) prodigious in the giving of your wealth, the importunate one presses you to dispense it all.
28. And when you loot the spoils of the tents, he who comes begging despoils you because of your bounty.
29. Your high status is the will of God who decrees man's fate, and according to the extent of your giving he gives you in return.
30. But you give to the mad and to the foolish. If you turn to face men who are robbers, then it is only war.
31. You are like a lion, and the sound of your reproof distinguishes you.
32. And in the hour of surprise and of rebuke, you follow a determined path to your commitment.
33. It is your habit, when the dust of war is thick, that with firm resolve you protect men's backs.
34. You resist the wound of the gun muzzle, and fear does not make you flee.
35. The reason for this is not fully known. You are so reckless in your courage. God preserve you.
36. In the battle of Garrūga,[1] O astrologer who awaits the star of fortune, the people who disparaged and who praised you
37. were convinced, so were the people of Arj and In Titām and the people of Tafalli and Innikīk.
38. And the Arabs of Jawl were convinced, and S͟hams͟hām, and your kindred were convinced. May God not cause you to perish!
39. And at the battle of Turbayk[1] you were 'weaned' from enemies who were burning you with their bullets.
40. You defended the backs of the Arabs of Raddām, and those of Taḥfazna and those of Zīk.
41. Your grey mare advanced to the sound of the war drum, in the hour of surprise and of confused tumult.

[1] Early in the nineteenth century.

42. And at the battle of Tanga[1] you attained an honoured status, your renown was greater than that of your foe.
43. The army was defeated and speedily routed when it fought you.
44. There it was that you stood in an advanced position, because you laid the enemy low.
45. You are firm with the ʿUbaydāt. They disapprove of you in a way which arouses your warlike passions.
46. So they regard you as a lion, stout and firm, with a hairy mane, and they cast rock and wood at you.
47. A raging destructive lion, angry in its roar, you have denied them your defeat.
48. And in the battle of Garṣa[2]—let speech be still—that battle when opposition to you ended,
49. the army of your foe looted the tents, and it was because of you that the army was defeated.
50. You became both father and uncle to the great camp, and you were the trial and despair of your foe.
51. The blood of their chieftainship and the basest of them, you banished them in disgrace and scattered them.
52. And by the cutting of locks and in the tumult like the clouds, you destroyed their might, and you oppressed them sore.
53. And at the battle of al-Fayʿīya[3] you were an Imām, your words infallible, may God keep you!
54. Your foe was treated like an ostrich. You put him to rout, and he fled herded together, from you.
55. Your battle is one of honour and dignity, a day of repairing and polishing your gun.[4]
56. It is the battle of the grey mare, which you stop from running away, and which you hold tight by the reins.
57. Its colour is darkened by the darkness, and this inflames your ardour and arouses your zeal.
58. As for its running against your will, that is denied. It halted with you to the south of the great camp.
59. It ran so fast that the hair on its neck could not be seen.

[1] A battle in Māli in the early nineteenth century.
[2] Early nineteenth century.
[3] A battle in Tagānit in 1324/1906.
[4] *tahwiid* means also 'judaizing': the poet connects the act of repairing the arms with the current legend that the artisans and smiths were Jews in origin. It is a play on words.

60. You were wounded while you guarded the tents, and the wound on your body is a mark of pride.
61. When a bullet of the enemy penetrated the knotting of your sleeves from in front, that did not deter you from your course.
62. He who was a witness in the battle remembers, and he is a sufficient witness for you.
63. The word of the woman of the great camps, the word of him who loves you and of him who loves you not.
64. Your praise surpasses (the talents of) poets and scholars alike, and you have firmly established the royal camp in your control.
65. The camp agrees with you in that. But if you are far away, it is defeated, and then the enemy is strong.

Targiiba—Epilogue to the kerza

1. It is your custom when you enter battle to acquire praise like booty.
2. The rudeness of battle does not harm you, nor are you repulsed by those who oppose you.
3. O Sīd Aḥmad, you have arisen. You surpass your contemporaries in everything.
4. You surpass the generation which will follow after you, in honour, in leadership, and in the repression of injustice.

The rasm *of Mḥammad wuld Ingdhay*

The *rasm* of the Trārza *īggīw* Mḥammad wuld Ingdhay has at least twenty-seven verses. The text is based on a written copy made by Mukhtār wuld Ḥāmidun, dictated by an *īggīw* familiar with the text, but the irregular sixth verse suggests that probably the *rasm* is incomplete. The translation of some passages has proved impossible, and the rendering in English given here is only an attempt at the approximate meaning of the original. The poem is a panegyric addressed to a prince of the Trārza. In fact, it is in praise of the Prophet, whose lineage forms the main part of the poem.

1. نَسْبَكْ بِسْمْ اَلْوَدُودْ x عَالْمْ اَلْجُودْ x

تَسَلْسَلْتْ اَلْمَوْجُودْ x مِنْ تْوَاسِيهْ

2. يَنْصُرْ رَسْمِ فِبْلُودْ x بِيهْمْ مَوْعُودْ x

طَفْلْ اَلشُّكْرْ اَلْمَعْهُودْ x نَاظْمُ فِيهْ

3. اَمْنْ اَلْغَرْبْ إِلَى امْبُودْ x رَافْدْ اَحْدُودْ x

دِ كْمْ اَدْكِيمْ اَلْبَارُودْ x وُنْدْ گَادِيهْ

4. اُهَنْدْ اَلشُّعْبْ اَلْمَجْهُودْ x سَاوْدْ السُّودْ x

كَضَرْبُ بِالْمَعْمُودْ x سَلْسْلَ فِيهْ

5. بَمِشَالِتْ حَسُودْ x سِيدْ وُجُودْ x

مَا ظَرُّوهْ اَلْجُنُودْ x مُنْتْ عَادِيهْ

6. عَبْدْ اَللَّهِ مَحْمُودْ x بُوهْ مَوْعُودْ x

بُو لَفْتُوحَاتْ اِكُودْ x [كُلّْ نَمْرُودْ x وَلَلِّ بِالتَّشْهُودْ x مَا مْنَ بِيهْ]

7. رُشْدْ اَرْشِيدْ اَلرَّشُودْ x بِيهْ سُدُودْ x

دَارْ اَدْيَارْ مِنْ اَشُودْ x نَاعْمَ بِيهْ

8. عَبْدْ اَللَّهِ مَحْمُودْ x بُوهْ مَوْعُودْ x

كَوْكَبْ غِلْظْ اَصْمُدُودْ x نَيّْرَ بِيهْ

9. اِبْنِ شَيْبَ صَنْدُودْ x بِالتّْجَاهُودْ x

عُكْبَ خَصْلَاتُ كَوْدْ x جُمْجْلَ بِيهْ

10. اِبنِ هَاشِمْ مَوْعُودْ x بِيهْ مَرْفُودْ x

اَلْفُمّْ اُشُكْرُ كَوْدْ x كُونْجْ اَعْلِيهْ

11. عَبْدِ مَنَافْ اَلْجُودْ x رَافْدْ اَلْرفُودْ x

بَطْلْ اَبْطَالْ اَلدَّدُودْ (?) x شَانْـهَ فِيـهْ

12. اِبْنِ قُصَىّْ اِكُـودْ x جَدّْ اَجْدُودْ x

عَبْدْ اِللّٰهْ اَلْمَحْمُودْ x عَنْدْ عَرْبِيهْ

13. اِبْنِ كِلَاب اِكُـودْ x غِلْظْ مَنْفُودْ x

عَدَّ اعْدَادْ اَلْمَعْدُودْ x مَا يْوَفِّيهْ

14. اِبْنِ مُرَّةَ كَـوْدْ x سَنْزْ سُنُودْ x

مَهْرْ اَلعَدّْ اَلْمَعْدُودْ x يَمْتْهَرْ بِيـهْ

15. اِبْنِ كَعْبْ اَلْمَقْصُودْ x وُلّْ مَعْهُودْ x

لُـؤَىّْ اُوُلّْ اِعُـودْ x مَايْدَ نِّيـهْ

16. غَالِـبْ سُلْطَانْ اِكُودْ x جُنْدْ جُنُودْ x

اِبْنِ فِهْرْ اَلْمَعْدُودْ x مِنْ جْدَادِيهْ

17. اِبْنِ مَالِكْ مَحْمُودْ x وُلّْ مَعْهُودْ x

نَضْرْ خَصْلَاتُ اِكُودْ x جُمْجُلَ بِيهْ

18. اِبْنِ كِنَانْ اَطْرُودْ x كُلّْ نَمْرُودْ x

كَزَرْزِ فِي عَكْرُودْ x عَنْدْ عَابِيهْ

19. اِبْنِ خُزَيْمْ اِكُودْ x شَالْ وُاشْهُودْ x

شَلْوْ اَبْطَالْ اَلْجُنُودْ x لَعْبْ رِجْلِيهْ

20. اِبْنِ مُدْرِكْ صَنْدُودْ x كَايْدْ اَكْيُودْ x

كَرْنْ اَكْثُرُونْ اَلْحُدُودْ x مُتَّوَ الِيهْ

21. اِبْنْ اِلْيَاسْ اَلْمَجْهُودْ x بَتّْ صَيْلُودْ x

غِلْظْ مَنْ اَرْفُودْ اَرْفُودْ x مِنْ كْثَنَانِيهْ

22. اِبْنِ مُضَرْ اَشْهُودْ x غِلْظْ مَنْفُودْ x

غِلْظْ اَلْحَسْبْ اَلْمَعْهُودْ x يَنْغَلَظْ بِيهْ

23. اِبْنِ نَزَارْ اَصْمُودْ x وُلّْ مَوْعُودْ x

مَعَدّْ اُوُلّْ اِعُودْ x مَايْدَ نِّيهْ

24. عَظْمْ اَلْغِلْظْ اَلْمَعْكُودْ x رَافّْد اَرْفُودْ x

عَدْنَانْ اُجَدّْ اَجْدُودْ x سَلْسَلْ بِيهْ

25. هُوَّ سِيدْ اَلْوُجُودْ x كَايْدْ اَكْيُودْ x

بِيهْ اَللّٰهْ اَلْمَجْبُودْ x يَنْحَبْدْ بِيهْ

26. لُلَ نُورْ مَحْمُودْ x بِيهْ مَرْيُودْ x

كَوْنْ اَعْبِيدْ اَلْمَعْبُودْ x مَايْكَا نِيهْ

27. شِيخْ اَنْجُوعْ اَلْمَوْجُودْ x بَتّْ عَزُودْ x

شُكْرُ كَادْ اَلْكُيُودْ x مَا تْوَفِّيهْ

1. I begin with the name of the beloved and bountiful Lord, who has created all things.
2. May he sustain my *rasm*, lauding the praise of one who is renowned in the land.

3. The limits from the Maghrib to Ambūd (ʻMbout) are 'neath his sway, by the power of his bullets. His gun is filled with powder.
4. The steel of the courageous serpent, lord of the serpents, 'tis his habit to smite it with the mace.
5. (This serpent) is like one who is envious of the Prophet, but the toughest troops of his foes in no way harm him.
6. ʻAbdallāh, the father of our Prophet, was often visited, and he (the Prophet) is the leader of every chief to victory (and by belief in the two declarations of faith—that God is one and Muḥammad is his Prophet).
7. He is the guide of him who is best guided among the guides. He is the abode where the cattle are fattened and nourished.
8. ʻAbdallāh, his father, was praised and frequented. He relied on the star of honour when he set ablaze (great enterprises).
9. He was the son of Shayba (ʻAbdu 'l-Muṭṭalib), heroic warrior in the faith, he whose deeds are praised was alone victorious,
10. The son of Hāshim, greatly visited, whose incomparable praise is in the mouths of all men,
11. (Son of) ʻAbd Manāf, the bountiful, carrier of burdens, hero of heroes who accomplished acts of great portent,
12. Son of Quṣayy, who has no equal, ancestor of ʻAbdallāh, praiseworthy in the eyes of his lord,
13. Son of Kilāb, who commanded the honour sought after, and who was endowed with innumerable qualities,
14. Son of Murra, leader and lord of lords, the uniquely endowed,
15. Son of Kaʻb, the sought after, son of renowned Lu'ayy, son of one who dishonoured not,
16. Ghālib, master of the troops, son of Fihr, distinguished among his forebears,
17. Son of Mālik, the renowned, son of the famous al-Naḍr, whose qualities are paramount and complete,
18. Son of Kināna, the banisher of every tyrant, and the crusher of the vagabond who confronted him,
19. Son of Khuzayma, the conquering chief, who has witness to the fact that he cut in bits heroic warriors. For him it was an easy task;
20. Son of Mudrika, the noble, more artful than the shrewd . . .?,
21. Son of Ilyās, the strong, like the hard stone, an honour inherited from the heights,

22. Son of Muḍar, the ideal pattern of honour pursued, the honour of a famous lineage wherein his pride resides,
23. Son of Nizār, the reliable son of the oft visited Maʿadd, son of him who is not base,
24. The seat of honour, bearer of burdens, ʿAdnān, the eldest forebear from whom the line descends.
25. The Prophet is the lord of men, the shrewdest. He is in God's hand, he is His well-rope.
26. Were it not for his famous light, needed for the creation of men, they would not have come into existence.
27. A lord for whom creation yearns, strong and mighty, his praise is beyond the tongues of those who praise. They are unable to match it.

The lineage of the Prophet as given by the grammarian Abū Muḥammad ʿAbdu 'l-Malik ibn Hishām is as follows:

Muḥammad was the son of ʿAbdullāh, b. ʿAbdu 'l-Muṭṭalib (whose name was Shayba), b. Hāshim (whose name was ʿAmr), b. ʿAbdu Manāf (whose name was al-Mughīra), b. Quṣayy (whose name was Zayd), b. Kilāb, b. Murra, b. Kaʿb, b. Lu'ayy, b. Ghālib, b. Fihr, b. Mālik, b. al-Naḍr, b. Kināna, b. Khuzayma, b. Mudrika (whose name was ʿĀmir), b. Ilyās, b. Muḍar, b. Nizār, b. Maʿadd, b. ʿAdnān, b. Udd (or Udad), b. Muqawwam, b. Nāḥūr, b. Tayraḥ, b. Yaʿrub, b. Yashjub, b. Nābit, b. Ismāʿīl, b. Ibrāhīm, the friend of the Compassionate, b. Ṭāriḥ (who is Āzar), b. Nāḥūr, b. Sārūgh, b. Rāʿū, b. Fālikh, b. ʿAybar, b. Shālikh, b. Arfakhshadh, b. Sām, b. Nūḥ, b. Lamk, b. Mattūshalakh b. Akhnūkh, who is the prophet Idrīs according to what they allege, but God knows best (he was the first of the sons of Adam to whom prophecy and writing with a pen were given), b. Yard, b. Mahlīl, b. Qaynan, b. Yānish, b. Shīth, b. Adam.

Poems from the Ḥassānīya Dīwān by Shaykh Muḥammad wuld al-Bukhārī wuld Ḥabīb Allāh wuld Bārakalla wuld Bā Zayd (d. 1282/1865)

Shaykh Muḥammad al-Māmī has received little mention in books and articles on the western Sahara. He lived most of his life in Tīris, the barren region bordering the south-eastern corner of the Río de Oro, and he is buried at Ayg in the same district. His remote abode may partly account for his neglect, since very few of his writings are available and most are known only by hearsay or repute. He was a prolific author, and his works in every branch of learning are numbered in hundreds. Many of these are short pamphlets or long poems, on grammar, rhetoric, or law.

The following Arabic works are regarded as being his most famous and among his best:

1. A poem expounding the text of the *Mukhtaṣar* of Khalīl, in 10,000 verses.
2. A poem called *al-Ṣadāq* on the basic principles of jurisprudence, in 1400 verses.
3. An *urjūza* on the genealogy of the ten companions of the Prophet to whom the reward of paradise was granted. This poem is in fifteen verses.
4. An *urjūza* on the companions who fought at Badr. There is said to be a commentary by the scholar and poet Zayn wuld al-Jamad.
5. Two famous odes:
   1. *al-Dulfīnīya*, a *nūnīya.* The poem is on historical and kindred matters.
   2. *al-Mīzābīya*, on the principles and arts of polemics. The poem is given this name because the word *al-mīzāb* ('sewer' or 'water-spout') appears in the second hemistich of the thirtieth verse. The poem is a *hā'īya*, of 162 verses, and is in *al-kāmil* metre.
6. A Qur'ān *tafsīr*.
7. *Mawrid al-ẓam'ān fil-maḥdhūf min al-qur'ān.*
8. An ode about the arrangement of the Meccan and Medinan *sūra*s and a detailed examination of the former in the light of the latter.
9. The *Kitāb al-bādiya.* This work is among the author's greatest compositions and is a series of rulings and judgements given in legal matters for the guidance of the Saharan community. It is this work which is held by many to envisage some relaxation in the rigid adherence to Mālikī jurisprudence.

   In the opinion of one great Mauritanian scholar: 'There is no other book like it, except the Rulings of the Jinn by 'Abd al-Wahhāb al-Sha'rānī, and between the desert and the jinn there is a kinship. As al-Mutanabbī says: "We are a party of riders among the jinn in the guise of humans, on birds in the form of camels." '

Apart from his Arabic studies, Shaykh Muḥammad al-Māmī took a special interest in mathematical and astrological theories, and at times these interests took him into strange by-ways. His contemporaries credited him with uncanny powers, and it is said that he possessed a book copied out for him by his pupils from the jinn, and that none could read it save he himself and the elect of his sons. He is also regarded as one of the very finest poets in Ḥassānīya. He used the dialect to express

Ṣūfī and abstract ideas, and he also composed a number of legal and theological works in colloquial poetry. He excelled, in particular, in poems of *istisqā'*—beseeching God to bestow rain on his parched and famine-stricken land. More than any other Moor, he contributed towards giving Ḥassānīya a literary genre, analogous in its way to that in Classical Arabic. It is unfortunate that most of his greatest poems are forgotten. The few examples given here are from written texts collected by Mukhtār wuld Ḥāmidun from members of the Ahl Bārakallāh, the poet's tribe.

Professor Th. Monod, however, has published two of the author's Ḥassānīya poems on secret scripts of Mauritania, the *ṣaryānīya* and the *'ibrānīya*, cf. *Contributions à l'étude du Sahara Occidental* (Gravures, peintures et inscriptions rupestres), Paris, Larose, 1938, p. 114.

1. اَنْتَ لَا حَجَّيْتْ اَمْسَوْحَلْ x وَاَفْرَغْ لِبْحَرْ مِنْ گَدَّامَكْ
2. اَثْلَتْ عِيمَانْ اَنْتَ تَرْحَلْ x اِرْدُّوكْ اَلْ بَلّْ اَخْيَامَكْ

1. If you sail westwards as a pilgrim, the open seas before you passing by,
2. Three years' voyage, without digression, will bring you home again to tent and tie.

This *gaaf* is in *lebtayt et-taamm* metre.

1. يَمُلَانَ جُودْ اَبْجُودَكْ x يَلِّ جُودِي مِنْ مَوْجُودَكْ
2. جُودَكْ فَضْلَتْ فِيهْ اَجْنُودَكْ x جُودْ اَبْجُودْ اَجْدِيدْ اِجِينَ
3. اَسْكِينَ مِنْ بَجّْ اَرْعُودَكْ x يَلِّ مَاهْ اَعْلِيكْ اَهْجِينَ

1. O Lord be generous with Your bounty, O You whose practice it is to show me bounty.
2. Your servants have great need of Your bounty. Be generous in giving us a new gift.
3. Water us with Your thunder-cloud. To You it is a matter of no consequence.

This *ṭal'a* is in *lebtayt et-taamm* metre.

1. يَمُلَانَ كَانْ اَلعِصْيَانْ x مَا خَلَّ لِمْسَارِبْ تَنْدَ
2. شَنْهُ ذَنْبْ اَلطَّلْحْ اَلْغرْثَانْ x اُذَنْبْ اَلْفَرْنَانْ اُلِعْلَنْدَ

1. O Lord, sins have not left an open space of land which is moist, or touched by rain.
2. What then is the sin of the thirsty *ṭalḥ*,[1] or the sin of the *efarnaan*,[2] or the *ʿelanda*?[3]

1. يَمُلَانَ شَمَّطْ لَحْشِيشْ x اُكُبّ اَلزَّرِيعَ ثَبْلْ آنِيشْ
2. وَاعْطِ لِعبَادَكْ بَاشْ اَتْعَيْشْ x مِنْ مَخْزَنْ مَا دُونْ عُكْدَ
3. غَلْبْ اَلْقنوطْ اُغَلْبْ اَلْفَيْشْ x اُغَلْبْ اَلذَّنْبْ اُغَلْبْ اَلرِدَّ
4. لُولَ تَرْيَاظَكْ بِتْرَشْرَيْشْ x اُمَّ تُغْرِكْ فِيهْ اَلْبَلْدَ

1. O Lord, bring forth the grass and cause the shoot to grow before the bud.
2. And give to men, so that they may live, the store of nurture which is Yours alone.
3. Your gift surmounts despair, it suppresses rivalry, it overcomes sin and apostasy.
4. Were it not for the way You send the rain in gentle showers, You would drown the whole land in it.

This poem, which may be linked to the preceding *gaaf*, is a *ṭalʿa* in *lebtayt et-taamm* metre.

1. لَثّْنَا لَكْ فِى ذِي اْلكَصْرَ x ثَدْحَانْ اَلظّْ يَمُلَانَ
2. يَبَلَّالْ اَعْرُوكْ اَلصَّدْرَ x وَاعْرُوكْ اَلْكِبْدْ اَلنَّشْفَانَ

1. In this time time of need we have offered You the vessels of faith, O Lord,

[1] *Acacia raddiana.* [2] *Euphorbia balsamifera.*
[3] *Leptadenia lancifolia.*

2. O waterer of the roots of the tree, and the dry and thirsty roots of the heart.

This poem is a *gaaf* in *lebtayt et-taamm* metre.

1. مَا يَڭْدَرْ سُلْطَانْ اَطَلَّڭْ x لَبْنُودْ اَعْلْ اَمْنَجْ اَمْغَلَّڭْ
2. فِي اجْوَالِيهْ اَشَيّرْ لَبْرَڭْ x وَاِصُوڭْ لِبْرَزْ شَعْشَانَ
3. يَسْحَمْهَ فِي اللّيْلْ اَبْمَرْفَڭْ x تَصْبَحْ بِالنِّيلَ شَرْڭَانَ
4. مِنْهُ حَدّْ اِڭَدّْ اِبُجْنَڭْ x زَنْدَوَاتْ اَفْ مُزْنْ اَمْلَانَ
5. مَا يَطْفِيهَ جَوْ اَمْرَڭْرَڭْ x يَڭُونْ اَنْتَ يَمُلَانَ

1. No power, save God, is able to unleash the thunderclaps of the dark cloud at forenoon,
2. in the depths of which the lightning darts, driving it on, o'er wide expanses, parched and dry,
3. darkening them in the night by a mountain,[1] they become like indigo at sunrise.
4. Who can make the torrent roar with lightning flashes like a tinder box?
5. No vibrant air is able to extinguish them. You are the only one, O Lord.

This poem is a *ṭalʿa* in *lebtayt et-taamm* metre. It may be connected with the preceding poem.

1. يَمُلَانَ فَرْغِتْ لَسْبَابْ x خَاطِ مَدّْ اَلْ جُودَكْ لَيْدِينْ
2. اَرْخِيهَ لِلْوَارِدْ وُالْغَابّْ x وُارْخِ شِدَّتْ لَادَمِيّينْ
3. اَرْخِيهَ بِالسَّيْلْ اَلْمَبْرُوكْ x اَلِّ ڭَرّْ اَنْزِيزْ مَدْڭُوكْ
4. اُبَدَّلْ لَاڭَرْڭَ بِالشَّوْكْ x وُالْحَالْ اَلْمِدَّفَّرْ بِالزَّيْنْ
5. وُالْوَادْ اَلِّ فُمُّ مَحْڭُوكْ x يَظْحَكْ بِالْمَكَرْ اُلْڭَحَاوَيْنْ

[1] Or an elbow?

1. O Lord, resolves have passed away, save one, the stretching forth of hands to crave Your bounty.
2. Open the heavens to the one who comes regularly to water and to him who does so rarely, and relieve the thirst and famine of the people.
3. Send forth the blessed torrent, like a closely embroidered garment in its pattern.
4. Bring forth the bud in place of the thorn; instead of a grievous state, favour us with beneficence.
5. And the river bed, the slopes of which are rough and dry, change it so that it may laugh and rejoice with *makr*[1] and chamomile.

This poem, in *lebtayt et-taamm* metre, is a *gaaf* followed by a *ṭalʿa*.

1. يَلْ بَانِ فِي الجَّوْاَسْمْ اَخْظَرْ : تَجْرِ فِيهَ الشَّمْسْ اُلْكُمَرْ
2. فِيهْ اَمْخَالِيكْ تَتْفَكَّرْ : وَانْتَ عَنْدَكْ كِيفْ اَلطَّاصَ
3. تَحْكَمْ عَنَّ جُنْدَكْ اْلَاكْبَرْ : لَا يَعْمَلْ فِينَ حَاوَاصَ
4. يَلِّ بَيْدِيكْ اَلنَّوَاصِي : اَبْحَرْ جُودَكْ مَا يَتْمَاصَ
5. لُو كَنْتْ اَحْكَمْتُ عَنْ عَاصِ : مَا يَحْظَرْ فِيهْ اُولِدْ مَاصَ

1. O, You who placed the blue sky in the heavens, where both the sun and moon pursue their course,
2. Your creation ponders deeply over it, but You are the one who knows the nature of the starry bowl.
3. Hold back from us Your mightiest host, the locusts, let them not take their spoils among us.
4. O, You whose hand grips the forelocks, let not the earth dry up the sea of Your bounty.
5. Were You to withhold rain from the sinner, no son of Māṣa[2] would enjoy a portion of it.

This poem is a *ṭalʿa*, followed by a *gaaf*, in *lebtayt et-taamm* metre.

[1] *Herniaria lenticulosa.*

[2] Māsa-Sī, a Bambára clan which dominated Dyāwara in Dyāra (Māli) in the eighteenth century.

1. مَا يَمْلِكْ دَوْلَ مِنْ لَمَزْونْ x

تَكْدَلْ مَشْيْ اَسْبُوعْ مِنْ اَلْجَّوْ

2. كُونْ اَلِّ يَقْصِدْهْ بِالْنُّونْ x

وُاْلكَافْ اَمْنْ اَلْظُّلْمَ لِلْظَّوْ

3. مُلْكْ اَمْحَمَّدْ شَيْنْ اُهَارُونْ x

اَلْرَّشِيدْ أَلَّا حَدُّ هَوْنْ

4. مَا فِيْهْ اَسْمَ كِيفْ اَلْفَكْرُونْ x

اِتْفَكَّرْ اَلِّ مَاهُ بَوّْ

5. اُرزِكْ اَلْخَلْكْ اَفْ كَرْشْ مَظْمُونْ x

تَوّْاِيْدِرّْ اِيتْمَرْكْ تَوّْ

1. None rules the riches of the rain clouds, filling a distance of a week of space,
2. except the One who, by a kāf and nūn,[1] wills it to be from darkness into light.
3. The realm of Muḥammad Shayn[2] and Hārūn al-Rashīd did not extend beyond this spot.
4. Here is not to be found a sky shaped like a tortoise. He who is not stupid[3] contemplates.
5. The livelihood of men is hidden within its belly. At times it gives milk and at other times it withholds it.

This poem is a *gaaf* followed by a *ṭalʿa*, in *lebtayt et-taamm* metre.

[1] *kun*—'exist', imperative of the Arabic verb *kāna*.

[2] Muḥammad Shayn wuld Bakkār wuld Aʿmar, ruler of the Īdaw ʿĪsh in the late eighteenth century.

[3] Or a stuffed camel hide for deceiving a she-camel when it is milked.

A prayer for rain addressed to the scholar saint Sīdī Muḥammad al-Kuntī, who lived in the fifteenth century and who lies buried at Faṣk on the edge of Azaffāl, the southern frontier region of the Río de Oro.

يَا مْرَابَطْ فَصْكْ عَنْدْ رَاصَكْ مِنْ كُلّْ اَشْوَارْ x اَتْلَاكَاتْ .1

جَايِّ مِنْ نَكْجِيرْ اَشْتَاتْ x اُجَايِّ مِنْ رَكْبَتْ كَنَّارْ .2

حَرْكْ اَلَهَ لَوْلَبْ مَعْلُومْ x بِيهْ رَكّْ اَسْمَاهْ مَرْدُومْ .3

كَانْ ذَاكْ اَللَّوْلَبْ مَحْكُومْ x بِيهْ وَسْخْ اَذْنُوبْ اَهْلْ اَلنَّارْ .4

ذَاكْ بَلّْ اَظْفَارْ اَسَلُّومْ x كَانْ فَمّْ اَنْكَصْرُ لَظْفَارْ .5

عَارْفِينْ عن ذَحَمْلْ اَثْكِيلْ x غَيْرْ يُومْ اَنْهَارْ اَزَبَّارْ .6

مَا يْكُومْ اَلْحَمْلْ اَلثَّكِيلْ x فِيهْ كُونْ اَمَلْيَ الصَّبَّارْ .7

يَلِّ بِيكْ اِكَرَّبْ لَبْعِيدْ x مَانِ حَامِلْ وَرْدْ اَكَادِيرْ .8

وَاَنْتْ اَكْرَبْ مِنْ حَبْلْ اَلْوَرِيدْ x وَاسْمَاكْ اَمْزَكَّرْ مِنْ لَغْدِيرْ .9

1. O *murābiṭ* of Faṣk, men have assembled at your tomb from every region,
2. coming in scattered groups from Nagjīr and coming from Ragbat Gannār.
3. Take a hand in their affairs, effect through intercession something profitable and through which their expanse of sky may burst (with rain).
4. Such action was denied, because of the vile sins of those who merit hell.
5. That is the place for the finger-nails of the courageous one, if other nails be cracked and broken.
6. We know that this is a heavy burden, but it is a day of intense heat.
7. Only a patient camel carries a heavy burden in it.
8. O God, whom the far distant one approaches, I cannot come to the well of Agādīr.
9. But You, o God, are nearer than the jugular vein and Your sky is filled with water pools of rain.

This poem (or poems) is a *gaaf*, followed by a *ṭal'a* (c c c b c b), another *gaaf* (d b d b), and a final *gaaf* (e f e f). The first *gaaf* and *ṭal'a* are in *bu 'umraan* metre. The second *gaaf* is in the same metre, but the final *gaaf* is in *lebtayt et-taamm* metre.

1. اَلْجُمْلَ مِنْ فَضْلَتَيْنِ x كَانْ اِنْدَفْعِتْ لَكْ لَا تَكْثَبَلْ
2. وُالْجُمْلَ مِنْ عُمْدَتَيْنِ x كِيفْ اِلْبَلْ جَاتْ اُجَاتْ اِلْبَلْ

1. Do not accept a sentence which is composed of two dispensable redundancies (e.g. *tamyīz* or *ḥāl*) if it be given to you.
2. A sentence consists of two indispensable supports, a subject and a predicate, as in the example 'the camels came', be that sentence nominal, or be it verbal.

This *gaaf*, which is an example of the scholastic tastes of the poet expressed in Ḥassānīya, is in *lebtayt et-taamm* metre.

This poem is a short Arabic grammar lesson. The poet states that the fundamental parts of an Arabic sentence are the subject and the predicate, whether the sentence is a nominal or a verbal sentence. Other parts of the sentence are *faḍalāt* 'redundancies', incidental to the fundamental structure of the sentence which is complete and intelligible without them. Thus جاء زيد 'Zayd came' is complete without the addition of راكباً 'riding', which is an example of a *ḥāl*, the state or condition of the subject or object of an act, or both, whilst the act is taking place. Another *faḍla* is the accusative known as *tamyīz* 'specification'. It is an indefinite substantive placed immediately after the proposition of which it limits or defines the predicate, e.g. زيد أكثر منك مالاً 'Zayd is wealthier than you are' (lit. 'Zayd is more than you in respect of property').

1. سُبْحَانْ اَلِّ بَيَّنْ لَشْوَارْ x اَلَارْتِبَطْ رَاصْ اَلْكَثَارِبْ
2. لَامَالِيفُ فِي السَّاحِلْ نَارْ x وَاْلفَ فِي الشَّرْكْ اَبْلَاصَاحِبْ
3. اَبْوُجْهُ كِثْبَلَ كِيفْ اَلدَّارْ x وَاكْثْفَاهْ اَمْكَاثِفِ يَا الطَّالِبْ
4. وَلَا عَنَّ دَرْكُ لَقْمَارْ x تَنْدَارْ البَطَّ لِلذَّاهِبْ

1. Glory to God who has specified directions, when seamen doubt the direction of their boat.

2. Lām-alif in the north-west is a light, while fā' is in the east and stands alone.
3. It faces southwards, like a tent, and its back looks northwards, oh you, the seeker.
4. And should the moons be hidden from us, then for the voyager, the compass should be set.

This poem is a *gaaf*, in *lebtayt et-taamm* metre.

The poet is in a light-hearted mood in this poem. He portrays a group of sea-men in a boat who are confused as to the points of the compass. To help them he indicates that the Arabic letters *lām-alif* (لا) point in a north-westerly direction, while the letter *fā'* (ڢاء) in Maghribī script points east, although the dot of the letter points south (the direction in which a tent is pitched), and the 'tail' of the letter points north. However, if there is no moon visible to guide the seamen they should use a compass.

CONTEMPORARY ḤASSĀNĪYA

I

The following poem, in lebtayt en-naageṣ *metre, represents a correspondence by letter between Shaykh Wuld Makkī and Shaykh Muḥammad wuld Muḥammad al-Yadālī*

Shaykh Wuld Makkī begins:

1. sallam li laʿd enjiik : ef leqruur enkaafiik.
2. ʿala munniina ḏiik : waʿla maana mayya.
3. waʿla ʿayya waʿliik : waʿla zaad ʿaliyya.
4. (u)ḵaṣṣas li laa tesġir : bislaami ʿayya sirr.
5. wemn el-gerraaḍ aḥḏar : waasiiha jebdiiya.
6. (u)sawwalha li ʿan zerr : en-naas eš-šargiiya.
7. (u)ʿan ḏaak el-ḥadd iyyaak : maa baddal ši biiya.
8. wel men ḏa fiih aġbaak : sawwal ʿannu ʿayya.
9. welli gaalet lak fiih : mašši li yan-naziih.
10. biih u laa yaʿlam biih : kuun enta ḵefiiya.
11. haaḏa layna twaasiih : igerr afṭan fiiya.
12. wejemmel wen kaafiih : maa zelt alha hiiya.

al-jawāb

13. laḥḥagt eslaamak fatt : liš-šaʿʿaar elli gelt.
14. wefṭan ʿanni ʿaddalt : talḥaagu bin-niiya.
15. waʿgebt eṣṣa jaabett : ʿanhem waḥdi ʿayya.
16. biiya ḏaak elli šeft : fek̲baar ej-jebdiiya.
17. (u)gelt alha ḏaak ez-zaad : gelt alha men lemraad.
18. gaalet li ʿannak gaad : fen-naas eš-šargiiya.
19. tadrak ši men lemraad : biš-šawṭ (šarṭ) aʿla ʿayya.
20. taʿjal wen waadeʿ zaad : en-naas el-gebliiya.
21. wel-ḥadd elli gelt uraak : ajbar lam ʿaaref haak.
22. menhem ġayr eṣṣa ḏaak : gad gaalet li hiiya.
23. maa nassa fiik u šaakk : ʿan sebbetha ʿayya.
24. wel-mekafaat ʿaṭayt : ferresla hahiiya.
25. nagbaḍ fiiha lajiit : men gebla lahḏiiya.

qāl al-S̲h̲ayk̲h̲ ayḍan:

26. salaamu kel-mudaam : wel-wardi wel-k̲uzaam.
27. (u)tejri bih leqlaam : menni wet-taḥiiya.
28. ila l-ak̲ el-humaam : u baʿdu inniiya.
29. fi k̲ayrin wekraam : wen laa baas aʿliiya.
30. wen elḥagna lektaab : er-raasel bej-jawaab.
31. biʾaḥsan el-k̲iṭaab : sajʿu aʿrabiiya.
32. anḍartu men laʿgaab : maa-ajmal ši fiiya.
33. mennu wanḍart efbaab : naḍm el-ḥassaaniiya.
34. (u)šeft anna fil-ʿarraad : maani jaaber mefaad.
35. duun ank̲alli ši ʿaad : bayn alaah aydiiya.
36. (u)jellejni ḏaak u zaad : ḥezmi guul el ʿayya.
37. welli fiih es-sedaad : men ḏa ʿaad aʿliiya.
38. laa budd emn anwaasiih : laʿaad agʿaad fiih.
39. es-sedaad ismi biih : wala ʿaad amjiiya.
40. fiih es-sedaad al-hayh : ʿaliiya faydiiya.
41. kent amjiyya saabeg : tarsel biiha ʿayya.
42. weš gaal ana saabeg : wajbert ed-durbayya.

al-jawāb

43. el-ḥamdu lil-gessaam : elli waasa leqlaam.
44. teġni ʿan leklaam : kaamel bil-kulliiya.
45. wes-saʿy aʿla leqdaam : muujab ḏil-qaḍiiya.
46. baʿd atamm es-salaam : huwwa wet-taḥiiya.
47. yaš-šayk̲ ana ḏaana : men karam mulaana.

48. saalim men lehaana	:	wen laa baas aʿliiya.
49. wanra zaad eflaana	:	hiiya lekṯar fiiya.
50. wan el-ḥadd elli kaan	:	šarg eḥziimu yemtaan.
51. men taṣriif es-subḥaan	:	hawn aṯbat faydiiya.
52. annu ʿaddal makaan	:	men ruuṣ aš-šargiiya.
53. waḥjab makaanu ḏaan	:	wafham ḏil-kayfiiya.
54. waʿref ʿanni muraak	:	rayt emmʷalli ši haak.
55. fahl afjaar u ḏaak	:	maa gaddu maziiya.
56. ḏa guuli ʿannak haak	:	ḵaṭra ḥaqiiqiiya.
57. annak maa kaan amʿaak	:	ḵaaṭer maahu hiiya.
58. wersil li billi fiik	:	ṭaari welli faydiik.
59. wayyaak yeradd (?) al-biik	:	baayed kaan ubiiya.
60. wel-ḥaal el-ḵalṭa ḏiik	:	el-muhaajiriiya.
61. wersil li billi raay	:	men ši kaamel fiyya.
62. waʿref ʿanni naglaay	:	u ḵayr el-ʿaṭiiya.

Shaykh Wuld Makkī said:

1. Convey my greetings. When I come to you, perchance I'll reward you.
2. (Convey my greetings) to Munnīna and to Māna Mayya
3. and to ʿAyya. Greetings to you and also to ʿAlī.
4. On my behalf—grant me your indulgence—greet ʿAyya in secret.
5. Be on your guard against the scandal-monger and be alone together when exchanging confidences.
6. Ask ʿAyya, for me, about the 'people of the east',
7. and about that one, whether she[1] has, or has not, exchanged me for another in her affections?
8. Be athirst to find out all you can. Ask ʿAyya about it,
9. and let me know what she tells you, oh blameless one,
10. and let no one but yourself know of it.
11. If you do this I'll be most grateful,
12. your service will be appreciated, and ʿAyya will be rewarded.

The order of this poem is unorthodox. It begins with a *ṭalʿa* (verses 1 to 3), followed by a second *ṭalʿa* (verses 4 to 6), then a *gaaf* (verses 7 and 8), and concluded by a third *ṭalʿa* (verses 9 to 12).

[1] Moors consulted agree that *ḥadd* means 'she' in this context. As *ḥadd* is an indefinite 'someone' (cf. Cohen, p. 165), it is eminently suitable for use in an intrigue of the kind manifest in the poem.

The answer of Shaykh Muḥammad wuld Muḥammad al-Yadālī:

13. I've conveyed your greetings to the *iggāwen* named by you,
14. and know that I've carried out what was intended.
15. Finally, for sure, I did exchange words of confidence away from them, alone with ʿAyya,
16. in view of the nature of the matter to be discussed.
17. I also spoke to her about your affair.
18. She said that among the 'people of the east'
19. you may obtain success in your affair, by keeping well in with (or on condition, according to) ʿAyya,
20. you should hurry up and bid farewell to (divorce) the 'people of the south'.
21. The one to whom you refer has found acquaintances.
22. In fact, that is what ʿAyya told me.
23. You are not forgotten, and I think ʿAyya is the cause.
24. As for the reward promised by you on account of the mission,
25. I'll take the gift, when you come from Senegal.

The poem begins with a *ṭalʿa* (verses 13 to 16), followed by a second *ṭalʿa* (verses 17 to 20), a third *ṭalʿa* (verses 21 to 23), and a final *gaaf* (verses 24 and 25).

Shaykh Wuld Makkī also said:

26. My greetings like wine, like the rose and lavender
27. brought by pens—my compliments,
28. to my brother of courageous activity—I am
29. in the best of health and circumstances.
30. I have received the letter, sending your reply,
31. excellently written in Arabic rhymed prose.
32. I've read it through and through. There is nothing dearer to my heart
33. than it. I've perused a passage of Ḥassānīya poetry,
34. and observed, that I can find nothing of advantage among women,
35. unless I give up something I already have.
36. That has both worried me, and increased my eagerness. Tell ʿAyya,
37. and tell her that I will have to do what suits my interests best.
38. If it is better that I stay where I am
39. then I'll concur, but if it is better for me to come,

40. then I'll come like a shot,
41. even before ʿAyya can say yes to me,
42. for I'm in a hurry and have both the will and the means to do it.

The poem begins with a *ṭalʿa* (verses 26 to 29), followed by a second *ṭalʿa* (verses 30 to 33), then a third *ṭalʿa* (verses 34 to 37), then a fourth *ṭalʿa* (verses 38 to 40), and concludes with a *gaaf* (verses 41 and 42).

The answer of Shaykh Muḥammad wuld Muḥammad al-Yadālī:

43. God, the Apportioner, be praised, who has caused pens
44. to dispense with uttered words, entirely,
45. and a journey on foot. With regard to this affair,
46. after all the greetings and the compliments,
47. O Shaykh, and being one who by the grace of God
48. keeps clear of shame, I'm very well.
49. So also is she. I've met her quite often.
50. The ardour of the one in the east grows yet greater.
51. Due to the vicissitudes which God ordains, I've proof at hand
52. showing that this one has set up home with somebody of high status in the east,
53. and thus is unapproachable. Understand the position,
54. and know that since we last left, I have found a pleasing thing for you
55. among the 'people of Afjār', and there is none like her in beauty.
56. I've been informed that you can pay a visit,
57. provided you and she are all alone.
58. Let me know your reactions, and how things fare with you,
59. so that both of us may find our peace of mind again (?).
60. Let me know how the company of the Muhājirīya[1] is getting on.
61. Send me all that you come across of concern to me,
62. and know that I am pressed, and make the gift a good one.

The poem begins with a *ṭalʿa* (verses 43 to 46), followed by a second *ṭalʿa* (verses 47 to 49), then a third *ṭalʿa* (verses 50 to 53), then a fourth *ṭalʿa* (verses 54 to 57), a fifth *ṭalʿa* (verses 58 to 60), and concludes with a *gaaf* (verses 61 and 62).

[1] Muhājirīya. According to Mukhtār wuld Ḥāmidun, the name Muhājirī (masc.) is used in eastern Mauritania to indicate a Ḥassānī or a *laḥmī* who has become a member of the Zwāya. Elsewhere he is known as a *tāyeb* (cf. p. 20).

II

1. emnayn ʿadt elli raaji : el-yuum šawf el-kiiraaya.
2. ya rabb kaṯra li nʿaaji : wel-maaʿz ef enwakaaya.
3. ayyaak nasman wen k̲arraf : wen ʿuud maani mutʾannaf.
4. wen ʿuud liṭ-ṭelḥ enšaggaf : baṭṭaaḥ fiḍ-ḍill eḥd̲aaya.
5. wen ʿuud kebši muʿarraf : birfuud zaad emsigaaya.
6. wet ʿuud leġnam tejriiti : wen ʿuud minha bmaaliiti.
7. wen ʿuud fiidi taadiiti : wen ʿuud ʿabdi waayyaaya.
8. faydiih sarraaḥ iiniiti : we-ʿuud yak̲baṭ zawzaaya.

1. When, today, I hope to see the shepherd's encampment,
2. O Lord, make my ewes and goats plentiful at Inwakāya,
3. so that I may become rich and abundantly supplied with pasturage and milk, and I will not be proud.
4. I will be a cutter of *ṭalḥ* and sleep in the shade near to the herd.
5. My ram will be well known for its carrying of my small water-skins.
6. My sheep will become my main enterprise, and through them I'll acquire great riches.
7. In my hand will be my wooden milking pail, and I will have my slave with me.
8. He will have a comb to remove cram-crams in his hand, and he will entertain by playing his flute.

The poem is a *gaaf* (verses 1 and 2) followed by a *ṭalʿa* (verses 3 to 5) followed by a second *ṭalʿa* (verses 6 and 7). The metre is *mraymiida*.

III

This poem, the significance of which is obscure and based on an interpretation of Muk̲h̲tār wuld Ḥāmidun, is a *ṭalʿa* (verses 1 to 4), followed by a second *ṭalʿa* (verses 5 to 7) and completed by a *gaaf* (verses 8 and 9). The metre of the poem is *lubb^{w}ayr agiilaal.*

1. tak̲liitek maa hanaatni : la nerged maa waʿʿaatni.
2. la nawʿa maa sahhaatni : biyya ʿandi taʿdaalek.
3. wek̲laagi maa hanaatni : fenwaasiiha lek haalek.
4. wek̲laagek maa k̲allaatni : ikuun anwaasiiha lek.
5. gelti ʿan haad̲u kaamlaat : jabru liʿyaal u d̲aak faat.
6. sebba liʿyaalek la nsmaat : hiyya sebba lefṣaalek.

7. tegder tetwaasa zaad laat	:	muuti ʿan gaaʿ ʿiyaalek.
8. ʿiyaalek yaʿref ʿilltu	:	kaan ak̲liik fiʿl el-maalek.
9. fil-maalek ḥatta gelltu	:	fiʿl el-maalek fil-maalek.

1. Your divorce has not left me tranquil. Whenever I sleep, it arouses me.
2. Whenever I awake cares trouble me, because of my love for you.
3. My soul troubles me. In granting you your divorce, I perish.
4. It is only for your sake that I have done it.
5. You said, 'All those other women have borne children.' That has happened (by God's will).
6. The bearing of children, were we to have spoken of it, would seem to be the cause for your divorce.
7. You may do it again. Do not die of sorrow on account of your family.
8. They could know the cause, whether your divorce was God's action with his subject,
9. and that your barrenness is likewise God's will upon his subject.

The poem concerns a wife who has compelled her husband to divorce her, although he loves her dearly, and he is grieved beyond measure to have to do so. It seems that the real cause which induced her to make him divorce her was never specifically discussed between them, although the husband suspects what it is. His wife had remarked that other women she knew had children, yet she had no children. The husband tells her not to grieve because of this. He thinks that she will ask for a divorce from other husbands because he believes that she is barren. The gift of children is something which God bestows or withholds from his creation, and there is no escape from his Almighty decree.

IV

A *tebraaʿ*, a poem improvised by Mauritanian women in a free style, often on the subject of love. The poetess is Maryam mint Agaylās.

1. maa nabġi d̲er-rajl ijiina	:	well aḥmad baaba kaafina.
2. menni maa k̲alla bagiiya	:	laylat wejdu d̲iik aʿliiya.
3. haad̲a raahu gern el-ʿašriin	:	laa yaṣlaḥ lak farḍ u laa diin.
4. well aḥmad baaba raaʿiini	:	nebġiik u laḥgak tebġiini.

1. I don't like the company of this group of men who come running after me. Wuld Aḥmad Bāba is quite enough for me.

2. He has not forsaken me. What remains of that night of his love for me still surrounds me.
3. This is the twentieth century, it is not suited to you, neither in obligation nor in religion.
4. O, Wuld Aḥmad Bāba, watch for me, I love you, so you must love me.

V

Another poem by a Mauritanian woman in a free style. The poetess is Ṣadgi mint al-Mas̲h̲ḍūfī of the Awlād ʿAmmʷanni of the Adrār. It is about her son. This poem, composed in January 1962 during the tense political situation on the frontier of the Ḥawḍ, between Mauritania and Māli, is, in the main, three *güfaan* (a b a b c b c (irregular) b b a b a).

1. yaa rabbi taḵli mašḍuuf	:	l-awwal menhem wet-taali.
2. welli beyya baʿd alla men ḵawf	:	yawʿdhem welli y-Allaa li.
3. ʿaddal fiihem ḏiik l-ḵaṣla	:	u laa waasa fiihem lemḥaali.
4. yaa rabbi jiibu led-dašra	:	u men ṣerwiiṣ allaa huuwal-ʿaali.
5. ṭra l-ġarb emmʷalli	:	weḵleg famm l-ḵawf.
6. kaafiikem men welli	:	jibuuh u tawf.

1. O God, get rid of the Mas̲h̲ḍūf, the whole lot of them.
2. Why?—My reason is simply one of fear, because my son goes towards them, O my God.
3. He has accomplished this great success to their detriment. He has acted chivalrously and he has done no harm to them.
4. O God, bring him back to the town (Néma) among the highest rank of civil servants.
5. (Dissidents from) Morocco are new down here, causing alarm along the frontier.
6. My son has done you good service, bring him back—that's all (I want).

VI

1. el-baareḥ yaa laʿla : nemt endaawi daa'i : saabeg laʿša raahu.
2. u men naama gebla : ṣalaati l-ʿišaa'i : laa naamet ʿaynaahu.

1. Yesterday evening, O Lord, I went to bed to treat my (love) sickness, before the ʿis̲h̲ā'[1] prayer,

[1] The evening prayer.

2. and he who retires before the 'ishā' prayer does not close his eyes in sleep.

This poem is in *mzaareg* (*el-mezaareg*) metre. It has a uniform rhyme scheme of three hemistichs in the pattern, a b c, a b c, etc.

VII

1. دار امجْي لڭويرب الاَوّلْ x تَمَّيْت الغروب انْنَسْفَلْ
2. لِجمْلَ شلّلْني مستَڭْبَلْ x وُانْكبْني لُوتِدْ وُاتْعيَثْرت
3. وُانْشِلْتْ احْذاي فمّ اعْجَيْلْ x مربوڭْ اَبْحَڭْبَه وانقطْعت
4. ڤَالتْ لِ ذِالْ نَفْنى نختلْ x غافسْني بَڤْرَتْنَ رظْعَت
5. وانْجِفْت ءُا جرجاني لِعْجَلْ x وانْشَلَّبت اشْوَي ءُا ظَحْكت
6. ڤلتْ الْهَا بِعْجِلْكُم يَعْزَلْ x ڤالت مَا يعزل وانت خفت
7. حَكَمْتْ وُذْنُ حلّيْت احْبَيْل x وارْبَطْت واتلَفّتّ ءُا ڤَلْت
8. لخوَيدِم لڤَدْيح الْ تُغْسِل x الْ نَحْنَ ڤالت لِ رَشَّخْتْ
9. افْ هاذ حَصْرِت ڭاع الْبِل x واڤْبظت اڤدَيحتْن وارْفَعْت
10. نَافدْ بلّي رَيْت الْ نختيْر x منُّ مَلْكْ عاسِرْ بشْولْت
11. ڭلّتْ منُّ ماريتْ آغيْر x خالكْ ش كطّيْت اتْفَكَّرت
12. دارْ امجي لڭويرب في الليْل x ليْله فيها لِفْرَاش اڭليل
13. بدّلتْ اصْرَيمِيَّ بكْفَيل x مِحْشي من كَاڭَه واتْڭْنْڭْلْتْ
14. حكّيْت اَثري مَسَّيْتَ طْفيل x راڤدْ واتْنَفّسْ واسَتْحرفَت
15. خايف ننشَاف ابهاذِ الحيل x امنين اصْرَدْعنّي رجّعتْ

1. When the first little boat came,[1] I was leading a hobbled camel at sundown.
2. It took me in a southerly direction. A tent peg knocked me aside, and I tripped a little.
3. I arose and found a calf before me, noosed by a rope of hair, and the rope was cut.
4. Then she, for whom I lie in wait and waste away, said to me in haste, 'My cow is suckling her young.'
5. I stepped aside, and the calf mooed and tried to butt me. Then I stepped back a little, and she laughed.
6. I said to her, 'Is your calf alarmed?' 'No,' she said, 'it is you who are afraid.'
7. She took it by its ear, and I loosed the rope, then tightened it. I looked about me, and I said,
8. 'That little calabash the slave girl's washing, why, it's mine.' My beloved said to me, 'What you have just said, everybody knows.'
9. While this was going on, the camels reached the pen. I grasped my little calabash and took my leave.
10. I took the homeward road. I found it an awkward time to meet my love, I felt uneasy.
11. 'Twas but a passing moment, but there was something else, and I recall it well.
12. It was when the little boat came in the night, a night when there were few cushions to lie on.
13. I laid down a bolster in place of a small ṣurmīya[2] cushion. It was stuffed with husk and bran and filled with bugs.
14. So I itched because of this, and I disturbed a sleeping child. I took a deep breath, held it, and turned aside,
15. in fear, lest I be observed in this predicament. And when the child no longer sensed my presence, 'twas then that I returned to where I was.

The poem is a *ṭalʿa* of nine verses, then a *gaaf* of two verses, and a second *ṭalʿa* of four verses in *lebtayt et-taamm* metre.

[1] Moors have, in the past, named the years after the arrival of certain boats, whether for collecting gum along the river or at ports on the Atlantic coast.

[2] *ṣurmīya*, a round or oblong-shaped cushion made of stuffed goat-skin and geometrically decorated and painted in earth colours by the Moorish women.

اللاحق او وقع مثال عول تحت امثلة جد الجهال كون افلكز بذا الكون
في باب الغرا المسائل منسوب لكبراء العول اغلطه فيه وا تعال
انكرها الذي ما انكوه امر حالت في بين العال بالمثال المثال كون
بو عمرو المقال زوج المرحوم وامه امثلة منها فبالمثال
اصل المسائل سته في ستاى تنزال لم الا تسكت فيه
انكبت تشير الحال للزوج اثلاث لمه والجد السخ سرا زيال
جات اخت الكسيم في منه ملات النص اجبال سمت لشلاثة صحيحهم
اتى تسع تثلال والجد اثنت الى الثمن عاد منهم اربعاى
ما تشالن يعويلهم والثلاث فالتسعاى حرام بها تحصيلهم
عشرين امع سبعاى لظ الكبيل او ليلهم ابيض فسقلثاى
معرفو سبيلهم اكاد ذمى لكراى الغرته وامى حله
منزعت الخلاى . الى عاد افكله في ما بين سبعاى
كيف الى عاد افعله اقم الهو من ام امعامهم فاذا الجد الى كله
طاع بين مزا منهم متوطن حيتهم وارد فيه الى كال
كاتلهم يكيبه سليهم سلب القيل الالل اوفيه لخي يلكوهم اخى
ميت ورثوه امر امثل مال فالزورق همز فلى ج الاول وارفع ثلث المال
والثاني ماض اعل شكى ثلث الباطي عن وافتال والثالث ج واتحر تجز

ثلث الباطي عن داك الكمال والرابع عن بيل الغم غرج واجمع الامزال
لزوج اجبر تسعاى ثلث التسعاى والعشرين والثاني لم السنا ي
ثلث الخمسة عشر اذ بيبي والثالث تحت اربعاى ثلث اتحسر ابكا واربعين
الحبر افهم ثم اغناى امعصب تحت الغوديى امنزكاه والزواى
واعظ كيه امر التبيبى امو الزام الشفيه والزلاى —

VIII

The case known as al-Akdarīya

الا ݣط اوقع محال عود x لخت امع اجد ابحال x كون افلكدريا الكود x
ذيك الغيّ المسال x منسوب لكدر ايعود x اغلط فيه واتعال x
انݣرها لك ما اتكود x امن حالت ذيك الحال x بالمثال المثال ݣود x
يوضّح المقال x زوج المرحوم وامه x امعاهم فالمثال x
اصل المسئال يمه x من ستّاي تتوال x لم الاّ تسكنت فمه x
اتݣبظ ثنتين اعجال x للزوج اثلاث لمه x والجد السدس اريال x
جات اخت اݣطعهم دمه x ملات النص اݣبال x ست لثلاث ضمهم x
اتج تسع تتلال x والجد الخت الّي الهم x عاد فم اربعاي x
ما تثالث يويلهم x واثلاث فالتسعاي x حد اضربهم تحصيلهم x
عشرين امع سبعاي x لصل اݣبيل او ليلهم x ابضرب فثلثاي x
هاذ هو سبيلهم x اكاف ذ من لݣراي x الغزته واعر حله x
هاذ لخت الخلاي x الى عاد افمحله x خ ما يجبر سفاي x
كيف الى عاد افبله x افم اخوت ام امعاهم x ذاك الجد الّ كله x
صاع يجبر مزاهم x هو لمدّ حجبهم x وارد فيه الّ ݣال x
كاتلهم يݣبظ سلبهم x سلب القتيل الال x افيه لغز يلݣوم اخر x
ميت ورثون امن اهل دال x فالزورق لحمدّ فكر x ج الاول وارفد ثلث المال x
والثان حاص اعل شطر x ثلث الباݣ عن وانشال x والثالث ج وانجر نجر x
ثلث الباݣ غن ذاك اݣبال x والرابع عن ذيك الغبر x غرّج واجمع ذا الّ
مزال x

لوّل زوج اجبر تسعاي x ثلث السبعاي والعشرين x والثان لم الستاي

ثلث اثمنطعش اذ يبين x والثالث لخت اربعاي x ثلث اثنعش ابگاو اربعتين

للجد افهم تم اغناي x امعصب لخت ال عودين x اهاذ كاف ول ازواى x

واخاطيه امن التبيين .

1. There has never been a sharing (of inheritance) between the sister and the grandfather,
2. except in the obscure and noted case of al-Akdarīya.
3. The question relates to al-Akdar,[1] who erred in it. Come to me,
4. and I will explain it to you so that it will not baffle you. How the circumstances arose
5. is shown by the example. The latter is the way to explain a statement clearly.
6. (There was) the husband of the deceased wife, and her mother. (The grandfather) was with them both in the example.
7. The initial basis of the case was six (divisions), one by one.
8. The mother kept quiet about it. She quickly took two shares (one-third of the six).
9. The spouse collected three shares (a half) and the grandfather one share of the six—a riyāla.[2]
10. Then came the sister. Her relationship to them decreased their shares. In fact, she was entitled to half.
11. So three were joined to six, and that clearly makes nine.
12. Those of the grandfather and the sister (together) add up to four in all.
13. Hers was not a third, oh woe!—Three when multiplied by nine
14. makes twenty-seven.
15. The basis of each is now apparent, through multiplying by three.

[1] This unusual case is the only one where the sister (whether the germane sister or half-sister on the father's side) was regarded as one of the *ahl al-furūḍ* together with the grandfather, instead of taking the rank of *ʿaṣaba* (p. 113, n. 2). The name of the case either refers to the word *akdar*, meaning 'obscure', 'dusky', or 'murky', or to the man to whom, it is said, the Umayyad Caliph ʿAbd al-Malik b. Marwān (685–705) submitted it for decision.

[2] *riyāla* is introduced here for the sake of the rhyme. In the region of Timbuctoo it is worth 5 francs, and it is called *ūgīya* in Mauritania, in general (Pierret, *Étude du dialecte maure*, p. 186).

16. This is how the division was made, and this explanation is sufficient.
17. The solution to this riddle is a difficult one. As for this sister,
18. were there a brother in her place, he would not get a *sufāya*;[1]
19. likewise, if there were in her place mother's brothers,
20. competing with that grandfather. He it is who sweeps them all aside, and gets their share,[2]
21. since it is he who brings about their being excluded. The maxim is applicable to him—
22. 'he has slain them and taken their booty'—the booty of the slain belongs solely to him (the slayer).
23. There is another riddle, oh my people, where a deceased had family inheritors.
24. In al-Zawraq[3] is a surprise for Aḥmaddu.[4] The first came and carried away one-third of the money.
25. The second quickly took the third of the remainder of it and departed,
26. and the third came, and, in fact, cut off the third of the remainder,
27. and the fourth was slothful regarding the remainder. He collected what was left.
28. The first is the spouse, who got nine—one-third of twenty-seven,

[1] *sufāya*, 0·05 of a franc (cf. Pierret, p. 186), a sou.

[2] Inheritors are of two kinds:

(1) *Ahl* (*aṣḥāb*) *furūḍ maḥdūda*, twelve heirs in all (e.g. husband, wife, sister) to whom a prescribed portion is allotted.

(2) The *ʿaṣabāt*, 'agnates' (e.g. sons, grandsons, father, uncles), take what remains.

The grandfather excludes the uterine brothers and sisters, unlike the father who excludes all brothers and sisters. He inherits in the same way as the father if the latter is not present. Uterine brothers and sisters are excluded by the father and grandfather of the deceased in the paternal line. One sister without a brother is entitled to a prescribed portion of one-half when she is an entitled heir. She is not one of the *ahl al-furūḍ* when the deceased leaves a corresponding brother or a paternal grandfather. She then takes the status of *ʿaṣaba*, and she inherits with the grandfather half of the man's share. She retains her status of *ahl al-furūḍ* in the presence of a grandfather in the peculiar case of *al-Akdarīya*, the subject of the poem.

[3] *Zawraq al-khā'iḍ fī ʿilm al-farā'iḍ*, according to Mukhtār wuld Ḥāmidun, is a work written by one of the scholars of the poet's tribe.

[4] Aḥmaddu is the nick-name for a person who appears in examples in the above text.

29. and the second (the mother) collected six, one-third of eighteen, this is clearly explained—
30. and the third (the sister) kept four, one-third of twelve, and two fours remained
31. for the grandfather. So understand. My poem is ended. By *taʿṣīb*,[1] from the sister, (the grandfather) had two shares.
32. This is sufficient for a Zwāya son, or other than him, by way of explanation.

Summary of the case

The following heirs were involved:

1. the husband,
2. the mother,
3. the grandfather,
4. the sister.

The initial basis of the division of the inheritance was 6.

1. the husband $\frac{1}{2} = \frac{3}{6}$
2. the mother $\frac{1}{3} = \frac{2}{6}$
3. the grandfather $\frac{1}{6} = \frac{1}{6}$
4. the sister $\frac{1}{2} = \frac{3}{6}$

In the above dilemma, by means of *ʿawl*[2] (a reduction of the inheritance), the basis for the division was reduced from $\frac{9}{6}$ to $\frac{9}{9}$.

1. the husband $\frac{3}{9} = \frac{9}{27}$
2. the mother $\frac{2}{9} = \frac{6}{27}$
3. the grandfather $\frac{1}{9} = \frac{3}{27}$
4. the sister $\frac{3}{9} = \frac{9}{27}$

The sister, however, had a claim to only half the share of the grandfather because of the rule which gives to the man the double of the woman, so the shares were combined, $\frac{4}{9} = \frac{12}{27}$, and were then divided, giving to the grandfather $\frac{8}{27}$, and to the sister $\frac{4}{27}$.

[1] *taʿṣīb* is where a female agnate who is one of the *ahl al-furūḍ* is converted into a residuary heir by a male relation of precisely the same relationship. This particular case is the one outstanding exception.

[2] *Encyclopaedia of Islam*, new edition, vol. i, 1960, p. 764.

The poem is a series of eight *giifaan* (1–5, 6–11, 12–16, 17–18, 19–20, 21–22, 23–27, 28–32). The first six are in *lubbʷayr* metre, the last two in *lebtayt et-taamm*. The poem is one of a series of résumés of the rules of Muslim succession in the Māliki *ma<u>dh</u>hab* and composed in Ḥassānīya on 17 <u>Dh</u>ū l-Ḥijja 1379/12 June 1960, by Aḥmad wuld Muḥammad ʿAbd al-Raḥman wuld Fatā for ʿAbdallāh wuld Aḥmad. The original copy is preserved in al-Me<u>dh</u><u>dh</u>er<u>dh</u>ra (Trārza). It is this original text which appears in Plate II. The version of the same text on pages 111 and 112 is unvocalized because of obscurities in the original. It may however, be of assistance to some in reading the original which is written in the form of Ma<u>gh</u>ribī script.

ZNĀGA POEMS

1. بَتُّ الَاصْبَطْ x تَنُّوْ مَشْتُ

2. تَنُّومَشْ بَطْ x الَاصْبَطْ بَتُّ

1. Batt (name of a woman) : al-Aṣbaṭ (name of man) : she loves him.
2. She loves only al-Aṣbaṭ : Batt (does).

This Znāga *gaaf* is in *ḥwaywiiṣ* metre.

1.
إنّ الشبابَ الذي تنْتِكْنَ نَوْبتُهُ x تِنتَكْنَ وَرْ نُمْرَ عن تَذْكَاره نِنَن

2.
أيّام إذْ نَجْتَني لِكْلْيّ نجْمَعُهَا x حمْرًا وإذْ نجتني تُو كنجأن شَكَن

1. Youth, the age of which is over, has departed. Until this very day I have not given up the recollection of it.
2. Days when I gathered the red fruit of the *legleyya*[1] and when I gathered the long pods of the *šegen*.[2]

(Metre irregular *al-basīṭ* ?)

[1] *Grewia tenax*. Vincent Monteil and Ch. Sauvage, *Contribution à l'étude de la flore du Sahara Occidental*, Institut des Hautes Études Marocaines, Notes et Documents, v, t. 1, Paris, Larose, 1949, p. 104, no. 351. Mu<u>kh</u>tār wuld Ḥāmidun describes the fruit as 'yellow', cf. *Précis sur la Mauritanie*, *I.F.A.N.*, 1952, p. 22.

[2] *Glossonema boreanum*, *ašakān*, cf. Monteil, p. 121, no. 416.

1.

بات الحُلَاحِلُ لـلاشواق يَنُّـكَرا x وبات إبليس فِي مزكُـوظـه إِغَرا

2.

حتى تبدّى له وجه الصباح يَرا x كـأنّـه بِـروْب من فـوقـه فَـرَىٰ

1. The master, filled with longings, spent the night, concealed, while Satan spent the night reciting in his ear.
2. Until the face of dawn appeared to him, and it was yellow, as though it was a bowl of skin-crowned, curdled milk.

This *gaaf* combines Znāga and Arabic. The metre is a form of *al-rajaz*. The poet is Muḥammad (Mḥammadh) wuld Aḥmad Yūra.

1. تَـمَـوْفِـرْ تـئِـذ تِتشَأْن اِتْسَنْ x بَـيْـذِ كْـنِـنْ ذَكْ اشَّمْكذِي

2. وَرْ ئِـنْ تُوْ كِـجْ يَغَيْرْ اتْسَنْ x آيشْ آءْ لِئّذ اعيَيْتْ اَيْكّذِي

1. That camping-site clothed in green with the *eššemkaḏi*[1] plant
2. does not recognize me, but it knows that I have often passed by that place.

1. بَـلِّـغْ سـلامـي ولا يَسْمَعْك مـن بـشـر x

إلى التي حبهُّا نِتّ آشَ اذْ امْدَر آري

2. اعـلـيـهَ بـالـمـارَ ما قد كنتُ اكتبه x

إشْ الـغُـبَـاري لـهـا ضحـى بأفـچّري

3. أُجْمَوَ تَـكْـتَـدَّ ما فِي الكَتْب من حِكَم x

أذْ وَرْ تَـشِـرْ ابـداً ما ليس يَـمْـجَـشِرِ

1. Convey my greetings, and let no one hear you, to the one who is my (heart's) ambition.

[1] *ašenkeḏ?*, in Ḥassānīya *Gynandropsis gynandra*, and *Cleome viscosa*, cf. Monteil, p. 67, nos. 209, 210.

2. Bear to her the token which I wrote for her, in *al-ghubārī*[1] script, at forenoon, at Āfajjār.
3. Were she to recall the wisdom in the writing, she would never mix together a mixture unacceptable.

(She never would associate with me, one whose association is unacceptable.)

The poet who composed this *gaaf* is Sīd Aḥmad Māmmīn. It is attributed in error to Muḥammad wuld Aḥmad Yūra, possibly because the latter was exceptionally versatile in this kind of love poem in Znāga and Classical Arabic. The poem is in *al-basīṭ* metre.

[1] The Mauritanian *ghubārī* script, read from right to left, is a form of *abjad*, where certain numerals, akin to European numerals, indicate letters of the alphabet, or where these same letters can indicate numerals. (The name al-Mukhtār, for example, is written: 2 1 4 6 4 3 1).

1. أيقش 1 111	4. دمت 4 44	7. زعذ 777
2. بكر 222	5. هنش 5 55	8. حفظ 888
3. جلش 3 33	6. وصخ 6 66	9. طضغ 99 9

10

FOLK-TALES OF THE TRĀRZA

FOLK-TALES in Ḥassānīya are a feature common to all the regions of Shinqīṭ, and the events, characters, and episodes appear again and again in both poetry and prose. The Trārza, for example, is the setting for many of these stories. In these fables and hagiographies the Moors express their ideas, their beliefs, their customs, and their wit. In the Trārza there has been preserved a cycle of short stories for children both Znāga and Ḥassānīya known as *tillis-n-Mīra* or *riwāyat Mīra*, episodes in the life of an imaginary Mauritanian woman, in which some moral or virtue is taught. The animals in all the stories have human virtues and vices. The hyena is a glutton, a coward, and unintelligent, while the jackal is crafty and a thief, a little like the hare; he is never very intelligent. At times these animals are given proper names. Social classes in Moorish society are often the subject of satire. The lower castes, particularly the īggāwen and the artisans, are gluttons or importunate, or cowardly. The warrior is always powerful, brave, and sometimes generous and noble, yet at the same time easily outwitted, vain, and wasteful, living from one day to the next and accepting what life offers with a smile. In the stories which originate among the Zwāya, the Ḥassānī Amīr is often a tyrannical figure, indifferent to religion and, in the end, always worsted. The Zwāya themselves are rich, lettered, pious, well fed, but often miserly. They use their skill to face, and finally overcome, their enemies.

ANIMAL LEGENDS AND FOLK-TALES OF THE SOCIAL CLASSES

The fight between the lion and the fly

An old lion was very hungry and exhausted by the heat. He tried to go to sleep but it was all in vain. A lady fly amused herself by tickling him in the eyes, the nose, and all over his body. Irritated beyond measure the lion exclaimed, 'You wretched little creature, leave me alone.'

'Since I am so small, you cannot feel my weight,' she replied. The lion was now very angry. 'Get away, your tickling disturbs me. If you continue thus, I'll use my tail to kill you.'

Quite unconcerned the lady fly threatened to kill him instead. 'You kill me?' asked the lion.

'Yes, oh king of the desert, the mountain, and the forest, and I'll prove it to you straight away.' On saying this, the lady fly entered one of his nostrils and flew towards his brain.

The lion was even more furious. He began to roar, to claw the ground, to tear the hair off his mane and his head, and to knock his head against the tree-trunks and against the stones. In the end he jumped about so much that he died of exhaustion. Then the lady fly came out from his brain, stood poised in victory upon his head, and said, 'Might is not always right, and it is thus that God punishes those who are vain.'

The last to be circumcised

One day all the wild animals of the bush circumcised their young. This event was marked by great feasting and celebrations. Every day the lion brought a camel or an ox to these young ones, while the jackal spent his time stealing sheep and goats. The young animals were treated like lords. It was unfortunate that the family of the grey, striped hyena were absent during the first days of the feast. When Muḥammad their son arrived and saw all this flesh in plenty he could not refrain from asking, 'How can I acquire some of all this fat and all this meat?'

He was told, 'Be circumcised and you will have a right to the feast.' He turned towards a woman seated beside him, and he ordered her to circumcise him. She grasped a great sharp knife, and she circumcised him. The blood flowed freely. Muḥammad felt himself growing quickly weaker and weaker, and he asked, 'Have you ever circumcised anyone who is still alive today?' 'Never,' she replied, 'I have circumcised nine, and they are all dead.' Muḥammad in agony sighed, 'Reckon me to be the tenth.' So his gluttony deprived him of his life, as well as his meat.

The adventure of the murābiṭ goat

A goat with a long beard who was learned, pious, and crafty went on pilgrimage to Mecca. All he had with him was honey and a water-skin. He knew that he could find something to eat all the way along the route he was to follow. Besides, his faith was such that it would give him the power to endure the most terrible hunger. One day he found himself face to face with a sick lion. The latter greeted him and said to him, 'Respected 'Atrūs, where are you going? It is rare to find one like you in this district.'

'I am going on the pilgrimage,' the murābiṭ goat replied. 'Am I on the right road?'

'Yes,' replied the lion, 'but if you are as pious as you look, you ought to cure me first of all.'

The goat was worried. He did not show it. He thought how he could play for time. He consented to the request, which was more in the nature of a courteous command.

He cut a piece from his prayer rug and wrote a talisman on it. Then he soaked it in honey and gave it to the lion. The latter swallowed it outright, licked his chops, and asked for more. He admitted, however, that he felt that this charm had had some beneficial effect. The goat gave him morsel after morsel, doing all he could to gain time. When he had given the lion the last piece, he thought of the hyena who had told him where to go. He pointed him out to the ever-demanding lion. The lion understood and did not stop to ask questions. With one blow of his paw he tore off a part of the back of the hyena in order to eat it. The hyena fled, pursued by the lion. The murābiṭ goat seized his chance and escaped.

It is wrong to swear, or The fortunes of a blacksmith

A blacksmith called Muḥammad, who was travelling with his wife, passed by an ebony tree. He swore to cut the tree. His wife said to him, 'Don't swear, since one is never sure of anything.' But he continued to do so regardless. He swore by his honour, and in the name of God, that he would cut this tree.

When they were enjoying their midday rest, the blacksmith picked up an axe, tucked it in his belt, left his wife, and went to cut the tree. When he began to climb it to cut it, he saw a panther at the top of it and a lion at its foot. Mad with fear and without thinking, Muḥammad leapt on the lion and gripped it by its ears. He remained lying on the back of the ferocious beast with his hands holding tight, while the startled lion fled, leaping and prancing again and again. Muḥammad still held tight while the lion went on running until it fell dead, but he still did not let go of its ears, even when men came and confirmed that it was dead, and they proved it by touching the dangerous beast. In order to make him relinquish his grip, those who had come to his rescue decided to act in a different way. One of them said, 'Kill a goat and cook its head and give it to a baby in front of the blacksmith. The baby will not know how to eat the head. Muḥammad will be unable to restrain himself, and he will jump off.' Events turned out as they had hoped, and in this way Muḥammad was saved since otherwise he would never have let go the lion's body. He began to cut off the right ear of the goat, then its left, and so on. When he came back home his wife repeated what she had said earlier to him, 'One should never swear to do anything.'

The murābiṭ and the shepherd

As was his daily habit, a shepherd sang with joy as he led his herd. A murābiṭ who had a long beard, and who carried a rosary in his hand, came up to him. The old man greeted the shepherd and asked him for news about pasturage and of nearby camps, how the animals were at that time, and he in turn gave the shepherd the latest news he knew. The murābiṭ spoke of the miseries of this world and ended up by saying, 'All of it is of no consequence. It is hell-fire that one should avoid by acting rightly, by praying, by paying alms and giving the *zakāh*. Our possessions can be of no better service to us than to save us from hell-fire and its torments and to lead us to the delights of paradise.'

The murābiṭ thought that he had softened the heart of the ignorant shepherd by his preaching, but when he saw the shepherd weeping and sobbing, he added, 'All, of course, can be redeemed, and it is never too late to do good.'

'That is not the reason why I am weeping,' replied the shepherd, 'but...' and he pointed his finger at the beard of the murābiṭ, 'it is your beard which reminds me so much of the beard my billy-goat had. A wild beast ate him last year. He was the finest in my herd.'

The murābiṭ, who was annoyed because he had failed, and also because he had been ridiculed in such a way by a rude and humble shepherd, took his leave.

Mīra and the lion

There once was a tribe which was about to set forth on its seasonal wanderings and among its members was a woman called Mīra. All was ready for the departure and the camels were saddled, and only Mīra remained unmounted. 'Go forth,' she said, 'and I will catch you up.' Her slave girl came to mount her in her saddle after the tribe had departed. She mounted her camel and placed her children beside her in her spacious saddle, and the slave girl led her forth. On the way she saw gum in a tree, and one of her children asked for it. Mīra ordered the slave girl to collect it for him. The slave girl said, 'It is a lion's eye.' 'Pluck it,' Mīra said. When the slave girl took it, the lion sprang forth and said, 'Give me something to eat, otherwise I will eat you up.' So Mīra gave him one of her sons. Then he said again, 'Give me something to eat, or else I will eat you up.' So she gave him her second son. Again the lion demanded meat, so Mīra gave him the slave girl. Then he said, 'Go away with me or else I will eat you up.' So she went with him, the lion leading her camel. Next he said to her, 'What are you looking at?' 'Nothing,' replied Mīra. 'May God blind you,' he said. He repeated his question, and this time Mīra replied that she had spotted an old woman at the mouth of a cave, and that she was churning milk in a skin. Again the lion cursed her with blindness. He brought her to the cave where the old woman was, and he made her enter it, while he prowled around outside preying on the cattle and other domestic animals to be found there. Then Mīra saw a slave pass by mounted on a camel, and he was urging on his herd of camels by repeating her name again and again. Mīra knew the slave. She called him, and he came to her. She told him what had happened to her and warned him against passing by that way lest the lion should eat him.

'Tell my young brother,' she said. The slave did so and along came all the brothers carrying their guns. The lion had warned Mīra that she should not leave the cave. The eldest brother, or his younger brother, stretched out his cloak to her for her to hang on to, but she refused. Then the youngest one of all stretched out his finger, and said to her, 'Remove this thorn for me.' She said, 'I am afraid lest we should go, and that the lion should come and kill me.' 'I don't want to take you away,' replied the brother, 'all I want you to do is to remove this thorn.' So she tried hard and pulled out the thorn. Then her brothers took her away, and the lion returned and found that she had left. He went in pursuit and found that the brothers had surrounded Mīra on every side to protect her, and that each one of them was carrying a gun. The lion began to pace about and say 'Mīra, Mīra, Yasrandaḥ,[1] you have drunk my milk, and you have eaten my bread and my meat.' The brothers said to the lion, 'Do not approach; if you do, we will kill you.' The lion said, 'Give her to me.' They said, 'We are afraid that you will eat her up.' 'I do not wish to eat her,' said the lion. Then they agreed to give her to him, and then kill the lion unawares. They gave her to him, and they erected a tent for them both, and they surrounded them. The lion forgot all about them, and when Mīra went in the tent to meet him, he insulted her and told her that he would eat her up on account of what she had done, and that he would begin with her breasts. But when he began to eat her breasts, the brothers shot at the lion, and they killed him.

THE MIRACLES OF THE TA<u>SH</u>UM<u>SH</u>A SAINTS

Muḥammad Wālid wuld Muṣṭafā wuld <u>Kh</u>ālunā[2] is the author of a noted Mauritanian work in Arabic on the lives of some of the most famous seventeenth-century saints of the Ta<u>sh</u>um<u>sh</u>a Zwāya, and in particular those of the tribe of the Banū (Awlād) Daymān. He was pressed to write this work by his relative, the scholar and mystic, <u>Kh</u>aylīd wuld Muttaylīya, and he unwillingly undertook the task. 'I agreed in spite of the lack of means and circumstances whereby the authenticity of a narrative might be verified. In general I rely upon men who are reliable, nevertheless I am slow of understanding and swift to imagine things.'

Whatever the author may say about his own work, it remains one of his most individual compositions. Amidst a long discourse on the concept of sainthood among the Moors and in Islam, there

---

[1] Or in Znāga—Čurungal. Both words are an exclamation.
[2] See note on p. 153.

are to be found a series of episodes in the lives of these saints, together with a description of their personal appearance and character. Once the author turns aside from theology, mysticism, or sermonizing, where his style is cramped within a rhymed prose in Classical Arabic, and when he concentrates on miraculous exploits, his narrative changes into simple description or sophisticated story-telling.

These stories stem from the folk traditions of his people, notwithstanding the fact that they are presented in Classical Arabic. In this way the author has preserved an early oral tradition, once in the vernacular, which might otherwise have been forgotten. The stories reflect the society of the acacia and gum woods of the south, a society still speaking the Znāga tongue and still retaining some of the customs of the Ṣanhāja.

An abridged selection of these stories is given here, based on an incomplete version of Wālid's text found in Mauritania. Copies of this work are very rare, but the task has been facilitated by also using a slightly different, shorter, Arabic version of the miracles of Abā Zayd and other saints of the Ta<u>sh</u>ums<u>h</u>a in *<u>Dh</u>āt alwāḥ wa dusur*. The majority of the stories summarized by Destaing in *Revue Africaine* No. 283, 1911, pp. 510–19 are included here.[1]

By way of an introduction it is essential to have some idea of the relationship of the saints and others who appear in these stories. All of them come from the five kindred tribes known as the Ta<u>sh</u>ums<u>h</u>a. All of them are related one to the other according to the genealogy shown opposite.

Abā Zayd

Aḥmad wuld Yaʿqūb al-Tā<u>sh</u>idbītī, known as Abā Zayd (1), gave all his possessions to the poor, but by way of compensation God caused men to bestow their gifts on him. The poet, Yagwa wuld Muḥammad al-Ad<u>kh</u>an al-Daymānī, has this to say of him, when invoking him:

> 'By Abā Zayd who gave away all his money and who had no fear of giving too little.'

One of the manifestations of his saintly powers was that one year blood fell as rain on the people, after that year had been one

[1] Cf. also the translation of a selection of these stories by Ismaël Hamet, *Revue du monde musulman*, vol. xiv, 1911, pp. 22–31.

TASHUMSHA

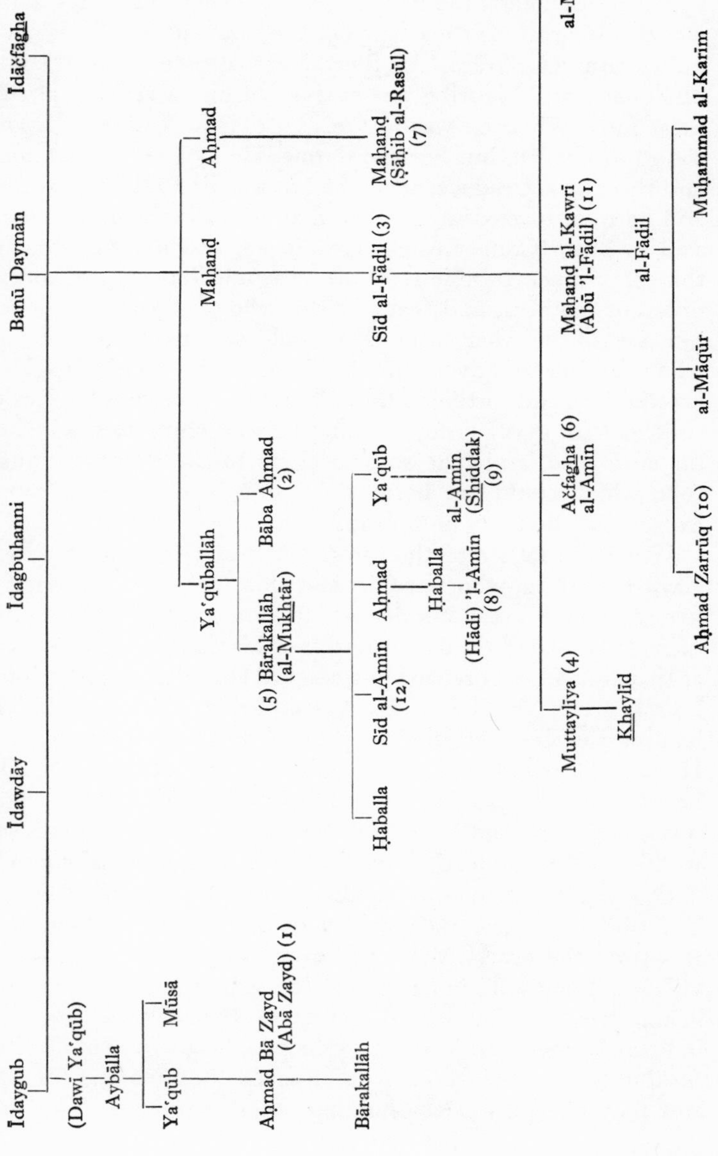

Īdaygub
Īdawdāy
Īdagbuhanni
Banū Daymān
Īdāčfāgha
(Dawī Yaʻqūb)
Aybālla
Yaʻqūb
Mūsā
Aḥmad Bā Zayd
(Abā Zayd) (1)
Bārakallāh
Yaʻqūballāh
Maḥanḍ
Aḥmad
(5) Bārakallāh
(al-Mukhtār)
Bāba Aḥmad
(2)
Ḥaballa
Sīd al-Amīn
(12)
Aḥmad
Yaʻqūb
Sīd al-Fāḍil (3)
Maḥanḍ
(Ṣāḥib al-Rasūl)
(7)
Ḥaballa
(Hādī) ʼl-Amīn
(8)
al-Amīn
(Shiddak)
(9)
Muttayliya (4)
Khaylīd
Ačfagha (6)
al-Amīn
Maḥanḍ al-Kawrī
(Abū ʼl-Fāḍil) (11)
al-Māḥi
al-Fāḍil
Aḥmad Zarrūq (10)
al-Māqūr
Muḥammad al-Karīm

which provided their sustenance and wants in abundance. They were afraid and troubled, and many of them declared that it was a sign of the beginning of the day of judgement. The people consulted the scholars, the pious, and the elders. Abā Zayd said that he was going to visit his Shaykh, Muḥammad wuld Daymān, for guidance and for grace. The Shaykh at that time was on the borders of Agnant, and his tribe was at Tin Yāshil. Abā Zayd hurried to meet him. When he was to the east of Tin Yāshil he heard the sound of a voice, but he saw no one. He looked to right and left, and then he noticed a tent pitched in the air a little below the sky, and he went towards it. He found an unknown woman there. She said to him, 'Come inside.' He did so, and she told him many things, and she prophesied that he would have thirty sons from different mothers, and that one son who was particularly dear to him would die when a lad. He would also have noble daughters who would be greatly favoured. Then he came to his Shaykh, who greeted him and fortified him, telling him to rely on God who was sufficient for every need, and that he who clung to God, clung to the sure hold, and that he who clung to the Prophet clung to a rope which could not be severed, since events never happened except they be the will of God.

When the father of the saint, Nāṣir al-Dīn, took a wife, Abā Zayd told those who were present that from this marriage there would come a great wonder which would astonish the minds of men. It is related on the authority of his daughter Maymūna that at that time he was repairing a sandal. He heard a girl trilling, so he asked why she did so. He was told that Abhanḍ wuld Yaʿqūb had married Haynīya, the daughter of al-Faqīh (al-Fagha) Awbik. He was surprised; what he was holding fell from his hand, and he cast aside his sandal. He used to play with Haynīya when she was a little girl, and he used to touch her fat stomach and say, 'A wonder will come forth from that fat little tummy of yours.'

One year the people were afflicted by a great drought. Abā Zayd had two daughters, each with a different mother. One of them was from the desert, the other from the people of the inhabited villages. They were both born at the same time. The family grew in number, and they lacked money. So the saint went to Gannār, in great hunger, and he came to the people at a time of destitution, seeking their succour. Their crier called for alms and for charity, and they filled a basket—holding about seven *aṣwāʿ*—with provisions. Abā Zayd took it, but he was perplexed as to how he might equitably distribute it amongst his dependants. He met Maḥanḍ Agdamussa al-Kumlaylī, who was a pious man, and he asked him for his opinion as to how it might be portioned out among his large and scattered family. The other said to him, 'If you are tired of having to decide how it should be distributed, then give it to the poor and destitute.' This was in accordance with the word of God, and so he concurred with this advice and returned home empty-handed. He came to the mosque and began to pray. Then all at once, a stranger prodded him with a camel stick, or the stump of a bush, and he looked towards him. The stranger indicated that he should arise and come with him. When they had crossed the open place of the settlement, Abā Zayd saw four fat cattle. One was an unweaned female, another was about to calve, one was on heat, and one was a bull. The stranger told him that they were his, and that he should make the one about to calve a foster-parent to the unweaned female, and that the cow on heat should be brought to the bull. 'They are yours to do with as you please,' the stranger added. Abā Zayd returned in joy to his people, and he met them, safe and sound, on the following night.

Once he spent the night at a nomad camp in the district of Tazyazt next to Jabal Marzubba. He was accompanied by his cousin Bāba Aḥmad al-Daymānī (2) and Yandaksaʿd al-Tās͟hid-bītī and others, and they were received hospitably and kindly. A man of the tribe went to great trouble to make them welcome and to show his bounty. He said to his wife, 'Oh mistress of the tent, offer something lavish, gather together the men of the tribe and near relations and give them the choice of our bringing them all together and giving them hospitality in the tent, or erecting special tents for them.' Now that was during a humid night of Jumādā, and it was so dark that a dog could not see a tent rope. The man slaughtered a ewe. The company longed to smoke tobacco, and his wife and others of the clan were in need of clothes. The saint began to pray supplementary prayers after the sunset prayer, and his companions slept, as is usual for the guest to do before he partakes of supper. When he saw that they were asleep, Abā Zayd disappeared when the skinning of the ewe had begun. He flew through the air as fast as he could, and he came to his wife Suk͟hna Yadaymrizk. She was at Gannār. He woke her up, and she arose frightened. He greeted her and said to her, 'Don't be afraid or grieved, it is only me.' When she had recovered from her surprise she said to him, 'Is this coming of yours mysterious and supernatural?' He said that it was, and he told her about all that had happened. She did all that was necessary that very hour. He departed from his family when they were asleep, and on arriving he found that the ewe was not yet roasted. The first who awoke from among his companions was Bāba Aḥmad, and he said to them, 'I smell the odour of the Trārza, or the Sūdān.' They looked about them, and there was Abā Zayd standing amongst them surrounded by provisions, and he neither looked tired, nor showed any trace of his journey upon him. Each one of them took what he wanted, and Bāba Aḥmad said to him in a teasing way, 'Perhaps you have been up to your tricks again, tonight.'

It was on that journey that a famous episode occurred between them and Sīdī Aḥmad al-ʿArūsī, who was outwitting the Zwāya, setting them riddles and deceiving them by his trickery until the people of the desert and the town flocked to him, and his renown was talked about at every gathering. His cunning, his learning, his judgement, and his generosity rivalled the ancient Arabs who were renowned for these qualities. He gathered around him followers who attained high positions in the land, dominating the people by their powers and the fear which they inspired.

Yandaksaʿd al-Tās͟hidbītī was greatly honoured by the people, and he was generous in paying the *zakāh*. When al-ʿArūsī came he was afraid that he would turn his companions against him by his tricks. Abā Zayd and Bāba Aḥmad were residing among the Tās͟hidbīt at that time, so he asked them to go to al-ʿArūsī to confound him. They left with a party of riders of the Tās͟hidbīt, handsomely attired. Abā Zayd said to the riders in the caravan, 'Make me your chief until we have finished with this al-ʿArūsī.' Abā Zayd said to al-ʿArūsī, 'I am the chief of all the people of the South.' 'I will better you', al-ʿArūsī said, 'since I have a *maḥalla*—a princely camp—and its chief, behind me.' 'So have I,' said Abā Zayd, 'four chiefs and a *maḥalla*.' Abā Zayd undertook to overcome the secret arts of al-ʿArūsī, while Bāba Aḥmad challenged his knowledge of riddles and his learning. He watched the camels as he waited his turn.

Al-ʿArūsī first began with his hidden tricks. In one hand he held a piece of charcoal, and in the other a date, without Abā Zayd knowing. Then he held out his hand which held the charcoal to Abā Zayd and he challenged him to tell him what he was holding. Abā Zayd answered him. Then al-ʿArūsī held out his other hand and again Abā Zayd told him what he was holding in his hand, and this in full view of all the people. Al-ʿArūsī, embarrassed, tried by trickery to change over what he had in his hands in order to refute Abā Zayd. However, the Banū Maghfar prevented him, one group taking one hand of his and another the other. They opened his hands and found it to be just as Abā Zayd had said.

Then al-ʿArūsī said, 'Where are your companions?' 'They are those men behind me,' Abā Zayd replied. Al-ʿArūsī next produced a leather bag of charms containing a copy of the Burda of al-Būṣīrī and a table of squares containing a riddle in the three letters f - j - sh, written incorrectly in an inverted order. Bāba Aḥmad was near to the camels, praying. Both Abā Zayd and al-ʿArūsī expected Bāba Aḥmad to solve the riddle. He was given the table, he looked at it and perceived an error in one of its columns. He explained that the first letter was at the end, namely that the first letter in a column was none other than the last letter in the preceding column. He also found another of its chequer-squares to be misplaced, and he rectified it. Then he looked at the Burda, and he smiled and laughed and said that only old folk read it. He recited it all to them and its contents from memory. Al-ʿArūsī said, 'The best of all this party of riders is their camel herder,' a saying which became a maxim. He and the Zwāya of the Banū Maghfar recognized the superiority of their adversaries. The influence of Abā Zayd and Bāba Aḥmad increased and ʿAbdallāh wuld Karrūm of the Banū Maghfar gave gifts to Bāba Aḥmad and his descendants for more than a century.

One day Abā Zayd left Gannār accompanied either by his sisters or his daughters (the narrator was in doubt on this point), making for their kinsfolk who were in Īgīdi, and he stopped with them at a barren spot. They had no food with them, and they spent the night where no people were. He said to them, 'Let each one of you choose what she would like for supper.' The first said, 'I want nothing but a dish of sopped bread, meat, and seasoned broth.' The second of them said, 'As for me, I want nothing but fresh meat, be it cut in strips and dried in the sun, or roasted.' The third said, 'As for me, I only want foaming milk. I prefer it to both broth and dried meat.' One of them mentioned a cloth bundle full of tobacco. Then he said, relying on God, 'Each one of you will have what she wishes if God so wills, and by His permission, so sleep my darlings until I wake you up to see your hearts' desires.' So they slept, and he began to adore God in diverse manners. One of them awoke and said, 'Father, when will what you say come to pass?—Bring us what you promise us, if you are truthful.' 'There is no doubt at all about it,' he replied. Then after a short interval he woke them up, and they saw the various kinds of food which they longed for, and which they had described to him. They supped on their hearts' desire, and the one who had wished for tobacco was given a bundle of hot *ṣandagīya* (?) tobacco. It was a surprising thing that one of them awoke when the others slept, and she saw her father holding a cluster of branches of the tree which was sheltering them, and he was moving his hands in turn, as though he was milking.

One day, after that, he folded his garment nine times, and they knew that it was for some important matter which he was about to undertake. Al-Faqīh (al-Fagha) Ḥabīballāh wuld Yaʿqūb interpreted this to them to mean that he would depart from them and dwell abroad for nine years, and so it came about. He journeyed backwards, with an iron-tipped stick in his hand. He came to Tagānit and met a Beduin woman looking after her sheep. He made his camel kneel at her sheep-pen, and she disapproved of him, and she said to him, 'Oh, Zwāya scholar, don't make your camel kneel here—are you mad?' He said to her, 'Let my camel kneel here, I wish to marry your virgin daughter.' She asked God's protection against him, and she said to him, 'That can never be, nor is it God's will that your head and hers should be joined together.'

They continued to exchange words, he to soothe her, and she with replies which were both uncouth and insulting. In the end she removed his camel saddle and baggage, and she honoured him with hospitality. He betrothed and married her daughter, and she was called ʿAshata bint Yaḥyā 'l-Hukārī, the mother of Bārakallāh fīh, and his sisters Āmina and Maymūna. He stayed there nine years. One day he heard that some Zwāya youths had been playing in his tent, and that one of them had fallen upon his dear little son who was called Sīd al-Fāḍil (al-Fāl) al-Daymānī. The boy had died on account of the fall. The father was angry because of that, and he hurled a meteor at the youths while he was in Tagānit. The episode of the meteor was revealed to Sīd al-Fāḍil (3) while he was in Īgīdi, and he grasped it and plunged it in the sea (or the river), and it was extinguished. Abā Zayd said to him after that,

'If you had not put it out, the people of the region would have been burnt by it.' Perhaps the death of his little son confirms what the woman in the tent in the air had said to him. His family used to visit him during his stay in Tagānit, and they said to him, 'Journey with us, so that you will not die here, a stranger.' He replied, 'Leave me, and have no fear of that. I shall be buried in Īgīdi.' It was as he said. He dwelt in Tagānit for nine years, as Shaykh Ḥabīballāh had foretold. Then he came to Īgīdi, and he died there. His tomb is at Tamghart. As the poet Ibn Jangī has said of him, 'There is no saint comparable with Abā Zayd, who lies buried to the left of the well of the old woman.' The poet Yagwa refers to this fact when he says, 'He told his people at the time of his absence that Īgīdi would be his tomb.'

One of the miracles of Abā Zayd was that on one occasion they were at Anguwayshim in the rainy season, and some of the camels of the tribe strayed. A party of men followed them on camels in the morning, and in the evening, and during part of the night march, running and ambling. The saint travelled some time after they had departed on a donkey of his which was noted for the slowness of its pace. He had a servant of his with him. When he reached In-Waylūṭ, he met the party who had arrived in a hurry after him, and they were astonished to see him, since they had left him in the tents, and he had come before them. He said to them, 'Do not pursue your camels, since they are now among the Trārza tribes in Inshīri.' They departed on their way, and he journeyed on his donkey. When they were close to Nouakchott (Anwākshūṭ), there he was, coming out from it, and he had filled his water-skin, and his servant was walking in front of him. They found this extraordinary, and he repeated what he had previously said. They left him, eager to find their camels, and they did not halt that night. On the following day they entered the region of the Trārza tribes, and there they found him in the first tent they passed, sitting in his corner, worshipping God, and he said to them, 'Perceive your camels.' These had gone out beforehand, among the camels of the Banū such and such, so the party found their camels amongst them.

One day a party of riders of the Banū Daymān visited him, and among them was Muttaylīya wuld al-Fāḍil (4) (Sīd al-Fāl). He cooked food for them, and he sat with them as they ate it. When they had eaten to their satisfaction, the remainder of his guests partook of it until they were satisfied. He said to them, 'The food will never be consumed entirely as long as my hand is placed in it.' He then called for his dependants and they were satisfied, then the guests of the tents which adjoined his own, then their dependants, then those who were in tents next to theirs, until the whole tribe came forth having eaten of it as had the rest of their guests, and the food remained just as it was, and it was as though no morsel had been taken from it. Perhaps his *baraka* took hold of them. The women of the Banū Yadām were too shy and embarrassed to come to him, and so they sent for the fare to come to them. He raised his hand, and he sent it to them, and they ate until none of it remained.

Dhū 'l-Nūn (Zanūn) wuld Dāmān slew a Christian of the Banū Dāmān, and the chief of the Christians was angry on account of that. It happened that Abā Zayd asked Aḥmad wuld Dāmān (d. *circa* 1045/1635) for three requirements: a skin of honey, tent posts, and a pair of shears, and Aḥmad sent him to the chief of the Christians with a letter of authority which insulted his parents and which asked him to fulfil the saint's three requirements. He said to the latter, 'I am sure that the cowardice of some of the Zwāya will prevent you from conveying my letter to him.' Abā Zayd prepared for his journey, and he came to the dwelling of Bāba Aḥmad al-Daymānī and found no one there. He laid hands on the skin prayer-rug of Bāba Aḥmad's wife, and he took it. Then he departed for the port, and with him went his servant. It is thought that his name was al-Aṭrash al-Agwaydisī, a relative of Abū Taktak. When they left the dwellings behind them, they met a woman from In-Yarzīg, and she said to him, 'Oh, Abā Zayd, escort me to the Christians so that I can sell these wares of mine, a skin of clarified butter.' He said to her, 'What is your name?' She answered, 'Tīẕayt'. And he interpreted her name as a good omen. He continued his journey, and he met another woman, and he asked her name also, and she said, 'Injillat', and he interpreted this as an ill omen. Then he continued towards the port and arrived there and delivered the letter of authority to the chief of the Christians. When he came to him and told him his story, the latter seized him and threw him into prison in revenge for all the Muslims, and his servant accompanied him into prison. While he was there, he sought God's aid, and God enabled him to escape from prison very quickly, but they were recaptured, and they were thrown into prison for a second time. The saint recalled, 'When we entered a second time we were with all the saints of the Zwāya, who were enjoying themselves in prison and playing a game (a kind of leap-frog or joust among youths carried pick-a-back?) called in Znāga, "Tin Yayyān Dhadhān", among them Sīd al-Fāḍil al-Daymānī and his pupil Akhtayr wuld Awbik al-Midlishī and others. My companion was in despair, and he was concerned about himself and about his sons, and he said, "If only I knew whether I will meet my son Muḥammad ʿAwḍ again?"' I said to my companion, 'Do not despair. God is with us. Have patience, oh Lagwaydisī, you will either come out of its mouth or from its side, and you will have the right to choose, if God permits. He will make things easy after all this hardship, and we will spend tonight at the abode of Dhū 'l-Nūn (Zanūn). He will do such and such a thing for us.' The servant said, 'I would prefer to depart from its mouth, because to come out through its side is inconceivable.' Abā Zayd continued, 'When we entered prison a second time, I asked my cousin Bārakallāh fīh wuld Yaʿqūballāh (5) for help, and he was at that time writing in Īgīdi, and he turned his back on me, though he did not doubt me. Then I sought the aid of al-Faqīh (al-Fagha) Awbik wuld al-Najīb al-Ḥājjī. He answered me, and he aided me, and after that Bārakallāh upbraided me because of it, and he said to me, "You embarrassed me when you sought my aid in your bondage." Then God aided me to escape in that I placed one of my feet over the side of the prison, and I reached over with the other, and I passed over the surface of the earth. Then I drew it back, and I placed it around the other. The chief of the Christians was astonished at that, and he said to the chief men round about him, "This man of learning is a magician," and he treated me hospitably and honourably, and he fulfilled my three wants, and he furnished me with other requirements. He ordered his servants to conduct us from their territory, and we returned in safety to our people. We journeyed to Dhū 'l-Nūn (Zanūn), and while we halted he offered us the milk of a she-camel, white or dark-coloured, abundant in milk. Then at supper-time he offered us a cauldron full of millet bread, just as I had told to my companion when he was in despair.' The saint said, 'I experienced hardship through this journey, and I think it is only due to the evil omen of laying hands on the skin prayer-mat of Umm Yūsuf.'

Once he left Gannār making for his family in the north, and with him went his servant and companion al-Kaddīrī, and when they had left the village behind them, the saint availed himself of a stick which he was carrying, and he mounted it, and he said to his companion, 'Come along, seat yourself behind.' He did so, and the saint added, 'Beware of looking round about you.' So they journeyed upon it at the fastest speed. The servant said, 'It was as though the face of the earth was coming to me in front at a rush—o'er hill and dale—until God decreed that I should glance around me, and lo, we were at Ṭalḥat Yatti in the region of Talfalli and Tijigilāten. My glances offended the saint, and he said to me, "If you had not looked around thus, we would have journeyed to our kinsfolk." Then we stopped and passed the night there, and I slept. When it was early on the morrow we heard the voice of a woman calling a goat, and saying, "'Ibrīsh", and repeating it. We set out for her people, and they were a small camp of white tributaries, and they showed us hospitality. Then we came to our people.'

Abā Zayd was once absent in the north among a party of riders, and when they had accomplished what they wanted there, they returned southwards. They had no provisions, and there were great tracts of desert and waterless waste before them. They advanced both swiftly or at a steady trot at all times of the day and night, until at the end of the first day when night came upon them, they stopped at a sheltered and uninhabited spot, and they slept from fatigue. The saint began to perform prayers and supplications, and while he was prostrating himself and standing in adoration during the night, the roasted meat of a sheep was placed before him, and he aroused the others, and they ate until they were satisfied. When it was daybreak they climbed into their saddles and rode off, and they continued through the desert, galloping and covering great distances or trotting. When it was the still of the night, they halted in a desert place, tired out and exhausted, and they slept. Abā Zayd arose to perform supererogatory prayers and, while they were sleeping, all at once he woke them up to see good roast beef, and they ate it until they were filled. Then when it was first light they mounted their riding beasts and continued across the desert as hitherto, until when night fell they found themselves at an uninhabited and awesome place frequented by wild camels and ostriches. They were so exhausted that no one could be found to unsaddle and unload their camels. They fell down, prostrated by their fatigue. The saint arose to pray, then he woke them up in order to eat tasty food, wheat or millet seasoned with delicious butter-like honey, and they ate until their hunger abated. When it was still dark and just before day-break they mounted once more and continued energetically to pursue their course.

One of his daughters, it is reported to be Umm Hāni', said to him one day, 'Bring me to my mother who is in Gannār.' (Her mother was Sukhna Yadaymrizk.) He answered her request. He arose, smoothed a spot, and spread a woolly sheep-skin there. Then he called her and sat her on the skin and said to her, 'Avert your gaze.' She did so, and he said to her, 'Open your eyes,' and she did so, and lo, she was joined with her mother in Gannār, and the distance from where they were grew shorter and then longer.

There was amongst them a poor fellow called ʿAbd al-Mannān who used to shepherd a flock of his mother's sheep. He was despised by everyone, and all spoke of him with contempt. He was bald and thin. Abā Zayd used to care for him, and he used to visit him in private, or openly, in order to share his company. Often he used to seek his blessing and to honour his shelter. He was young at that time, and the saint said to him, 'Oh, ʿAbd al-Mannān, when you visit the holy sanctuary and meet such and such a person of the people of Mecca, the blessed and bright, convey to them my greetings and respects, and when you go to Medina to visit it, then convey my honours and respects to the occupant of the spacious tomb.' Whenever he spoke in this way the people were surprised, and they disapproved. Then, after a long interval, God decreed that ʿAbd al-Mannān should perform the pilgrimage to the holy sanctuary, and, through God's good grace, he returned to his land and to his people, and the first one who met him from among the people of the Trārza was al-Faqīh (al-Fagha) al-Amīn wuld Sīd al-Fāl al-Daymānī (6), and he was carrying his baggage including a sheep-skin filled with butter. Shaykh al-Amīn asked him how he had fared, and about the distances, the routes, and the halting-stages, and the landscape on the route to Mecca. He gave him a satisfactory answer to all his questions, and one of the wondrous things which he told him was that when he entered Mecca he met two white-haired old men. As soon as they saw him they came running to him and they showed their happiness in their expressions. It was as though they recognized him as one of their own sons. The first thing they asked him was, 'What has prevented the saint Aḥmad wuld Yaʿqūb (meaning Abā Zayd) from coming to us?' Everything they asked him revealed the longing and the affection which they felt towards him.

Maḥanḍ wuld Aḥmad, 'the companion of the Prophet'

Maḥanḍ wuld Aḥmad al-Daymānī (7) was a noted figure among the Moors and the Negroes. He was honoured by the masses and dearly loved by the select. He had only to be seen or his name to be mentioned, and he would be given gifts because of the favour which God had bestowed on him. Because of this the Banū Daymān and others used to travel with him and escort him, seeking his blessing, and to curry favours through him, and endeavour to transact commerce on account of him among the rulers of the Negroes and the Banū Ḥassān. They took their gifts and their rewards, because the saint was an abstemious man in this respect. He had no concern for any kind of worldly possession. He was quite content with simple fare for his journey and a God-speed to go with it. He was satisfied with enough food to keep body and soul alive, with coarse and shabby garments, a patched and sleeveless shirt, and a worn skin prayer-mat for his prayer. After his death he bestowed some of his *baraka* over a long period and to a wide degree upon Mūsā al-Mamlūk, a client of the Banū 'l-Faqīh (al-Fag͟ha) Awbik al-Tawkamlī, and he used to be absent for long spells in various countries, unaccompanied by goods or wares. He used to accumulate much wealth without recompense, because he had only to pass by someone who knew Maḥanḍ Aḥmad and they would give him charity because they were accustomed to his accompanying him. Everyone who saw him used to say, 'This is the friend of "the companion of the Prophet"'.

One day some of Maḥanḍ wuld Aḥmad's grandchildren, Awlād al-Sayyid wuld ʿAbdallāh, travelled with him seeking his *baraka*. They made their camels kneel for some purpose of theirs, and one camel rolled him in the dust, and his thigh, or his leg, was broken. The news was spread abroad among the people, and by the riders in the provinces, and it was rumoured in distant places that he had died from a camel fall. Bakkār wuld ʿAlī al-Braknī heard of it. He was chief of the Banū Mag͟hfar, and he loved the holy man greatly, and was a benefactor of his. The news reached him when he was in the remotest part of Tagānit, and he was furious. He rode his swift horse, intent on avenging the death of his murābiṭ. He rode very fast, exchanging one tired horse for another, or he took a camel, until he reached the place where the holy man was. He swore a terrible oath that he would take his revenge on those who had caused his death, and that he would take his bloodwit from the people of the Trārza. When he tried to assault those who were responsible, he was told that the saint was not dead at all. His anger cooled after he was told that the people were innocent of what had befallen him. Then the Awlād al-Sayyid bore him to their people, and they set his broken limb, and they erected a structure for him in the courtyard of the house, and they furnished a number of splints and bandages. They supplied tent ropes, so that his leg could be kept straight, and they made his body light with the aid of supports. This was to make him comfortable, and so that he could rest easily on his right side, and on his left. They went on treating him and making him happy until heavy rain poured down on them one night. This was followed by a flood, and a thunder-storm which uprooted date-palms and swamped the desert tracks, and the wild beasts and domestic animals were brought into close proximity to each other, so torrential was the wind and the rain and so tempestuous were the elements. It was as though the heavens were rent in twain. The like of it had never been seen before. While all this was going on, the saint continued to murmur and to persist in his invocation of God, and to be in an anxious state. His chest made a sound like the bubbling of cooking pots or the buzzing of bees, until they were conscious of his absence, because this sound from him suddenly stopped. They said, 'For some reason or another, he has discontinued his invocation, and the rumbling of his chest has ceased.' They called him, and he did not answer, so they came running to him, and they did not find him in his place. They were grieved and perplexed, and they were in a predicament. They began to blame each other for some error they had committed, and in the way they had fed him or in his treatment. They could do nothing except to say that they had come from God, and that they would return to Him. They were in a tumult over the holy man's affair, baffled as to how he had come to disappear. One said that the angels might have taken him away, another that the earth had swallowed him up, another that the flood had carried him off. They agreed that if a viper had bitten him, then his body would have remained, or that if a thunderbolt had struck him, they would have found portions of him. While they still remained perturbed, unable to do anything more, all at once, as they were watching (he reappeared) and they heard his chest make its accustomed sound. They rejoiced at his coming, and it was announced in the tribe that he had returned. Everyone came to see and from the furthest part of the settlement there came a man, running. He said, 'He has given you the task of nursing him for a month, then he has caused you anxiety through his disappearance for an hour, and this is a man in whose treatment there is recompense. You have fulfilled his wants in food and provision, and God is sufficient for him, and He is his healer. Glory to God who has covered you with His bliss, both outwardly and inwardly.'

When they gathered around him and uttered expressions of welcome and joy and relief, they found him just as he had been, surrounded by his tent ropes and his supports. They approached him and inquired as to what had befallen him. He turned away from them, and they asked him again, but he did not reply. They pressed him, and he made veiled allusions. This did not satisfy them, so they besought him, knowing that he would not refuse an earnest appeal. Then he said, 'I went away to pray and to prostrate myself in Mecca.'

Bārakallāh (Bārakalla) fīh wuld Ya'qūballāh (al-Mukhtār)

Saint Bārakallāh (5) had an ass which was very slow. The ass was humble, ugly to look at, but beautiful and sweet in temperament. To experience and to know, it was the most delightful of creatures, but to look at unbecoming and repulsive. The saint used it to cross the deserts and the open spaces. He used to give it a pack-saddle and water-skins and send it off on its own. It sought its way to the well, even if it had not seen it before, by inspiration from God. If the ass found somebody at the well who knew it, that person would fill its water-skins and lay them upon it. If it found a stranger at the well who would not attend to it, then it entered into the lower water-cistern and created a commotion, striking out with two of its legs to right and to left, and rebelled against whoever tried to come near it, be he man or beast. It would not let anyone approach the water-channel until the people knew that it wanted its skins to be filled. Then they would fill them for it, load them on its back, and it would set off on its own until it came to its master's house. If it found someone who would unload the water-skins, it would let him do so, otherwise it would kneel down, then lie down rolling on the ground, until the water-skins fell off its back, gently and easily.

When its master died, and was buried near to Ablaykh al-Taydūm, his donkey came to the tomb and stood with its head bowed. His family missed it. They were anxious about it, and they knew that it had failed to appear for some serious reason, because it never used to stay behind. It used to come to the family on its own, at morning and evening. A girl went to look for it, and she found it there. Then she wanted to drive it, and it refused, and she went round to its head and took the side of its neck, wishing to lead it. The ass was stubborn and intractable, so she left it and came to her people and told them what had happened. They sent somebody else who chided it to make it walk, but it refused. He waved a stick at it, but it would not be driven. The man struck it, but it remained where it was; then he lashed it, but all to no effect. When it was clear to them that handling it would not make it move, they left it on its own there, and they brought it water and food. Some time after that they had to depart on a journey, and they came to it. They were a large band, and they coerced it by driving, and it stoutly refused, then by leading, but it sat down on its back legs. So they turned their backs on it. Then, when the day of departure came, they found a company of men from various clans, both freemen and slaves, tough and strong, some capable of pulling a young camel, and they had various instruments with them, whips, ropes, and sticks. They came, and they took their ropes, and they tied its limbs with ropes, and they competed and co-operated in pulling the ass, and they used up all their strength. Then they tried every trick and ruse, but all to no effect. It was then that they knew, when the ass had foiled them for every explicable reason, that there was a supernatural power here which could not be countered. They were in despair, and they cast aside their ropes and their sticks, and they left the ass in order to make their departure. They left it standing in its place like a tree-trunk, and they broke camp. Then after that the bones of the ass were seen lying at that spot.

One day saint Bārakallāh wuld Yaʿqūb left his family to make a journey. His family had a noble cow, abundant in milk, the only one they milked at that time. It was called Tunmu'ḍu, a Znāga name, which means in Arabic, 'the woman blacksmith'. The cow missed the saint while he was away, and one of its bones broke, and normally no beast lived in such a state, and the people sought to purchase it. The saint's wife refused, and she said to them, 'Leave it until its master returns, then you can discuss it.' They erected a shelter for it, and they fed it well and watered it. They did not expect it to live. Then its master returned, and when he was seen approaching his sons ran out to meet him, and one of them said to him, 'Father, it has had a mishap which has disabled it, the doctors have wearied over treating it. Have no hope of it living, there it is, next to the dwelling. It has suffered long.' He told him all that had happened. The saint replied, 'There is no evil portent to be gathered with regard to it—God forbid.' When he came to the cow, he smote it, and he pointed his hand towards it, reciting a verse (86) from the Burda of al-Būṣīrī:

> 'How often has his hand by its touch cured him who is sick, and has unloosed knots from the noose of him who is slightly deranged.'

or another verse (47):

> 'If his miracles, in grandeur, were to correspond to his worth, then his name, when invoked, would give life again to decaying bones.'

The cow got up, shaking as if it had been untied from a halter or a noose. The bone had been set, and the swelling reduced through God's grace, and for no apparent reason. His brother Bāba Aḥmad saw the cow on the following morning, healthy, standing up, and being milked, and he said, 'Perhaps my brother al-Mukhtār came last night.' He was told that this was the case. By the healing of the cow he deduced that his brother had returned.

His friend Mahanḍ wuld Mi'jan al-Ingādisī, and his kinsmen, came to him at a time of famine, and there was neither food nor drink to be found. When he saw their sorry plight he was filled with compassion for them, and he asked them to go with him to his own people, and they helped him, and they journeyed with him, at speed, until night fell upon them at Umm Rashīd, a waterless place, and they rested exhausted there.

Al-Ingādisī and the family slept, but the saint did not. He busied himself in prayer and adoration until he awoke them early in the night to see a cauldron filled to the brim with excellent food, well seasoned, and they ate of it until they were filled. They put the cauldron near them, and they protected it with their vessels. In the morning it was not in its place. Al-Ingādisī was astonished over the affair of the cauldron. They resumed their journey until night-fall, and they spent the night in an extensive stretch of ground, quite uninhabited. When a portion of the night had passed, and they were more tired and exhausted than they had been the night before, they fell asleep, while he, the saint, made supererogatory prayers and recitations until he aroused them, deep in the night, to find the same fare as the first, or even better, and they ate until their thirst and hunger left them. Al-Ingādisī said that he would find out about this cauldron, and where it came from, since that night it was not the same as the first. He said that he would not go away until he knew where it went. So his wife said that he should hide it, and she would not get hold of it. He took what rope he found there, and he tied each rope to the cauldron until it was held fast, and then he went to sleep. In the morning it was not there, although the knots and loops were untied in their place, and he knew that it was a divine act impossible to fathom.

One day the saint went from Tin Daksammi making for the *qṣar* of the Īdaw Fāl and riding on his slow donkey. When he arrived before the tribal settlement, ʿAbdallāh wuld Āmūki, the chief of the Kutaybāt, caught up with him, and he had with him his companion Maḥanḍ wuld Mi'jan wuld Hummad, the chief of the Ingādis. They were both going the same way as he was, and they were both riding noble camels, one camel was a young stallion and the other camel was gelded. They asked him where he was going, and he told them. That time of year was the rainy season when it was very hot, and the sun blazed fiercely, and the land was deserted. When they met him and his donkey which was slowly carrying him along, the Kutaybī said to his companion, 'Tell your lord to send back his donkey and come with us. We will carry him on one of our camels, so that neither he nor his donkey will perish from hunger and thirst in the uninhabited desert.' Al-Ingādisī then did as his companion had suggested, and he said to the murābiṭ, 'The distance is far, and the ground is full of scrub and difficult to walk in. The *qṣar* is some way, it is hot, and your donkey is stupid. Send back your donkey, then you will not die of thirst. Come along, we will take you as an extra rider on one of our camels, if you so wish, and you can travel with us in safety and comfort until you reach your destination, and where you wish to go, neither tired, nor hungry, nor thirsty.' The saint politely declined the offer, so they turned aside and left him, and they journeyed on until at high noon they reached Tin Aḍbayʿ, and they rested in the shade of its *dūm* palm. Then they continued in the afternoon, and they reached the *qṣar* at evening time. They both saw the donkey pasturing about the houses of the *qṣar*, and they argued over the resemblance it bore to the donkey of the saint. Then all at once they saw its master, and he was sitting under a tree in the open court of the *qṣar*, worshipping God and sheltering in its shade, apparently since early in the day. The two camel-riders asked the people of the *qṣar* concerning the hour when the saint had arrived, and they were told that he had arrived in the forenoon.

Sīd al-Amīn wuld Ḥaballa wuld Aḥmad wuld Bārakallāh wuld Yaʿqūb

Saint Sīd al-Amīn (8) lost a calf. It strayed when they were at the well of Ti<u>sh</u>kurkur, and he sought it at nearby wells, but he could not find it. Then he looked for it to east and to west, to south and to north, but he still did not find it. He returned in despair to his people, and he saw his cattle at the well, thirsty, going around the water-channels persistently, and driven from well to well. He began to water them, when a slave belonging to the kinsfolk of Maḥanḍ al-Faqīh (al-Fa<u>gh</u>a), called A<u>gh</u>ayr Ki'<u>dh</u>, hotly disputed with him the right to the first bucketful, and each one of them refused to concede it to the other. The slave shook the bucket to fill it, and each one of them stood at the mouth of the well, watching the large bucket appear, and each one wanted to grab it for himself. When the bucket came near to the top of the well each one of them came close to take it, and, lo, there was the lost calf, tied by a rope for everyone to see. Sid al-Amīn took it, and the slave was left embarrassed and dumbfounded.

Once he went away with his cousin, the saint Sīd al-Fāḍil al-Daymānī, beyond the Senegal river, and when each had done what he intended, they returned, and when they came to the river they stopped at its southern bank, and they sheltered there awaiting a ferry-man to take them across the river, or a bridge to cross over by. While they were sitting there, delousing each other's heads, all at once they found themselves on the opposite bank of the river. Each of them attributed to the other the honour of that unintentional miracle, each one saying to the other, 'This miracle is only due to you, since we were on yonder bank of the river and are now on the nearer bank.' God said it was His will.

A miracle reported by the scholar al-Mukhtār wuld al-Sharghi

Once I travelled in Gannār, and I met Mawlūd wuld Muttaylīya. One day I was sitting in the courtyard of one of the nobler dwellings ready to return to my family. All at once I espied him walking amidst the dwellings, and he had a bag of provisions in his hand, collecting charity in it from the people of the village, neither praising him who gave it nor blaming him who withheld it, quite unconcerned about distinguishing one class of men from the other. He simply gathered all he found, millet, beans, cucumber, and flax, and mixed them together in one vessel. When he saw me getting ready to travel, he came to me and sat opposite, and he asked to go with me and I answered him in the affirmative. I said, 'Where is your camel? Bring it near and make it kneel.' He said, 'I have no camel, I only have a thin slow donkey.' I was loath to have him accompanying me, and I said to him, 'My Lord, we are not companions. How can we agree when I have a huge beast, which, by God's grace, is strong enough to halt where I wish, or come to my people at noon, and you are not in the same position. You are not a rider like me so that we can be compatible, nor are you just a traveller on foot so that I may carry your cloth for you and seat you behind on my camel, nor have you a companion who will meet your requirements.'

[This story seems to be incomplete. According to Mukhtār wuld Ḥāmidun it probably ends with the arrival of the holy man on his donkey, before the narrator of the story on his camel.]

Sīd al-Amīn wuld Ya'qūb (Shiddak)

Sīd al-Amīn wuld Ya'qūb (9), who was nicknamed Shiddak, travelled away from his people, making for the salt mine, and he had a donkey train with him, and there was no companion with him. He came to the mine, filled his receptacles with salt—or nearly did—and then returned, driving his asses on his own, and whenever a provision bag of his fell off, he carried it without a helper. Likewise, if he stopped at a place where no one was to be found, when he wished to load, he brought each animal close to its carrying bag and he used to load its back without a visible helper. He would load the part of the carrying bag which was near to him and then load the other part of it, through God's grace. Thus he continued until he came to his people. It was strange that during that journey of his, he passed the night in a desert stretch. His provisions were consumed, and he rested, tired out and exhausted. He said to himself, 'I will savour the salt, following the *ḥadīth* of the Prophet—"Live, even if it be on the portion of a date."' He took a piece of salt and chewed it, and it had a flavour very different from the usual flavour of salt, so he took another piece of it, and he tasted it, and it was just like the first. He took a third piece and ate it up, and he found it to be similar. He took a handful of it, or he filled his outstretched hand, and he ate it up. He trusted in God's grace, and he slept satisfied, his thirst quenched on account of this splendid food and delicious drink.

Sīd al-Amīn Shiddak was walking one day on his own in the forenoon in the centre of Īgīdi, and he was wearing a patched mantle. A man assailed him. This was an evil character from the Awlād Ghaylān, a warrior called Mannān wuld al-Muzarghaf (?), and he stripped him of his mantle, unjustly—may God cause him to perish and rid the land of such as him. There was a companionship between this Ghaylānī and Aḥmad Zarrūq wuld al-Fāḍil al-Kawrī al-Daymānī (10), and on that day he had gone to him and done what he wanted—woe to him—and had taken this mantle as spoil, or so he thought, and he carried it over his shoulder and brought it home with him. He gave it to his wife, and as soon as she wore it, she began to itch violently in her body. She could not stand it, and she was very frightened, and she took it off. She said to him, 'What is the matter with this garment of yours which you have brought?' So he took it from her, and he had not finished putting it on when his skin was irritated and an even more violent itching than that of his wife tormented him. He took it off, and he told her about it, and he said, 'I took it by force from a poor beggar of the Zwāya, and perhaps he is of those who are unapproachable. Well, here it is, look, what do you suggest, how are we to dispose of it? In my view the only thing to do, wife, is for you to take it and hide it safely with your clothes until its owner comes for it, or we find someone who will take it to him.' The woman was a coward, and she said to him, 'No, by God, it will never come in my house, nor come anywhere near my possessions.'

A heated domestic argument followed, and finally he took the mantle and put it on top of a spear, and he hid it in a corner of the room of the house. News of the theft spread among the people. It brought him abuse, and he was ashamed in their midst. It was then that the itching which afflicted him through wearing the garment led to painful and ugly sores and horrible boils and black pimples and fever of various kinds, and he fell grievously sick, confounding the doctors and distressing those who were dear to him. In the end his condition was so acute that he was neither dead nor alive, and in dire distress, twisting and turning from side to side, and nothing seemed good to him, he lost his sense of taste, and the medicine did nothing but aggravate his condition. His body and clothes stank with putridity, he was fouled by the oozing of his boils and abscesses until he presented a shocking spectacle. He loathed life itself, and his people despaired of him, when they had tried every medicine they could. All the time his sickness grew worse and worse. In the end they neglected him. He told them one day to take him to his murābiṭ to cure him, in an apparent or some secret way. He was transported in an enclosed and curtained litter, and the stolen mantle was carried along with them, and they put him down before the holy man, Aḥmad Zarrūq. He then sought his aid and said to him, 'My lord, since I last saw you I have been thus, alive without a soul and dead without a grave. What a sorry lot is mine. My soul is nigh unto death.' Then he said, 'Perhaps a joy and relief will soon come after the affliction which I have fallen into. It is matter for God, and then for you, since all other arts and skills have failed me. One must needs complain to one who is honourable, who will console or comfort, or who feels compassion. Succour me, or else reckon me doomed to perdition.'

The holy man wept with tenderness and mercy, and he said to him, 'May the Pardoner come to your aid. You can only be given it by the murābiṭ whom you stripped. God's will is unalterable. You dared to do that which no human being nor jinnī has dared to do. What made you do that rapacious act, and so find ill most grievous and lasting in this world and the next?' The robber replied that he had done his evil act when he had erred in his ways, without taking heed of the consequences, and that it was the devil's doing. Aḥmad Zarrūq then scolded and reproved him, and he left to consult Shiddak. When he came to him he said, 'Oh cousin, may God cool your eye, and sever not your tie. This robber who has acted thus with you—may God heat his eye and may his flow of milk be stopped—used to treat me kindly, and were it not for the threat which befalls because of this friendship, then what has happened to him grieves me. Now restrain your anger and come to him with me, perchance I can secure for you a regular payment on his charge.' He relented and accompanied him, and when he appeared before the robber he said to him, rejoicing at his misfortune, 'What do you want from me, and what made you strip me and disclose my imperfection amidst the Muslims?' The robber was silent for a while and did not answer. Then he confessed his guilt and repented and regretted deeply that he had not honoured him instead, at that time. He swore that if God cured him then he would pay the saint and his descendants a *gharāma*. The murābiṭ said that he wished for no payment. All he wanted was that he should swear never again to injure a Muslim. Then the saint arose, took dust, and recited over it, 'Truly we sent it down, and truly it has descended'. That was all he said. Then he scattered the dust upon him, and the robber was healed. When it was dark the latter arose, completely cured, and he returned in joy to his family.

Abū 'l-Fāḍil al-Kawrī wuld Sīd al-Fāḍil (*Fāl*) (11)

A commander of the Arma—the half-breed descendants of the Moroccan invaders of the Songhai empire—came to them when they were at Atwaygammit. It is a very ancient well near to In Tawffukt where the saint Shaykh Muḥammad al-Yadālī lies buried. He imposed on them all kinds of intolerable excesses and injustices. For example, he said to them before he got down from his camel, 'Come along, hurry up, and make my camel kneel for me, hurry up, oh sons of dogs. Have I not addressed you?' A man of theirs came to him and said, 'Sir, may God prolong your might and grant you a long and easy life. These are Berbers who have no knowledge of how to deal with kings, and they can barely understand a word, so pray be patient until they are aware how you should be treated.'

The other replied, 'You have uttered words in vain, oh slaves of slaves. If you do not do what I command you, there will be a serious situation between us after I have dismounted. You must take me to a great tent and prepare another tent for my companions and a sumptuous chamber all for myself. In it there must be soft, raised beds and rows of cushions and spread carpets and vessels, and you must bring my companions roast meat and delicious drink. I want broth and meat and fat, and you must make it quickly.' A group of men from among them came to him, and they said to him, 'Excuse us. These are poor people of servile status of the dependants of the Caliph Ismā'īl.'

The commander resigned himself, and they took him into a fine, newly pitched bridal tent of Bārakallāh wuld Abū 'l-Māḥi. The news of all this reached the saint Abū 'l-Fāḍil al-Kawrī wuld Sīd al-Fāl. He was an old man. He called his grandson Aḥmad Zarrūq wuld al-Fāḍil, and he said to him, 'Oh, Aḥmad, let me accompany you to this Arma and sit with him and address him.' Aḥmad Zarrūq replied, 'Grandfather. It is no aim of yours to go to him, neither would it be of any advantage to meet him, lest taking as a model the tradition—'the most virtuous of acts is to speak the truth to an unjust ruler'—you would confront him with something disagreeable, and you would confront him with the truth, and he would be emboldened against you, and that would lead to a major scandal and a feud. As for your fighting with him or a battle taking place, I can hardly tolerate his injuring you in front of me.' The Shaykh said, 'My grandson, what God has ruled must be, His alone is the power. You need not go to him. I have lived my life-span, and I have only done good to you, God be praised, and perchance I may continue to do so in the future.' In the end his grandson agreed to take him to him, and they left. The saint held a camel stick in his hand, and he supported himself on it, until they came to the Arma. His grandson greeted the latter, and the old man uttered greetings and salutations, but upon the Prophet, on the company present, and upon the servants of God who acted righteously, and he paid no attention to the Arma. The Shaykh sat down to one side in his place and the grandson drew near until he sat before the Arma. He began to address him in a flattering way and utter pleasing words and expressions. The Shaykh dozed, dropping his head in his lap, and he remained thus for a while, half asleep and half awake. Then all at once he raised his head and said to the Arma,

'Oh so and so, son of so and so,' by his name and the name of his father. 'I met your mother this very noon—so and so, the daughter of so and so.' The Arma said to him in astonishment, 'What means this?' The Shaykh continued, 'I have just met her—a tall woman, black, and one-eyed. One of her breasts was bigger than the other, and in her courtyard was a high date-palm, a support for the seated. I told her all about your affair, and what had taken place between you and the Zwāya, and she said to me, "Convey my greetings and salutations to so and so, and tell him that I am as he likes, but he is not as I like, since he has harassed the Muslims. And remind him of what happened between us on the day he left with his expedition, when I went out with him to see him and the camp depart, when I grasped him by his collar by one hand, and I raised one of my breasts with the other, I said to him, 'My son, I beseech you, by God, the Merciful, and by the milk of this breast of mine, that you harm not the Muslims, and that you come back to me and assure me of it.' Then he did the act which he has committed and I am responsible for him who breaks a promise and who shames a covenant." '

When the Shaykh had finished, the Arma was silent for a while, then he sighed deeply and said, 'Verily we have with us some like you, oh my lord! There are some like you among us.' The Arma repeated this phrase a number of times. Then he got up, startled and in fear. He called his kinsmen and servants, and he said, 'Bring us our mounts at once.' Those of the Zwāya who were present delayed him and asked him to tarry, and they said to him, 'Oh, prince, we will never be happy with you or with ourselves if you leave us thus, openly and without due payment; favour us with your presence and give us pleasure through your company, at least for a portion of the day, until your wants are satisfied, then depart in peace.' 'No,' the Arma replied, 'by your lord, I shall not rest here, and by the right of my lord I shall not eat of your food, let alone take payment from you. I only ask you for a prayer and a charm, and that you write an epistle for me, and that you be magnanimous towards me with regard to what has occurred.' Then he left. He had eaten nothing, and he travelled at midday without causing them the slightest loss, even of drink, and this through God's grace and through the *baraka* of Abū 'l-Fāḍil al-Kawrī.

The Ingādis were men of power and great courage, and they attacked and assaulted the people. Once they raided some of the

Zwāya of the coastal region, and a group of those whose possessions had been seized came to the Tashumsha to seek their aid, because at that time the Tashumsha were the elect amongst the people. A group of the Tashumsha—among them al-Faqīh (Ačfagha) al-Amīn wuld Sīd al-Fāḍil (6)—rode forth with them. They journeyed until they came to the robbers, who received them with abuse and foul language. They stayed with them about a week, and the robbers quite openly took turns to abuse them with vile words. When they despaired of obtaining anything from them, they returned disappointed. They came to their people, and they discussed the matter and pondered it deeply. Al-Amīn said to his brother Abū 'l-Fāḍil al-Kawrī (11), 'Oh Maḥanḍ, these are poor folk, you have a duty towards them with regard to these possessions of theirs. All attempts which I have made have failed, all that is left is for the initiative to come from your side. Perhaps you can recover their possessions. Be neither apologetic nor indifferent. Be responsible for their recovery, for if you pursue your goal, you will end up by successfully obtaining them.' Al-Kawrī said to him, 'Did you not pursue it? You are not like me.' 'Yes,' replied his brother, 'I sought their return in an apologetic and indifferent manner. I endeavoured to find them, but God did not make it an easy matter for me. How different we are. I am not like you, because you are of a fighting temperament.'

Al-Kawrī went forth with God's blessing, barefoot and with only one man with him, and they came to the Ingādis and stayed with them. The tribe refused to entertain them, so they remained in front of the tents, thirsty and hungry and wandering in destitution and sheltering under a tree. It was a stormy day, when great gusts of wind were blowing. When it was evening a man of the tribe passed by them. He was a dim-witted, empty-headed fellow, and he came close to them to help them. When he saw al-Kawrī he was astonished at the beauty of his appearance. He tarried a while looking at him with delight, oblivious of the world around, then he passed on his way and came to his people. He said to them, 'Oh my people, today I have seen a wonder.' They asked him what it was. 'It was simply that I passed by two men. They could not have been human. They were either angels or sons of God (God forbid!).' One of their company said to the others, 'Why don't you meet this scholar, speak to him, and deal with him in accordance with your code of chivalry, and in accordance with your duty to meet him and treat him hospitably? Act as seems fit to you regarding what he wishes from you.' Some of the people supported him, and they said, 'This person has indicated a wise course to you.' They discussed the matter and eventually they adopted his point of view. A group of their men came to al-Kawrī and his companion, and their chief approached them, and he was called al-Khāl (or Khājkhāj). He was arrogant and ill-tempered, and he said to them both, 'What is your business?' Al-Kawrī replied, 'We have not come out of love of you, nor to delight in you, oh enemy of God. You know what we want. We have come in search of our possessions which you have wrongfully stolen. We sent our lords after them, and you abused them, and treated them yet worse, and you denied them their possessions.' Al-Khāl replied, 'As for the possessions, there is no means of access to them, for they are as far distant from you as the Pleiades. They belong to people who are strangers to you. Had we known there was some sort of connexion or relationship between you and their owners we would not have approached them nor come nigh unto them, let alone denied them to you. As for you, oh lord and kinsman, be welcome among us, and if you have any wish, then let us know. God willing it will be speedily carried out.' Al-Kawrī said to him, 'Know—may God in no way favour you—that the others of the Zwāya are my dependants and that they are of more concern to me than myself, and that however remote they are, they are all like me. He who shows me honour and acts in an evil manner towards my dependants, his abode is not honoured, and he is no concern of mine.'

Then they left them, and returned to their people, and it happened that al-Khāl fell sick before he reached his house. His flow of urine stopped at that time. He was in great pain on account of it, and he nearly died. He was distressed beyond measure, and he began to flounder in blood and totter between the door and the house, coming and going and turning restlessly to right and to left. His people said, 'My God, if al-Khāl dies, you both will die for him. Your brother will certainly taste death first, so your heart will be grieved sore by it, and your anguish and sorrow will be the greater, then you will die.' And when the matter grew yet worse with al-Khāl and he was on the brink of death, crying out loud and moaning and groaning, and his complexion was grey and ashen, and when he knew that there was no refuge other than God, he said, 'Aid me, oh sons of dogs. Go to the holy man and bring him quickly and make him happy by giving him all he wants, perchance God may help me and relieve me of this torment.'

A party of them came to Abū 'l-Fāḍil al-Kawrī and spoke to him about their master. They sought his help and abased themselves before him until he relented and went with them. He came to al-Khāl and said to him, 'How about you?—to hell with those whose dwelling is hell-fire. I have come to you, oh evil-doer, and were it not for your kindred I would not have come. Where is your strength and the multitude of your people? Have you not protected yourself or your people defended you?' Al-Khāl replied, 'I confess my impotence, my lord, and my trickery and the error of my ways are plainly manifest. I am a man smitten with the evil eye, oppressed in his heart, and wronged in both worlds. I admit that I am weak, and I know that I am broken and engrossed in the "days of ignorance".' Al-Kawrī said to him, 'What you have unlawfully and unjustly seized of our cherished possessions, for all to see, has come home to roost.' Then he poked him with his toe in the pubic region, and he said to him, 'Arise, oh donkey of hell-fire.' Al-Khāl urinated freely, by the grace of God, and he experienced an immediate relief from his agony. He returned all the possessions to al-Kawrī, and he was embarrassed on account of what had befallen him in the eyes of his people, his relations, and the womenfolk. The story is referred to in a verse of Yagwa: 'and by al-Kawrī who said, "the Zwāya, all of them, are my dependants" '.

Sīd al-Amīn wuld Bārakallāh fīh

Sīd al-Amīn wuld Bārakallāh fīh (12) one day heard an argument between the disease Consumption and Vinegar, or between Consumption and Honey within him, and this is how it happened. When he felt that he had Consumption in his chest he drank Vinegar or Honey in order to cure it. 'When I drank it', he said, 'it stayed in my chest, and it seemed to me—I was quite sure of it—that it said to the Consumption, "Depart from me, oh sickness," and Consumption replied, "You go away from me, for I shall not depart. I was here before you, and you found me sheltering here." Then Honey said, "This is not the way to answer a guest when he has alighted at the abode of one who is generous. He ought to make him welcome—now go away from me, as you wish, go in peace, for no illness has ever stood in my path. Either you depart or else I will scale your defences, and you will become like scattered dust or like strewn ash. You will be utterly destroyed and vanish to nothing. I annihilate everything which is established, and I remove everything which is firm. I am the supreme ruler, the medicine for every disease, and the cure for every malady." Then Consumption replied, "This is not the way for a guest to talk when he knocks at the door of those who are generous. He should only bring with him gentleness, kindness, easiness, flattery, self-control, peace, and quiet, until he is given accommodation. But the guest, if he is impatient or greedy, knows his end—so keep away from me and return whence you came, for I will never turn aside for any medicine, nor will I ever see it scale my defences, for I warn you, should you dare to tackle me, I shall not leave my place. Either you retrace your steps or stay where you are and be disgraced. Go away wherever you wish. You cannot dislodge me. You will see how affairs are determined by their results and matters by their consequences." '

Both parties continued their heated and ominous discussion in this vein for quite a time, and the saint heard all that was going on about him. Then God decreed that Consumption should dumbfound the other, and that their argument should no longer worry him. Their affair neutralized the effectiveness of the medicine. To God be the glory, in whom alone is might and power. None can contravene His predestination, and none can amend His judgement.

Sīd al-Amīn said to the people one day, 'A man has only to behold my face, whoever he may be, and he will be pardoned of his sins, even if the latter be like rabid sheep, or as countless as the sandhills of Arabia.' This saying was noised abroad among the soldiers and those who joined with them from among the Arabs at the time of the war of Sharr Bubba. So each man came leading his people, mounted or on foot, and there was a mighty throng until the night time, and the last of those who came were women from the Intāba —a tribe of the Awlād al-Nāṣir settled among the Zwāya.

A NOTE ON THE WORKS BY WĀLID WULD AL-MUṢṬAFĀ WULD KHALUNĀ AL-DAYMĀNĪ (d. 1212/1797)

If Wālid wuld Khālunā is a lesser figure than his master, Shaykh Muḥammad al-Yadālī, his literary works are almost as wide in range. In many ways he is more obviously Berber in his sympathies and in his outlook. Very few of his works in Arabic are at present known. Those most famous are:

1. *al-Waʿz wal-ʿibar wa dhikr al-umam al-māḍiyah wal-duwal al-sālifah*, an historical poem of over 1,000 verses.
2. His commentary in two volumes on Khalīl, commonly known as *al-Muʿīn* but named by the author *Shifāʾ al-ghalīl.*
3. *Kitāb al-ansāb*, setting out the origins of Znāga families in the Trārza and some of the leading Zwāya tribes, and showing the male and female ascendancy in the paternal and maternal lines.
4. His *urjūzah* of sixty-two verses recording the deaths of chiefs, kings, and scholars and notable events between the years 1092/1681 and 1180/1766.
5. *Khawāriq awliyāʾ Tashumsha*, 'the miracles of the Tashumsha saints'.
6. Two Znāga poems on the subject of intercession with God and the beseeching of his favours. The poems are described as being Ḥassānīya in measure, namely that they are in the metre of *al-batt lekbiir*, and they are closely modelled on the pattern of the Ḥassānīya *kerza.* The poems, which are now being studied, are the longest written in Znāga and are undoubtedly masterpieces.[1] They are written in Arabic script. The first is called *el-Makzuuz.* There are a number of Arabic words throughout the poem. It has about 280 verses. The text includes a comprehensive list of Arabic texts prized by the Zwāya of the eighteenth century. The second poem of some 150 verses is now barely comprehensible save to one or two Znāga speakers. Its vocabulary is archaic. It is called *el-Mazruufa.*

These two manuscript texts, probably the only early Znāga texts in existence, are more substantial than the simple folk-ditties

[1] The texts are now with my colleague, Dr. J. Bynon.

so far published. Their composition by a scholar of the calibre of Wālid wuld Khālunā, combined with his other historical works, conclusively show him to be the author best qualified to portray the Ṣanhāja of the eighteenth century. It will not be long before they are the sole record of an extinct society.

11

TWO ARABIC MANUSCRIPTS ON THE SUBJECT OF MAURITANIAN MUSIC AND SAHARAN FOLK POETRY

al-Tadhrīb—(al-mīzān fī māʿrifat lebtuuta wa mā yuqāribuhā min buḥūr wa ḍhuur f-azawaan)

By
Muḥammad Maḥmūd wuld ʿAbd al-Fattāḥ wuld Abyayr
who died in the nineteenth century
and by
Muḥammad wuld Muḥammad al-Yadālī
a scholar still living
on the subject of *azawaan*

F. 1 بسم الله الرّحمان الرّحيم   وصلّى الله على سيّدنا محمّد وآله وصحبه

ميزان الغناء أي الشّعر الحسّانيّ وهو أي الغناء ما وُزِنَ من كلامهم قاصدين وزنه فى بتّ من لِبْتُوتَ فما لم يُوزَنْ فيها أو لم يُقْصَدْ وزنه لم يكن غناء لبتوت وهي كثيرة والمشهور منها أربعة ويليها في الشّهرة ما أشبهها ممّا سيُذْكَر معها إن شاء الله ولمعرفتها فائدة لامتداح النّبيّ صلّى الله عليه وسلّم والخِيَرَة من أمّته ومجيء الوعظ والحكم والتّوسّل فيها ولدخول الغناء في حديثَيْ إنّ من الشّعر لحكمة ومن مدحني ولو بشطر كنت له شفيعاً وفي قول عمر رضي الله عنه تعلّموا الشّعر وعلّموه أبناءكم فإنّ فيه العفّة ومكارم الأخلاق لإنّ الغناء هو شعر أهل هذا الزّمن وهي للغناء بمنزلة البحور للشّعر يوزن الغناء فيها كما يوزن الشّعر فى البحور إلّا أنّ المعتبر فى وزنها المتحرّكات دون السّواكن ويعدّون ما حُرِّكَ لإلتقاء السّاكنين او بنقل حركة همز إليه وهمز الوصل إن ابتدئ به متحرّكًا بخلاف الهمز العاطف عندهم تِفِلْوِيتْ على

[1] *batt* is used in Ḥassānīya to mean metre, cf. Chapter 5. The plural is either *btuut* or *btuuta*, as in the manuscript. Cf. Socin, Diwan aus Centralarabien, Leipzig, 1900–1, vol. iii, p. 247, which gives *batt* (*btuut*) as a verse (Zeile) of a poem (viz. in the colloquial (nabaṭi) poetry of Nejd), and as a thread (Faden).

MANUSCRIPT I

Folio 1

In the name of God, the Merciful, the Compassionate, may God bless our Lord Muḥammad, and his family and his companions.

The poetic measure of *ghinā'* (*leġna*, Ḥassānīya poetry). *Ghinā'* (is the name given to) the measured speech of those who intend that it should be measured in a *batt* from *lebtuuta*.[1] That which has not been measured in the latter, or where no metre has been intended, is not *ghinā'*. *Lebtuuta* are of many types. Four of them are well known, and there are others like them which come close to them in renown, and are to be mentioned in their context, if God permits. A knowledge of them is useful in the praising of the Prophet—the blessing and peace of God be upon him—and of the élite of his community, in the delivering of a sermon, maxims, and fervent entreaty and (in addition), on account of the inclusion of *ghinā'* in two traditions: 'Wisdom is to be found in poetry'[2] and, 'He who praises me, though it be with a hemistich, I will be his intercessor', and in the saying of 'Umar—may God be pleased with him—'Learn poetry and teach it to your sons, for indeed both chastity and noble traits of character are to be found in it'. Because *ghinā'* is the poetry of the people of this time and they (*lebtuuta*) fulfil for *ghinā'* the same purpose as metres for Classical Arabic poetry, (*ghinā'*) is measured in them as Classical Arabic poetry is measured in its metres, except that the determining factors in its scanning are vocalized letters without regard to those which are unvocalized.[3] They deem to be a vocalized letter that (letter) which has been given a vowel on account of the meeting of two unvocalized letters or because of the transfer of the vowel of *hamzat al-qaṭ'* to it, or *hamzat al-waṣl* if it should be at the beginning, as opposed to the *hamza* which, according to them, fits one hemistich with another, and which falls before a vocalized

[2] The first *ḥadīth* appears in the *Ṣaḥīḥ* of al-Bukhārī, *Kitāb al-Adab*, Bāb 90, which relates that which is sanctioned and disapproved of in the forms of poetry and their metres. The *ḥadīth* is quoted on the authority of al-Zuhrī.

[3] *Kitāb al-Wasīṭ*, 1958, p. 73.

أخرى الكائن قبل متحرّك فلا يعدّونه متحرّكًا مثاله / أَنَ يَسِّيد إِلَى

كَانِ / عَن الأَحْوَاش اِقْعدَتّ اِفْتِشْبَاشْ // عِدتِّ الِّ فِي اشْطُونْ إِرَانِ /

ڤَلْبِ سَاكِنْ هَوْنْ اِفْلَحْوَاشْ // فالڭَاف بمنزلة البيت والتِفِلْوِيتْ بمنزلة

المصراع والكلمات بمنزلة أجزاء التّفعيل والكَرْزَهْ بمنزلة القصيدة وما

دون الكرزة وفوق الڭاف بمنزلة القطعة فالكرزة على هذا مؤلّفة من

الڭِيفَانْ والڭيفان من التِّفِلْوَاتِنْ والتّفلواتن من الكلمات والكلمات من

الحروف الحسّانيّة ولها أي لبتوت بحور وظهور تقابلها فِزَوَانْ لِبْتَيْتْ بحره F. 2

الطّويل وظهره الأكحل بَيْكِ والأبيظ لِعْتيِكْ وتوزن تفلواتنه بثماني

متحرّكات وهي الأعلى فى وزنه وينسفل إلى متحرّكين والمنسفل منه

هو الذّي فيه أَشْوَارُ الغناء ولكن لا يُطْلَقَ اسم لبتيت إلّا على ذي ثماني

[1] *Wa*, 'and', always counts as a short syllable unless it falls at the beginning of a verse. This rule is sometimes rather loosely observed.

[2] This poem, which illustrates the type of conjunctive *hamza* referred to in the text, is a *gaaf* of four hemistichs in *lebtayt et-taam* metre. In the second hemistich, *ʿan el-aḥwaaš* must be pronounced *ʿan l-eḥwaaš* in order to preserve the eight syllables of this metre. The aḥwā<u>sh</u> are the straw huts used by <u>Sh</u>ay<u>kh</u> Sīdyā and others among the Zwāya as schools and centres of Islamic learning. An Arabic poem by Abū Bakr wuld Muḥammad wuld Abū Bakr (d. 1921) on one of these dwellings is published by Muḥammad Yūsuf Muqlid in *<u>Sh</u>uʿarāʾ Mūrītāniyā*, Beirut, 1962, p. 598.

[3] The *gaaf* is the simplest form of Ḥassānīya poem, cf. Chapter 5. In Arabic poetry each verse (*bayt*) consists of two hemistichs. In Ḥassānīya poetry the author conceives of four hemistichs to the verse.

[4] The author of the *Kitāb al-Wasīṭ*, p. 73, is unaware of the derivation of this word which he spells *taafelwiit*. The root of the word in Berber indicates a door.

[5] The *kerza* (pl. *kerz* and *kerzaat*) is especially employed for panegyrics. It is a very long poem and is usually, although not invariably, an extended form of *gaaf* known as *kerdaadya* (pl. *kerdaadyaat*). It is also known in Znāga poetry.

[6] On the difference between *azawaan* and *leġna*, cf. Chapter 8.

letter, and this they do not consider to be vocalized.[1] An example of this is:

1. O Sīdna wuld Shaykh Sīdyā, if I am late for the *aḥwāsh* and in a state of longing,
2. I reach a point where only solicitude comforts me. My heart is at peace here in the *aḥwāsh*.[2]

The *gaaf*[3] is the equivalent of the *bayt*, the *tifilwiit*[4] is the equivalent of the *misrāʿ*, and the words are in the place of the components of the *tafʿīl*. The *kerza*[5] is the equivalent of the *qaṣīda*. That which is shorter than the *kerza* and longer than the *gaaf* is the equivalent of the *qiṭʿa*. So, according to this, the *kerza* is composed of *giifaan*, the latter of *tifilwaaten*, the *tifilwaaten* are composed of words and the latter from Ḥassānīya letters. The *lebtuuta* have corresponding Classical Arabic metres and *ḍhuur* in *azawaan*.[6]

Folio 2

Lebtayt.[7] Its Classical Arabic metre is *al-ṭawīl*,[8] its *l-aḍhar el-akḥal* is *baygi*, and its *l-aḍhar el-abyaḍ* is *liʿtiig*.[9] Its hemistichs are measured in eight vocalized letters, these being the maximum number in its metre, which is reduced to two vocalized letters and the reduction of it is the medium for the *eŝwaar* of *ghināʾ*. However, the name *lebtayt* is only given to that which has eight vocalized letters. The rest have other names: seven (vocalized

[7] *Lebtayt*, the little *batt*, cf. Chapter 5, has been defined by Mukhtār wuld Ḥāmidun as the term employed in Ḥassānīya poetry to classify separately those metres which, as a feature, preclude two adjoining unvocalized letters in their hemistich. This definition embraces not only pairs of unvocalized consonants, but an unvocalized consonant preceded by a diphthong or a long vowel, cf. Chapter 5, and Leriche pp. 713–14. *Lebtayt* is loosely used:
(*a*) to denote all metres which are of the type described above;
(*b*) to denote specifically *lebtayt et-taamm*, which has eight vocalized letters in its hemistich. This is how it is defined by the author of the manuscript;
(*c*) to denote, particularly in the Adrār and Tagānit, the fourth and final *ḍhar* of *azawaan*, often called *baygi* in other parts of Shinqīṭ.

[8] There is no connexion between the metre or metres of *lebtayt* or *al-ṭawīl* according to informants consulted. They know of no *rapport* between the quantitative measure of Classical Arabic poetry, and the numerical syllabic system of Ḥassānīya poetry. The author appears to mean by his statement that within *baygi*, in *azawaan*, sung Ḥassānīya poems are measured in *lebtayt*, and sung Classical Arabic poems in *al-ṭawīl*. Nowadays, these pairs of corresponding metres are largely ignored.

[9] It is curious that the author makes no mention of *aʿaḍḍaal*, since the name is an ancient one. It is well known, and it is mentioned in the second manuscript.

متحرّكات وما عداه له أسماء أخر / سَبْعَ مِنْ مَسْرُومَ / سِتَّ هُومَ لِبْلَيْدَ /
وُالْخَاطِ ذَ تَيْدُومَ / ماهِ ابْتَيتْ اِتْوَاحِيدَ / ولا يلتقي فيه ساكنان إلّا ما كان
من ذلك فى وقف التّفلويت فإنّه مغتفر فى جميع لبتوت ولا عبرة بكثرة
السّواكن وقلّتها فى هذا البتّ كغيره من لبتوت مثال أعلاه / يَلِّ
شَوْرَكْ فِي النَّظْرَ زَيْنْ / اِمْنَ اشْوَارَ اوْلَادِ الْعِلْمَ // جَيْتِ انْدُورِ الدّْنِيَ
وُاَلدّيِنْ / وُالْعِلْمِ النَّافِعْ وُالْحِكْمَ // ومثال أدناه / جَيْتَكْ / رَاجِ // عَنْدَكْ /
حَاجِ // لُبّيِّرْ بحره الخفيف وظهره الأكحل سِنّيِمَ والأبيظ اِلرّْبَابِ وتوزن
تفلواتنه بسبع متحرّكات بلا زيد ولا نقص ولا بدّ أن يلتقي ساكنان
بعدهما متحرّك واحد فى الأولى منها ونظيرتها في التّقفية كالثّالثة مثلاً
دون الثّانية ونظيرتها كالرّابعة ويقال لذات السّاكنين اِمْكَرِسْعَ ولغيرها
مَسْرُومَ لسرمها من السّاكنين مثاله / أَنَ عَنْدِ يَسيِدْنَ / لِمْشَابِهْكُمْ
بَحْوَالِ // تِكْظِ هَمّ وَادْ زِيدْنَ / شِ مَا كَانِ افْتِحْجَالِ // ومثل لُبّيِّر
اِنْتَاطْرَارْتْ إلّا أنّ السّاكنين يلتقيان فى جميع تفلواتنه مثاله / عَنّكْ بَعْدِ
الَى كَانْ خُوكْ / اِمْنِ الذّنْبِ الّ طَالْعُ // شَكَا لَكْ وَجّهْ بِيهْ بُوكْ / فِكُّوهْ

[1] If the author is here referring to *masruuma* in *lubb^{w}ayr*, then this cannot be in *lebtayt*, since *lubb^{w}ayr* is a metre with a pair of unvocalized letters.

[2] *leblayda*, the little place, is a *šawr* of *faağu*, cf. Leriche, p. 736. It is also a Mauritanian women's dance.

[3] *tayduuma* refers to *tayduum*, a metre of seven consonants in *lebtayt*.

[4] The poem is a *gaaf* of four hemistichs, in *lebtayt et-taamm* metre.

[5] The poem is a *gaaf* of four hemistichs, in *batt aṯnayn* metre.

[6] *lubb^{w}ayr* means 'the little well', cf. Chapter 5 and Leriche, p. 725. Each hemistich has seven syllables, and there is a pair of unvocalized letters before the final vocalized letter in the first hemistich of each verse.

[7] *siññiima*. Chapter 8, Leriche, pp. 739–41. This *ḍhar*, the third in *azawaan*, is the most commonly performed. It is transitional, combining the pride and

letters) is called *masruuma*,[1] six (*lebtayt sitta*) is called *leblayda*,[2] the rest is tayduuma,[3] *btayt* is not one term.

Two unvocalized letters do not meet in it (*lebtayt*) except in the pause of the hemistich and this is excused in all the *lebtuuta*, and it is of no consequence whether there be many unvocalized letters or few in this *batt* as in the others. An example of the maximum is:

1. O thou to whom it is better to look towards, than it is to the sons of learning.
2. I have come seeking earthly things, religion, useful knowledge, and wisdom.[4]

An example of the minimum is:

1. I have come to you beseeching,
2. What I need is thine.[5]

Lubbʷayr.[6] Its Classical Arabic metre is *al-khafīf*, its *l-aḏhar el-akḥal* is *siññiima*[7] and its *l-aḏhar el-abyaḍ* is *rrbaabi*.[8]
Its hemistichs are measured in seven vocalized letters, neither more nor less, and there must be two unvocalized letters meeting, followed by one vocalized letter, in the first hemistich and its equivalent in the rhyme scheme, the third, for example, but not the second and its equivalent, such as the fourth. The hemistich which has two unvocalized letters is called *emkarisʿa*[9] and the other *masruuma*[10] because it dispenses with the two unvocalized letters. An example of *emkarisʿa* is:

1. O Sīdna, I regard myself as a fitting person to seek
2. your fulfilment of my need and that you should add something extra which has not occurred to me.[11]

Entaaṭraart[12] resembles *lubbʷayr* except that the two unvocalized letters meet in all of its hemistichs, for example:

1. If your brother complains to you about a sin which he has committed before God,

ferocity of *faaġu* and the sadness of *baygi*. According to some Moors the name is derived, together with the style of singing, from Bawwār in Māli.

[8] *rrbaabi* means 'rebec'. Chapter 7 and Leriche, p. 740.

[9] According to an informant *emkarisʿa* in Ḥassānīya means, 'systematically arranged or organized'.

[10] *masruuma*. The traditional form of *lubbʷayr* incorporating these two types of hemistichs, is known as *agiilaal*, 'that which has the cut tail'.

[11] The poem is a *gaaf* of four hemistichs, in *agiilaal* metre.

[12] *entaaṭraart* is a Znāga word indicating the plant *psorata plicata*. The author of the manuscript distinguishes this metre from *lubbʷayr*. Others hold that this and *agiilaal* are forms of *lubbʷayr*. This view is shared by Mukhtār wuld Ḥāmidun.

اَمْنِ الِّ خَالْعُ // ومثل اِنْتَاطْرَارْتْ تكَادْرِينْ إلّا أنّها تارة يكون ساكنا
تفلواتنها جميعاً بعدهما متحرّكان وتارة يكون ساكنا أُولاها ونظيرتها
بعدهما متحرّكان وساكنا ثانيتها ونظيرتها بعدهما متحرّك واحد
وناقصتان عن أختيهما بمتحرّك مثال النّوع الأول / اَعْذَرْنِ يَسّيِدْ فِي
امْجِيكْ / اِفْكِلّتْ الَادَابْ وَيَّاكْ // هَمّ فِيكْ اَكْثِيرْ وُاعْلِيكْ / حِمْلُ مِنُّ
رِيحْ يَرْعَاكْ // ومثال النوع الثانى / هَوْنَ امْرَاضِ اعَاوْدُونِ / مِنْهُمْ عَقْلِ
فِي الظّْيَاعْ // وَلِّ مِنْهُمْ نَاوْشُونِ / يَكَانِ نِتَاشْ ثَاعْ // اِمْرَيْمِيدَ بحرها F. 3
الوافر وظهرها الأكحل كَرْ والأبيظ مَكَّ مُوسَ وتوزن تفلواتنها بسبع
متحرّكات لا تزيد ولا تنقص ولا بدّ أن يلتقي في كلّ منها ساكنان قبلهما
متحرّكان وبعدهما خمس متحرّكات ويكتفى عن السّاكنين فيها وكذا
غيرها من لبتوت بالسّاكن المشرّد مثاله / مَا ثَطّْ رَيْنَ حَدِّ اكُونْ /
فَخْلَاقْ بَخْلَاقُ شِبْهَكْ // اِعْلِيكْ بِسْمِ اللَّهِ هَوْنْ / وُاعْلِيكْ بِسْمِ اللَّهِ
هَكْ // ومثل اِمْرَيْمِيدَ بُعُمْرَانْ إلّا أنّ ساكنيه قبلهما متحرّك واحد
مثاله / هَوْنْ حَدِّ النَّفْسُ عَايِفْ / شَافْ مِن جُودَكْ بَاشْ اِجِيكْ // جَاكْ

[1] This poem is a *gaaf*. A source attributes it to a poet called Durayd ʿAlī of the Īdaw ʿĪsh.

[2] *tigaadriin* is of two kinds, *tigaadriin et-taamma*, with the variation indicated in the text, or *sġayyer tigaadriin* where the even numbered hemistichs have only five syllables instead of seven, cf. Chapter 5 and Leriche, pp. 726–7.

[3] The poem is a *gaaf* of four hemistichs.

[4] The poem is a *gaaf* of four hemistichs.

[5] *mekka mūsa* (*muusa*). According to Mukhtār wuld Ḥāmidun, many Mauritanians think that this name may be associated with a monarch of Māli, perhaps Mansa Mūsā, King of Māli, whose pilgrimage to Mecca in A.D. 1324/5 is famous. But there is some doubt as to what '*mekka*' signifies. Is it Mecca, or is it maize?—either is possible. The form '*makkat mūsa*', which might be expected, is not unknown, but it is so rare as to suggest that '*mekka*' is probably a form of the

2. you should obtain for him the favour of your father, and free him from that which makes him afraid.[1]

Tigaadriin[2] is similar to *entaaṭraart* except that at times the two unvocalized letters of all its hemistichs are followed by two vocalized letters and at times the two unvocalized letters of its first and corresponding hemistichs are followed by two vocalized letters, and the two unvocalized letters of its second and corresponding hemistichs are followed by one vocalized letter and are a vocalized letter shorter than their sisters. An example of the first kind is:

1. Pardon me, o Lord, for coming to you in so unseemly a way.
2. I have great need of you, but to you the bearing of my need is a light thing, as a wind. May God watch over you.[3]

An example of the second kind is:

1. Here are my infirmities, heal me. On account of them my mind is astray.
2. Catch and save me from them, I may be caught indeed.[4]

Folio 3

Mraymiida. Its Classical Arabic metre is *al-wāfir*, its *l-aḍhar el-akḥal* is *kar* and its *l-aḍhar el-abyaḍ* is *mekka mūsa.*[5] Its hemistichs are measured in seven vocalized letters neither more nor less, and there must be two unvocalized letters meeting preceded by two vocalized letters and followed by five vocalized letters in all its hemistichs. However, a displaced unvocalized letter may stand in place of the two unvocalized letters, here as in the other *lebtuuta*. An example of it is:

1. I have never seen one whose character is like yours,
2. blessing be upon you here, blessing be upon you there.[6]

Buʿumraan is like *mraymiida* except that there is one vocalized letter before its two unvocalized letters. An example of it is:

1. Here is one who despises himself and who has seen on account of your bounty a reason to come to you.

Mandinka name 'Magham'. Delafosse notes the name كاي مكّ, Kaya, son of Mekka, who is supposed to have reigned in Ouagadou (a region of Kumbi) and to have founded a dynasty at Ghāna (Maurice Delafosse and Siré Abbâs Soh, *Chroniques du Fouta Sénégalais*, Paris 1913, pp. 255, 269). Yet another theory supports a Māli origin for this name. It was a type of playing invented by an *iggīw* called Mawlay Ismāʿīl, a poet of the Ahl al-Labb wuld Bū Sayf of the Awlād Mubārak who introduced it via the Ḥawḍ from Digna (Tāghutu) in Māli. The word seems to be Bambára, and in all probability its origin is now totally unknown in Mauritania.

[6] The poem is a *gaaf* of four hemistichs.

يِرْجِفْ قَلْبُ خَايِفْ / فَلّْشْ مِنْ خَوْفْ يَنْجِيكْ // اَلْوَاكْدِ بحره الرّمل
وظهره الأكحل فَاقْ والأبيظ عَرَّايِ السُّرُوزْ وتوزن تفلواتنه بعشر
متحرّكات ولا بدّ أن يلتقي في كلّ واحدة منها أربع سواكن ساكنان فى
أوّلها قبلهما متحرّكان وساكنان في آخرها بعدهما متحرّكان أيضاً ولا
تكون تفلواتن گيفانه إلّا اثنتين متّفقتين في الرويّ وهو الحرف الّذي
تتوارد عليه التفلواتن بخلاف لبتوت غيره فأقلّ تفلواتن گيفانها أربع
وأعلاها لا حدّ له فقد تكثر حتّى تكون گرزة مثاله / يَسِيدْنَ يَلِّ لِلْعَانِي
افْرَاجَ / اَرْعَاكْ نَمْشِ مَا زِلْتِ انْدُورْ حَاجَ // ومثل الواكد فى ذلك كلّه
اِنْگَادِسْ ولِمْسَكَّمْ إلّا أنّ تفلواتن گيفانهما أربع وقد تزيد متحرّكاتهما
على عشرة وقد تكون تسعة وقد ينحرف السّاكنان فيها عن مكانهما في
تفلواتن الوَاكْدِ كما قد شاهدنا ذلك ولا أدري أسائغ فيهما ذلك أم
من لحن المغنّين مع أنّي قد قال لي الخبير بهذا الفنّ إنّ أصل وزنهما
كوزن الوَاكْدِ فتارة يغيّرونهما وتارة يأتون بهما على الأصل ويدلّ
لهذا أنّي رأيتهم يغيّرون الوَاكْدِ عن وزنه المتداول المذكور آنفاً والله
تعلى أعلم واستغفره وأتوب إليه لأسلم ويقال لهذه الثّلاثة وما أشبهها
لِبْتُوتَ لِكْبَارْ والمستحسن عند حذّاق المغنّين في تفلواتن گيفان لبتوت

[1] The poem is a *gaaf* of four hemistichs.

[2] According to Mukhtār wuld Ḥāmidun, *el-batt lekbiir* is of several kinds. *El-waakdi* is one of these. It differs from the others, firstly by the position of the unvocalized consonants in its hemistich of ten syllables, and secondly by the fact that its *gaaf* differs from that found in all other metres. It is composed of only two hemistichs, instead of four, and both the hemistichs have the same rhyming letter.

2. He has come in fear to you, his heart trembling. Protect him from his fear, may God save you.[1]

El-waakdi.[2] Its Classical Arabic metre is *al-ramal*, its *l-aḍhar el-akḥal* is *faaġu*[3] and *l-aḍhar el-abyaḍ* is *'arraay essruuz.*[4] Its hemistichs are measured in ten vocalized letters. In each hemistich four unvocalized letters must meet, two at its beginning preceded by two vocalized letters and two at the end followed by two vocalized letters, also. The hemistichs of its *giifaan* must be two of the same *rawī*, and this letter is the rhyming letter of the succeeding hemistichs, contrary to the other *lebtuuta*. The minimum number of hemistichs of its *giifaan* is four, and there is no maximum limit. They may develop into a *kerza*. An example of it is:

O Lord, who art a release for the distressed, do not let me go as long as I wish a favour.[5]

Entirely similar to *el-waakdi*, in that respect, are *engaades*[6] and *lemsaggam*[7] except that the hemistichs in their *giifaan* are four, and that their vocalized letters may exceed ten. They may be nine, and the two unvocalized letters in them may be shifted from their place in the hemistichs of *el-waakdi*, as we have already observed. I am not aware whether this is permissible in them both, or whether it is due to an error of the singers, although the expert in this art has told me that their basic metre is the same as that of *el-waakdi*. Sometimes (the singers) alter them and at other times perform them according to the original. Evidence for this is the fact that I have seen them changing *el-waakdi* from its prevailing measure, afore mentioned. God knows best, I seek his pardon, and I repent to him, so I may be saved. These three, and the likes of them, are called *lebtuuta lekbaar.*[8] Among the skilled singers, the

[3] The name *faaġu or faaqu*, the second *ḍhar* in *azawaan*, may come from an Arabic verb, *afāqa*, meaning 'to arouse', or 'to stir up'.

[4] *'array essruuz* (*sseruuz*), or *ssruuzi*, indicates the one who leaves the saddles empty. Those who once occupied them have died in battle.

[5] The poem is a *gaaf* of two hemistichs.

[6] The name *engaades* is probably connected with the tribe of the same name (Ingādis) now extinct, but which formerly dwelt in the Trārza. Wālid wuld Khālunā refers to them in his biographies of the Tashumsha saints, cf. Chapter 10.

[7] It has not been possible to obtain information to indicate in what respect *lemsaggam*, 'the straightened', differs from *engaades*.

[8] The author quotes almost all the forms of *el-batt lekbiir*. Others, such as *al-mawmaaya*, are little known and, in view of the unpopularity of the lengthy panegyric in modern times, are likely to be forgotten.

غير الوَاكْدِ أن تكون أربعاً ثمّ ستّاً ثمّ ثمانياً ثمّ عشراً كل مرتّبة دون ما
قبلها في الحسن وما زاد على ذلك فتطويل وتثقيل لا سيّما في الطَّلْعَة
والطّلعة ما كانت الثّلاث الأوّل منها مقفّاة بتقفية واحدة ومحلّ هذا في
F. 4 الكِيفان حيث لم يُقْصَدْ تطويلها جدّاً حتّى تكون كرزة وإلّا فالكرزة
مستحسنة عندهم تنبيه قد يُوجَد متحرّك وساكن في قوّة السّاكنين فلا
يُحَسَب المتحرّك في عدد المتحرّكات الوزنيّة لأنّ أصله السّكون ويقال
للتفلويت الواقع فيها هذا مملوخة ولا يقع في لبتيت إِذْ لا يلتقي فيه
ساكنان وصورة ذلك أن يكون فى الكلمة بمحلّ السّاكنين حرفان
ساكن فمتحرّك فيُحَرَّك السّاكن ويُسَكَّن المتحرّك ولا يفسد معناها
مثاله فى اِمْرَيْمِيدَ مثلاً / مُرِيدْ لَازِمْ حَضْرِتْكُمْ / مَا يَرْغِبْ اِرَاهَ حَضْرَ //
وِسِيدْ فَرْظْ اِبْخِدْمِتْكُمْ / لاَ يَجْبَرِ افْدَهْرُ كَشْرَ // خاتمة يُستحَسن فى الغناء
ما يستحسن في الشّعر من المحسّنات كالجناس والإستخدام والتّوجيه
والتّورية ولزوم ما لا يلزم ونحو ذلك مثال الأوّل منها / يَلَّ يَسْوَ فِي

[1] *mamluuka* means 'pulled away' or 'pulled off'.

[2] The poem is a *gaaf* of two verses. The point of the author seems to be that the second and fourth hemistichs are eight syllables and therefore one in excess of that normally permitted in *mraymiida*. This has come about because a displaced unvocalized letter stands in place of two unvocalized letters.

[3] *istikhdām* is a figure of speech wherein an expression which has two meanings is used in one sense and the other sense is recalled by a pronoun which agrees with and relates to that expression, e.g.:

إذا نزل السماء بارض قوم x رعيناه وإن كانوا غضابَا

'When rain falls on the land of a tribe, we have grazed on it although the tribe be angry with us', where سماء in the sense of 'vegetation' is recalled by the pronominal suffix of رعيناه. M. Garcin de Tassy, *Rhétorique et Prosodie des* approved (arrangement) in the hemistichs of the *giifaan* of the *lebtuuta* other than *el-waakdi*, is that they should be four, then six, then eight, then ten, each rated inferior to its predecessor in beauty. Anything which exceeds that is long-winded and burdensome, especially in the *ṭalʿa*. The latter has its first three hemistichs in the same rhyme and the place of this in

Folio 4

the *giifaan* is where a lengthy prolongation of the *giifaan* has not been deliberate to the extent that it would become a *kerza*. Otherwise, the *kerza* is esteemed by them (the singers). Note that a vocalized letter and an unvocalized letter may have the force of two unvocalized letters, so that the vocalized letter is not deemed to be in the number of vocalized letters of the measure, because, basically, it is unvocalized. The hemistich in which this occurs is called *mamluuḵa*.[1] It does not occur in *lebtayt* since two unvocalized letters do not meet in it. An illustration of that is, that in the word there may be, instead of the two unvocalized letters, two letters, a vocalized and an unvocalized, and the unvocalized is given a vowel and the vocalized letter loses it. The meaning of the hemistich is not faulty. An example of it in *mraymiida* is:

1. A disciple constantly in your company who wishes none else.
2. The duty of serving you is uppermost. He finds no ill fortune in his lifetime.[2]

Conclusion. The qualities which are appreciated in Classical Arabic poetry are equally appreciated in *g̱hināʾ*, the pun for example, and *istiḵhdām*[3] and ambiguity and double-entendre and supererogation, and so forth. An example of the first is:

1. O thou in whose direction both Zayd and Yaḥyā come as equals,

langues de l'Orient musulman, Paris, 1873, p. 91. My colleague Jarīr Abū Ḥaydar has kindly furnished me with the following example:

أراعى النجم فى سيري إليكم x ويـرعـاه من البيداء حصاني

'I gaze at the star in my journey to you, while my horse pastures on the desert pasturage'; where the word نجم meaning both 'star' and 'grass' is used. Cf. S. A. Bonebakkar, *Some Early Theories of the tawriya*, (Mouton, The Hague, Paris, 1966), p. 19.

امْجِيكْ اِفْشَوْرْ / زَيْدُ يَحيى جيتَكْ عَانِ // دَايِرْ يَحْيَى ثَلْبِ بِالنُّورْ/ نِشْرِبْ مِن بَحْرِ الْمَعَانِ // ومثل الآخر منها / جَيْتَكْ مِحْتَاجْ / لِلِّ نَجْبَر // ثَلْبِ مِرْتَاجْ / مَا فِيهِ اصْبَرْ // وَلِّ عِلْمِ انَّكْ / ذِى النَّاسْ اِتْلَافَ // اِبَطِّ عَنَّكْ / ذِيكْ الْخِلَافَ // ويعاب في قافية الغناء ما يعاب في قافية الشّعر كالإتيان بألف قبل الرويّ تارة وحذفه أخرى كالعالم والعلم والعمّ والعامّ كتعاقب الألف مع الواو والياء مثل ثام وثوم جاك وجيك وغير ذلك من العيوب ويكون سرقة في الغناء ما يكون سرقة في الشّعر أيضاً وما لا فلا وتتفاوت السّرقة في القبح فأقبحها أن يسرق غناء غيره لفظه ومعناه ثمّ معناه كلّه ثمّ بعضهما وما لا يجوز أن يكون رويّا في الشّعر لا يحسن جعله رويّا في الغناء كهاء الضّمير وكافه وهاء التّأنيث ونحو ذلك والله تعلى أعلم وأحكم وأستغفره ممّا علمت وما لم أعلم . هذا ما أمكنني أن نأتي به من ميزان الغناء لأنّي لست من فرسانه ولا من أهل شأوه وميدانه لكن تطفّلت على هذه النّبذة منه الكافية عمّا يتشعّب عنها المعيشة للمبتغي أكثر منها بهمّة ابن شيخي حين ندبني إليها تذريباً للأفهام ومؤانسة فى الكلام راجياً من الله تعلى أن ينيلني ما منها قصدت ويغفر لي ما فيه عثرت ومعتذراً لذوي الألباب الإخوان من ذي **F. 5** شيبة يعدو جواده بذا الميدان فعسى الله أن يجعل لي فيه خيراً كثيراً

[1] The poem is a *gaaf* of two verses in *lebtayt et-taamm* metre.

[2] This poem consists of a *gaaf* of four hemistichs in *btayt arbaʿ* (*ḥwaywiiṣ*), followed by a second *gaaf* in *btayt ḵamsa* (*ḥaṯu jjraad*).

2. I have come to you on purpose, wishing for the quickening of my heart by the light and to drink from the sea of ideas.[1]

An example of the last is:

1. I come to you in need of what I find,
2. my heart is quaking, there is no endurance in it.
3. So I know that these people are needy.
4. May He (God) delay your succession, (the death of your father whose successor you will be).[2]

Defects in the rhyme in Classical Arabic poetry apply equally to *ghinā'*, for example the bringing of *alif* before the *rawī* at times and omitting it at others such as *'ālim* and *'ilm* and *'amm* and *'āmm* or, for example, the following of *alif* with a *waw* or a *yā'*, such as *gām* and *gūm* and *jāk* and *jīk* and similar faults. Plagiarism in *ghinā'* is the same as in Classical Arabic poetry. The same applies to that which is not regarded as such. There are degrees of plagiarism, some being worse than others. The very worst case is where one takes and uses the *ghinā'* of another, both in letter and in meaning. A lesser theft is the theft of all its meaning, then some of its letter and meaning. The rules governing the approved use of a *rawī* apply equally to *ghinā'* and to Classical Arabic poetry. Examples are *hā' al-ḍamīr* and *kāf al-ḍamir* and *hā' al-ta'nīth* and so forth.[3] God, the Sublime, knows best. He is the most wise, and I ask His forgiveness for what I have come to know and that which I know not. This is all that I have been able to produce about the poetic measure of *ghinā'*, because I am not familiar with it, nor one of the company of those who excel in it, both in object and in scope. But I have intruded on this small part of it (to provide) a sufficient basis for what may branch forth from it, the sustenance of him who wishes to pursue the matter further. (I have done this) through the eagerness of the son of my *Shaykh* when he assigned me to it as a means of sharpening the faculties and for a study, hoping God, the Almighty, will obtain for me that for which I have striven and pardon me where I have erred.

Folio 5

I apologize to my brothers in learning, to the venerable one whose charger gallops in this field; perchance God may grant me much

[3] For a discussion of these matters, cf. Wright, *A Grammar of the Arabic Language*, Cambridge, 1955, vol. ii, pp. 352–3.

ببركة من ندب إليه وأبيه وأشياخه ومن نالوا البركة منه سيّدنا ومولانا محمّد صلّى الله عليه وسلّم وعلى آله وصحبه وسلّم تسليماً وسمّيت هذا المخترع التّذريب أو الميزان فى معرفة لبتوت وما يقاربها من بحور وظهور فَزَوَانْ .

انتهى بحمد الله وحسن عونه مخترع محمّد محمود بن عبد الفتّاح بن عبد الله بن أحمد بن بُدّ بن أحمد بن الفاضل ابن امرابط مكّ بن أبيير من خطّ هرون ابن الشّيخ سيدي عن خطّ المؤلّف .

بسم الله الرّحمان الرّحيم الحمد لله وعليه الإعتمادْ ومن فيض كرمة الإستمدادْ والصّلاتان والسّلامان الدّائمان بدوامهْ على محمّد أفضل خلقه وأكرمهْ وبعد فلمّا كان علم كلّ شيء أفضل من جهلهْ لا سيّما للحاذق النّبهْ ومن حكم عليّ بن أبي طالب وألفاظه العجائب النّاس بزمانهم أشبه منهم بآبائهم طلب منّي بعض الأقارب الأشرافْ والقرناء الظّرافْ وهو يعقوب بن محمّد ابن الشّيخ سيدي رحم الله السّلفْ وبارك في الخلفْ ولم أطل في تعريفهْ لشهرة تالده وطارفهْ شيئًا يعين في فهم طرق الغناء في هذه البلدان المعروف عند أهله بأَزَوَانْ فأجبته إلى ذلك اذ لم أجد بدّاً من هنالك وإن لم أكن من أهلهْ ولا يضرب لي بسهمهْ لكن استعنت بالله في أمره وما توفيقي إلّا به وقد اشتغل بهذا قبلي

good in it. Through the grace of him who assigned it, of his father and his Shaykhs and those who have acquired their grace from him, our Lord and Master, Muḥammad—God's blessing and peace be upon him, upon his family and his companions. I have named this original composition 'The sharpening of the faculties', or 'How to acquire a knowledge of *lebtuuta* and their equivalent metres in Classical Arabic poetry and *ḍhuur* in *azawaan*.'—Here ends, God be praised, and through his good help the original composition of Muḥammad Maḥmūd b. ʿAbd al-Fattāḥ b. ʿAbd Allāh b. Aḥmad b. Budd b. Aḥmad b. al-Fāḍil b. Mrābiṭ Makka b. Abyayr (copied by the hand of Hārūn b. al-Shaykh Sīdyā from the original hand of the author).

MANUSCRIPT II

In the name of God, the Merciful, the Compassionate, praise be to God, upon whom be trust and from the flow of whose bounty support is found, and two blessings and salutations be for ever upon Muḥammad, the most excellent and noblest of God's creation. Since knowledge of all things is superior to ignorance and especially to the man who is percipient and understanding, and since among the wise sayings and wonderous utterances of ʿAlī b. Abū Ṭālib is to be found, 'People more closely resemble their contemporaries than they do their forebears', one of my noble and resourceful relatives, Yaʿqūb b. Muḥammad b. al-Shaykh Sīdyā—may God have mercy on the forebear and bestow his blessing on the successor—asked me, and I tarried not in acquainting him, on account of his renown both acquired and inherited, with something which would assist in the understanding of the ways of singing in these countries, and known by those familiar with it as *azawaan*. I answered his request since I found no way of avoiding it, and although I am not familiar with it and have no expert acquaintance with it, I have sought God's help in the matter and my success is due solely to Him. Two other contemporaries of mine have worked in this field before me but I have not followed their lead in this matter in view of the way the art changes with

رجلان من أبناء هذا الزّمان ولم أقفهما في أمرهْ لتغيّره بتغيّر دهرهْ فأقول وبالله التّوفيقْ والهداية لأقوم طريقْ . أمّا هذا الفنّ المطلوبْ وإن لم يكن عند بعض النّاس بالمحبوبْ فقد اشتغل به كثير من أهل الزّمن ليسوا في طرقه على سنن لكن نذكر ما هو غالب أمرهم عند حديثهم وقديمهم أمّا أوّل ابتدائه عندهم فهو طريق يقال لها كَرْ وفيها من الفروع الوَافِرْ وسَيْنِ فأمّا المناسب لها من الشّعر فليس بمستقيم على حالة لكنّ أكثره ابن وهيب ومدح المصطفى صلّى الله عليه وسلّم أمّا ابن وهيب فكقولهم / آيات طه / ليست تُبَاهى / ولا تناهى / على الدّوام // وأمّا المدح فكقولهم / أفي الرّسل من بالهاشميّ يشبّه / حرام عليه النّار قلب أحبّه // وأمّا ما فيه من الشّعر الحسّانيّ فلا يتغيّر أمّا فى

F. 6 أصل كَرْ فمثل اِمْرَيْمِيدَ كقوله / كَانْ حَدّْ اِبْقَ يَتْنَهْوَلْ / بِيهْ هَوْلْ

اَمْنَادِمْ نَهْوَالْ // ذَاكْ بَاط اَلِ لَا يَعْجَلْ / مَا اسْمَعْ حِسَّكْ فَانَيْوَالْ //

[1] The author is referring to Muḥammad Maḥmūd wuld ʿAbd al-Fattāḥ and to an earlier author, Muḥammad ʿAbdallāh wuld al-Bukhārī wuld al-Filālī of the Ahl Bārakallāh. The latter composed a Ḥassānīya *kerza* on *leġna*. The poem is divided into several sections, on *gnaydiiya*, *faaġu*, *baygi*, and *siññiima*.

It begins with the following *gaaf*:

Within *kar* are five divisions. When you have in mind the 'White' way; *mekka mūsa* (*muusa*), and *al-faayez*, which arises out of it.
(*Entemaas*), is the chief 'black' way, and *sayni* (*kar*).

The poem explains:

(*a*) that *enweffal* (*kar* in *gnaydiiya*) is outside the divisions referred to above;
(*b*) that in *faaġu* the 'black' way is *tenaččuuga* and *sayni faaġu*, the 'white' way *et-teḥzaam*, and *ssruuzi*, and that *faaġu lekbiir*, in *gnaydiiya*, is a link between the other two;
(*c*) that *eññaama* and *rrbaabi* are the divisions of *siññiima* in the 'white' way;
(*d*) that *el-ʿitiig* is the 'white' way of *baygi* and that, in *gnaydiiya*, *baygi lekbiir* is also called *baygi jjraad*.

Other parts of the *kerza* refer to the way strings should be plucked in each the times.[1] I say—and my success is through God, and guidance to the straightest path—that as this art about which information is asked, though it be disliked by some, many people of the time have been engaged in it. They follow no established correct usage in its methods but I shall mention their prevailing practice of both nowadays and in times past. As for the primary way they perform it, it is known as *kar*, in which there are branches including *al-wāfir* and *sayni*.[2] There is no fixed rule at all as to what type of Classical Arabic poetry is suitable for it, but it is mostly Ibn Wahīb and poetry in praise of the Prophet, the blessing and peace of God be upon him. As for Ibn Wahīb, they say, for example, 'The miracles of Ṭāhā have no peer in excellence nor do they ever come to an end'.[3] As for the praise of the Prophet, they say, for example:

1. Is there among the Messengers of God one who compares with the Hāshimite?
2. A heart which loves him is immune from the fire of hell.[4]

As for Hassānīya poetry, there is no variation. In the case of *kar*, in its original form, an example in *mraymiida* is:

Folio 6

1. If a man loves to be entertained, on account of the voice of a singer,
2. that man will not be eager until he hears your voice in *anaywaal*

jaamba, but the text is unintelligible without a commentary or explanation by an *īggīw* with his instrument.

[2] According to Leriche, p. 735, *al-wāfir* is a combination of the 'black' way of *kar* and poems, *mraymiida* in metre, are sung to it. He also mentions *sayni 'ṭ-ṭaari* as a recent combination among the Trārza musicians. It seems likely that the author is using *sayni* here to mean *sayni kar*.

[3] Ibn Wahīb is a name used to denote poetry of praise, in particular praise of the Prophet. The name is a corruption of Ibn Mahīb. It is, or was, a custom of the scholars of Shinqīṭī to study in Ṣafar the poems by the Andalusian poet Abū Bakr Muḥammad al-Mahīb in praise of the Prophet, each poem being based on a letter of the alphabet, and there are many manuscript commentaries on these poems in Mauritanian libraries. The author quotes as his example the thirty-sixth verse of the poem by Muḥammad al-Yadālī (Chapter 4) cf. *Kitāb al-Wasīt*, p. 223, and *Revue du Monde musulman*, vol. viii, June 1909, 'Un poète Saharien' by L. Massignon.

[4] *Dīwān al-wasā'il al-mutaqalliba fī madḥ al-nabī*, by 'Abd al-Raḥmān al-Fāzāzī al-Andalusī with the *takhmīs* of Abū Bakr Muḥammad al-Mahīb, (Dār iḥyā' al-kutub al-'arabīya bi Miṣr), p. 8.

وُانَّحَيْوْ اُظَهْرْ اَكَادِيرْ / ذَاكْ بَلّ اِخْبَيْطَكْ لِكْبِيرْ // اُزَيْنَ عَنْدَكْ زَادْ

اِتْعَاسِيرْ / رَوْقْ رَدّاتْ اِبْتَيْتْ اَكْحَالْ // اُرَوْقْ زَادْ اَمْعَاكْ اِتْشَوْعِيرْ / كُلّ

حَدّْ اُمَلِّ مُحَالْ // وأمّا ما في سَيْنِ فبُعُمْرَانْ كقوله / نَجِعْ لِعْنَاىَ

وُالتَّشْطَاطْ / سَوْحَلْ اِلْمَبْرُومْ اِللَّىَّ // اُكَالْ سَاحَلْ عِكْثْلِتْ لَنْبَاطْ / اُكَالْ

شَرْكْ اِلْمَدَاحِىَّ // اُنَجِعْ رَفْعِتْ مِسْلِمْ مَظْلُومْ / شَامْ مِنْ دَرْكَلْ لَدَرُّومْ //

لصَّمَامِيطْ اُلتِّنَيْمُومْ / لَرِظْ كِلِمْسِ وَاللَّىَّ // اُصَدّْ رَاحَلْ بَاشْنَاه اَلْيُومْ / لَا

اعْرَيْبَاتْ اَلرِّوِىَّ // وأغلب طرقهما في أرْدِينْ والتِّدِنيتْ مَكَّ مُوسَ والفَايِزْ

وأمّا ما يقال في سَيْنِ من الشّعر العربيّ فلا قاعدة له إنّما هو شعر

ينتخبونه كقول بعض الشّعراء / ألا إنّ أشهى الطّيّبات جميعها / محادثة

الخلّان غير الأراذل // وضرب كبود العيس في كلّ ليلة / إلى البيض أشباه

[1] This poem is a *gaaf* of two verses followed by a *ṭalʿa* of three verses. There are references to the following musical forms in the poem:

(*a*) *anaywaal*, in its several forms, is a combination of the 'black' way of *kar*, cf. Leriche, p. 734;

(*b*) *annḥayw* is not mentioned by Leriche. It is possible that the term *neḥya* is meant here, cf. Leriche, p. 732.

(*c*) *agaadiir* is a *šawr* of the 'white' way of *faağu*, cf. Leriche, p. 739, and of the 'white' way of *siññiima*, cf. Leriche, p. 743.

(*d*) *btayt lakḥal* is the 'black' way of *baygi*.

[2] The complete text of this poem, with variations as established by Muḥammad wuld Dāddāh, is a *gaaf* of two verses (repeated twice as a refrain) followed by a *ṭalʿa* of three verses, separated from another of the same length by the refrain. The metre is *buʿumraan*, but in certain hemistichs a vocalized letter and an unvocalized are substituted for two unvocalized letters, and there are several hemistichs where an initial conjunction in both hemistichs is not reckoned to be among the vocalized letters.

1. The camp of divine solicitude and of great enterprise, has gone to the north with her, she with the tressed hair.
2. The camp has pastured to the north of the water hole at Lakhlāṭ (to the north of Wādān) and pastured to the south of al-Maddāḥayya (near to al-Ḥank).
3. And the isolated mountain of Mījik (north-west of Fort Gouraud) and the little isolated mountain of al-Ghayn. They have pastured at the camp of the payment of the debt (blood money).

3. and *annḥayw* and the *aḍhar* of *agaadiir*, that which is proper to your fervent playing.
4. You delight also in the difficulties of experimenting in melodies of *btayt lakḥal*,
5. and anyone who tries the art of singing poetry along with you cannot do so.[1]

In the case of *sayni*, they employ *buʿumraan* as in the words:

1. The camp of divine solicitude and of great enterprise has gone to the north with the one with the braided locks.
2. It has pastured to the north of the waterhole of Lanbāṭ and the south of al-Madāḥīya.
3. The camp of the exalting of an oppressed Muslim has gone from Dargal and Addarrūm
4. to al-Ṣamāmīṭ and Tinyammūm, to the edge of Galamsi and the Layya
5. and has come back travelling today with pride to Aʿraybāt and al-Rwīya.[2]

Their prevailing ways of playing on the *ardīn* and the *tidīnīt* are *mekka mūsa* and *el-faayez*.[3] As regards Classical Arabic poetry used in *sayni* there is no fixed model. It is simply poetry which they select, as the saying of one of the poets:

1. Indeed, the most pleasant of all good things, is the discourse of companions who are not base,
2. and the strenuous riding of camels of good breed, every night, to the white-complexioned women, like gazelles holding back from the herd.[4]

4. And Ajwayr and ʿAglat Turīn (between Fort Gouraud and Fort Trinquet), they have pastured among the people of bad intentions (the enemy).
5. Consuming, all alone, the yield of the maturing of the male date-palms and at Aftāsa (western Adrār), and at al-Argīya (north of the Tīris).
6. The camp of the succour of a Muslim, a victim of injustice, has gone from Dargal (west of Tijikja), and Adarrūm.
7. To al-Ṣmāmīṭ (Adrār), and Tin Yammūm (northern Adrar), up to Aʿraybāt and al-Arwīya (Tīris).
8. And has come back travelling today, with pride, to the land of Gilimsi and al-Layya (near to Tijikja).

These verses, which are a challenge by the Idaw ʿĪsh of Tagānit (hence the points of orientation) to the men of the Adrār, are attributed to Muḥammad wuld Muḥammad Shayn who died in 1236/1820. A version of this poem with variations in both text and translation appears in D. Cohen, *Le dialecte arabe ḥassānīya*, Paris, 1963, pp. 242, 243.

[3] *el-faayez*, 'the successful', 'the winner', is the subsidiary form of the 'white' way of *kar*.

[4] These verses appear in an ode by the Mauritanian poet Mḥammadh wuld al-Wālid al-Daymānī who lived in the eighteenth century.

الظّباء الخواذل // و كقوله / والله ما فعلنا من المحرّمات شيئًا / إلّا وبتنا
في الثّوب مقترنان / دنت منّي ودنيت منها / واستراحت نفسي بذاك
التّداني / وبعد هذا طريق يقال له فَاقُ وفيها فرعان التَّحْرَارْ والتَّحْزَامْ
فأمّا الأصل الّذي هو فَاقُ فجنسه من الشّعر الحسّانيّ نوعان أحدهما
لِمْسَكّْمَ والآخر البَتّْ لكِبْيِرْ فأمّا لِمْسَكّْمَ فكقوله / سِيدِ اعْلِ جَيْتْ اِمْسَافرْ /
مِن بِعْدْ اِجَيْتَك دَافْرَ // اِنْدَوَّرْ خَادِمْ كَافْرَ / مِنْكِبْهَ كِدّْ اِزْبَارَ // يَشْبَهْ عَنْدِ
لِمْغَافْرَ / كِبَاراً وَصِغَارَ // وأمّا البتّ لكبير فكقول الآخر / سِيمْ وُالْمَرْفَكْ
وَوْهَامْ / وُالْوَادْ اُتَمَيْظَورِيهْ // وُالعَاتِكْ وَاشْرَمْ وَاحْكَامُ / وُاَيَّاظْ اَكَّانْ
اِلعَالِكْ فِيهْ // مَحْصَرْهُمْ شِيخُ وَاكْلَامُ / مِنْ يُومِنْ عَادْ اِجَمَّعْ فِيهْ //
أَحْمَدُّ شِعْبِتْ جَرَّامُ / كَنَاي اِسْلُوكْ اِلخَيْلْ اِعْلِيهْ // فَيْتَاكْ اَعْزَامُ لَوَّامُ /
غَلَّاكْ اَلْفُمّْ اَلبَايِدْبِيهْ // عَادْ اَعْوِينُ مِنْ تِكْسَامُ / عَنْ لِعوِينْ اَلثَّانِ
غَانِيهْ // غَيّْرْ اِعْجَبْلِ فِيهْ اَيَّامُ / يُومْ اِتْخَاوِ حَسَّانْ اَعْلِيهْ // نَغْمَاشْ اُمِنْ
حَاشْ اَوْهَامُ / بَابْكَا كِرتُ وُابْزِ كْرِيهْ // أُعَايِدْ يَتْمَثّْلْ[a] كِدَّامُ / (حِلفُ)
كَاعْ اَلِّ مَا يَرْخِيهْ // اِنْكَرْ طَبْلُ تَوّْمْكَامُ / دَارْ اَلْكُورِيّْنْ اِنْوَاصِيهْ // فِي

[a] يتنمّل

[1] This poem appears to be an adaptation, or corruption, of a poem by ʿUmar b. Abū Rabīʿa. It is similar to a verse of his in the *Kitāb al-aghānī*, and quoted by Th. Noeldeke, p. 17, *Delectus Carminum Arabicorum*, Wiesbaden, 1961.

[2] *et-teḥraar*, the 'freeing', is the subsidiary form of the 'white' way of *faaġu*. Baroja notes that *faaġu* is divided into two parts, *faaġu* proper which is long, high-toned, and difficult to perform and sung at the moment of battle, while *et-teḥraar* is sweeter, shorter, and at time amorous in character, *Estudios Saharianos*, p. 415. *Et-teḥzaam*, the action of tightening a belt and the waist in order to prepare for battle, is included in *faaġu* in the 'white' way in the Trārza, but elsewhere it is sometimes reckoned to be in *siññiima*.

and:

1. By God, we did nothing forbidden, except that we passed the night in the garment in close association.
2. She drew close to me, and I to her, and my soul was refreshed by that closeness of one to the other.[1]

After this is a way called *faaġu* in which are two branches, *et-teḥraar* and *et-teḥzaam*.[2] As for *faaġu* in its basic form, there are two kinds of Ḥassānīya poetry used in it. One of them is *lemsaggam* and the other *el-batt lekbiir*. An example of the first is:

1. O Sayyid ʿAlī, I have come as a woman traveller from afar.
2. I have come to you needy, wanting a slave girl who is strong, and whose shoulder is the size of a sand dune.
3. O best among the *Maghāfira*, both great and small.[3]

As for the second:

1. Sīmu and al-Marfag and its surroundings and the valley and Tamayda Wirīh
2. and al-ʿĀtig and Ashram and its districts and Bayāḍ Agān which is near to it.
3. The chief of their great camp and its spokesman since the day they began to gather in it
4. is Aḥmad—the verdant plant of its watercourse, collector of squadrons of cavalry upon it.
5. He breaks the will of his reprover, and shuts the mouth of the one who is afraid of him.
6. He has increased his wealth through distributing gifts. He has no need of any more wealth.
7. But, for me, the most marvellous of his days there was the day when Ḥassān banded against him.
8. Nughmāsh and he who gathered around him from the Banū Bakkār and from the Banū Buzakrī
9. and the Banū ʿĀyid running (like ants) before him. His allies did not forsake him.
10. He beat his drum at the time of his sojourn, and he placed the negro between his forelocks

[3] If this poem is *lemsaggam*, it does not agree with the definition of the first manuscript, since the hemistichs are only of seven syllables and there is a pair of unvocalized letters before the final vocalized letter, in the manner of *lubb^{w}ayr*. The poem is a *gaaf* of three verses, each hemistich of uniform rhyme, and it is likely that it is due to this and not to the syllabic form that the poem is attached to this particular metre. Sayyid ʿAlī is possibly the Brākna Amīr Sīdī ʿAlī (son of Aḥmad I) who died in 1893.

اكْتَمْ دُجَنْبِرْ وُاغْمَامُ / وُلَجْلَاجْ الِّ يِدْرِمْ فيهْ // (يُوْمْ اَتْخَالِيفْ[a] اَلُوْنْدْ
اَعْلِيهْ / اُبْرُدْ وَاشْكَاهْ اُتِزْمَامُ) / مَزلِتْ اَنْفَيْدَدْ فَاقْدَامُ / نَرْفِدْ عَيْنِ مِعْرِفْتِ
F. 7 بِيهْ // لَوَّلْ يِغْشِينِ تِبْسَامُ / مَشْكْ اَلْخَصْلَ مَزَالْ اَعْلِيهْ // والشّعر العربيّ
لا قاعدة له فيه كما قلنا لكنّهم ربّما غنّوا فيه بما يناسب للحرب
لمناسبة ذلك للمقام كقول الشّاعر / ليس الشّجاع الّذي يحمي فوارسه /
عند اللّقاء ونار الحرب تشتعل // لكنّ من غضّ طَرْفاً أو ثنى قدماً / عن
المحارم / ذاك الفارس البطل // وقول الآخر / بأيّ يوميّ من الموت
أفرّ / أيوم لم يُقدر أم يوم قُدِرْ // وأردين والتّدنيت انّما يدخلان هذه
الطّريق بشيء يقال له عَرَّايْ اَسُّرُوزْ وبعضهم يقول له اَسُّرُوزِ وأمّا التَّحْرَارْ
فيدخلانه بشيء يقال له اَلْحِرّْ ولا قاعدة تلازمه من الشّعرين العربيّ
والحسّانيّ إلاّ أنّه أكثر ما يستعملون فيه اِبْتَيْتْ سِتَّ كقول القائل /
اَمَّاسِمْ ذِي اجَّدْلَ / فِي ادْلِيلِ مِنْخِزْنِينْ // كَيِفْتْ خِزِنْتْ نَزْلَ / مِنْ
تَاكُنَانِتْ بَيْنْ // اَكُمَّاطْ اُشَهْلَ / نَوْبِتْ لِمْحَالِيِينْ // وأكثر ما ينشدون

[a] The rhyme scheme requires that the second hemistich should come first.

---

[1] This poem is a *kerza* of fourteen verses. It is in praise of the Amīr of the Brākna, Aḥmad wuld Sīdī ʿAlī, who died in 1841. René Basset, *Mission au Sénégal*, pp. 524–5, discusses the battle of Youga.

(*a*) A *maḥṣar* is a camp of upwards of forty tents.

(*b*) 'He placed the negro between his forelocks' (verse 10) refers to the custom of sending a negro skilled in magical charms capable of bringing about the defeat of the enemy, in front of the chief.

(*c*) 'The wisp of the lock of hair' (verse 14) means that the signs of victory were manifest in his countenance. The lock of hair is a symbol of victory and noble virtues.

The poem is an example of Ḥassānīya panegyric at its best.

11. in the gloom of December and its hail clouds and the intense cold which enveloped it,
12. and his cold and fatigue and hunger when the gunpowder was in disagreement above him.
13. I went on hurrying after him. I raised my eye and recognized him,
14. and the first thing that came upon me was his smile and the wisp of the lock of hair that was still upon him.[1]

Folio 7

There is no fixed model for the Classical Arabic poetry used in *faaġu*, as we have said, but often they sing in it (poetry) which is suitable for war, as that is apt for the occasion, as for example the words of the poet:

1. The valiant one is not he who protects his knights at the encounter when the fire of war is ablaze.
2. Rather it is he who averts his glance or stays his foot from those acts which are forbidden. That knight is the hero.

or:

In which of my two days shall I flee from death. Is it a day decreed or a day undecreed?[2]

Both the *ardīn* and the *tidīnīt* enter this way through something called *ʿarraay essruuz*, which some call *ssruuzi*. As for *et-teḥraar* they, (the two musical instruments) enter it by something which is called *el-ḥirr*,[3] and there is no fixed model for it in either form of poetry, Classical Arabic or Ḥassānīya, save that the measure most frequently employed by them is *btayt sitta*, as, for example:

1. The brand marks of this virgin are concealed in my heart,
2. like the self-concealment of a camp of Tāgunānit between
3. Agummāṭ and Shahla at a time when robbers are at large.[4]

[2] This latter verse of poetry is attributed to ʿAlī b. Abū Ṭālib.

[3] *el-ḥirr* or *el-ḥurr*, 'the noble', is according to the īggāwen, simply another name for *et-teḥraar*, the subsidiary form of *faaġu labyaḍ*.

[4] Nowadays known as *lebtayt en-naageṣ*. The non-warlike nature of the subject matter is compatible with the observations of Baroja, cf. p. 197, *Estudios Saharianos*, p. 415. The poem is a *gaaf* of three verses. Its provenance is the Trārza, since the place-names are well known, cf. Leriche and Mukhtār wuld Ḥāmidun. 'Notes sur le Trārza' *Bull. I.F.A.N.* tome x, 1948, p. 516.

فيه من الشّعر العربيّ مثل قول الشّاعر / ملاحة خدّه لمّا رأتها / لدى
إسرائه حور الجنان // صنعن كما صنعن نساء زليخا / لرؤية يوسف
البهج الحسّان // وأمّا التَّحْزَامْ فطريقه في التّدنيت وأردين صَالَ وأكثر
ما يناسبه من لِغْنَ نوع يقال له الْمِصَّارِعْ كقوله / عَنْدَ تَنَاكْ / رَيْتْ اَلِّ
حَاكْ // اَمْرَ مَجْعُولْ / اَعْلِيهَ هَوْلْ // تَمْدَغْ مِسْوَاكْ / وُاتْسَّوْكْ هَاكْ //
تَظْحَكْ وُاتْكُولْ / رَظْعُ لعْجُولْ // ومن الشّعر مثل قوله تجنّب لقاء النّاس
والزم مكانكا / وقيّد بقيد من حديد لسانكا // ولا تنس ذكر الله في كلّ
ساعة / ولا تضيّع في الملاهي زمانكا // واعلم بأنّ الموت يأتي بغتة /
وأنّ ادّكار الموت يحيي جنانكا // وبعد هذا طريق يقال لها لِكْحَالْ
وإنّما خصّت بهذا الاسم وإن كان في كلّ ما ذكرنا لِكْحَالْ ولِبْيَاظَ لكثرة
استعمال هذا الاسم لها وطريقها الكبرى سِنّيِمَتْ هَيْبَ وهي سِنّيِمَ
الْكَحْلَ وفيها من التّدنيت شيء يقال له لِقْيَامْ وآخر يقال له اِنّيَانِ وفيها
من لِغْنَ نوع يقال له اِسْغَيّرْ كقوله / مَلْكَ مِنْتْ اُمَّانْ ذَالّ / بيِهْ اَلْحَزْمْ
اَلّا اكْطَلّ // دِرْتْ اِنْصَلّ مَا احْجَلّ / في اصْلَاةِ عَجْلَانْ // وُالْمُرُورْ اِبْذَا

[1] These verses appear in an ode in praise of the Prophet by Aḥmad wuld Muḥammad Sālim al-Midlishī (d. 1320/1902).

[2] *ṣaala*, 'bridge', is also known as *egaṣṣaar*, a dance, usually a warlike men's dance of slow rhythm. It is a *šawr* of *et-teḥzaam*.

[3] *el-meṣṣaariʿ*, connected with the root *ṣaraʿa* or *ṣarraʿa* 'to put two hemistichs to a verse', appears to be a poetic form combining *hwaywiiṣ* (four syllables) with *lebtayt et-taamm* (eight syllables) to form a *gaaf* of two verses.

Most of the Arabic poetry they sing in it is like the poem:

1. When, at the time of his nocturnal journey, the dark-eyed maidens of paradise saw the beauty of his cheek,
2. they used their arts just like the women of Zulaykhā for a sight of Joseph, the handsome, the beautiful.[1]

As for *et-teḥzaam*, its way in the *tidīnīt* and *ardīn* is *ṣaala*[2] and the most apt form of Ḥassānīya poetry for it is a kind called *el-meṣṣaari'*, for example:

1. At Atanāk, I have seen one who delights, a woman beloved, full of beauty.
2. She was chewing a tooth-pick, moving it thus, laughing and saying, 'the calves have suckled'.[3]

As an example of Classical Arabic poetry:

1. Avoid meeting people and keep to your place, and fetter your tongue with an iron fetter.
2. Forget not to mention God's name every hour and waste not your time on amusements.
3. Know that death comes unexpectedly, and that keeping death in mind gives life to your soul.[4]

After this is a way of playing called *lekḥaal*[5] and it has only been given this special name, though there be in all that we have mentioned a *lekḥaal* and *lebyaaḍ*, on account of the frequent use of this name for it. Its principal way is *siññiimat hayba*, otherwise *siññiima al-kaḥla*. Within it the *tidīnīt* plays something called *leqyaam*,[6] and another called *eññaani*, and the type of Ḥassānīya poetry used in it is called *sġayyer*, for example:

1. The meeting of Bint Ummān is the means whereby passion beguiled me.
2. I have desired to pray, but prayer would not quickly come to me.
3. Indeed confusion has come upon me, and my prayer is invalid.

[4] These verses are from an ancient Ṣūfī poem. Mukhtār wuld Ḥāmidun has seen it quoted in a document written by Aḥmad wuld Muḥammad of the tribe of the Īdaw al-Ḥājj (d. 1220/1805/6).

[5] The author does not mention *siññiima* as one of the *ḍhuur*. Instead he uses *lekḥaal*, and mainly concerns himself with the 'black' way of *siññiima*.

[6] *leqyaam* is perhaps the same as a *šawr* called *legya*. It is certainly a *šawr*. *Eññaani* is a *šawr* of *siññiimat hayba*.

احْصَلِّ / هُوَ وُالْبَطْلَانْ // وَانَ ذَالِّ مَا انْصَلِّ / ثَقْلَ يَا لسُّبْحَانْ // كُدِّ
اَنَّوْخَظْ مَا انْصَلِّ / مَلْكَ مِنْتْ اُمَّان // وقول الآخر / غَيْظِكْ نَاعِتْ فِيهْ
عِذْرِ / اُفِدْوَ غَيْظِكْ مَا انْشَفْرِ // اُكَدَّ اَلِّ يَا لرِّيمْ يِبْرِ / غَيْظِكْ مَاهُ خَاصّْ //
اِمْنْ اَلْمَرْظَ وَامْسِكْرِ / وَاَلْكَبّْ اَعْلَ الرَّاصْ // وامّا الشّعر العربيّ فكما
F. 8 قبله إلّا أنّهم أكثر ما يستعملون فيه الخفيف كقول القائل / ووفى قدر
بيضة من نضار / دين سلمان حين حان الوفاء // وتغدّى بالصّاع ألف
جياع // وتروّى بالصّاع ألف ظماء // وبعد هذا طريق يقال لها اِزَّرَاكْ
صغيرة واسمها مشتقّ لأنّها ملفّقة من لِكْحَالْ ولِبْيَاظْ ولا قاعدة لها في
الشّعرين وشَوْرُها في التّدنيت وأردين يقال له اِرَّبَابِ إلّا أنّي سمعتهم
أكثر ما ينشدون فيها / الموت باب وكلّ النّاس داخله / يا ليت شعري
بعد الموت ما الدّار // وقوله / في ليل صول تناهى العرض والطّول /
كأنّما ليله باللّيل موصول // لا فارق الصّبح كفّي إن ظفرت به / وإن
بدت غرّة منه وتحجيل // ما أقدر الله أن يدني على شحط / من داره
الحزن ممّن داره صول // وبعد طريق صغيرة أيضاً ويختصّ به أهل هذا

[1] *sġayyer*, 'the very small', is a metre in which the hemistichs alternate between seven and five syllables, and the last two vocalized consonants must be preceded by two unvocalized consonants. The author's example is a *ṭalʿa* of five verses. The hemistichs which have *lām* as their *rawī* are seven syllables, those with *nūn*, five. The final hemistich repeats the opening of the first hemistich of the *ṭalʿa*, so the poem 'bites its tail'.

[2] The poem is a *ṭalʿa* of three verses and as it has no *gaaf* it is incomplete. The hemistichs which have *rāʿ* as *rawī* are seven syllables, those with *ṣād*, five.

[3] *zzraag* (*ez-zraag*), 'spotted', or 'motley', is a name given to a type of playing which combines 'black' and 'white' in *siññiima*. It seems to be known only in Western Mauritania.

4. I am he who prays not, it is a heavy burden, O God.
5. As long as I continue meeting Bint Ummān; I can not pray.[1]

and again:

1. As for your anger I have shown my excuse for it. To cure your anger I will not waver.
2. The ability which, o gazelle, will cure your anger is not lacking,
3. whether it be by appeasement (with money) or by my excuse and by leaning over backwards.[2]

As for Classical Arabic poetry, it is the same as before (i.e. there is nothing laid down) save that they mostly use *al-khafīf* for it.

Folio 8

as, for example:

1. He paid the worth of an egg of pure gold, the debt of Salmān when the time of payment fell due,
2. and a thousand of the hungry lunched by the Ṣāʿ and the thirst of a thousand was quenched by the Ṣāʿ.

After this is a way called *zzraag*.[3] It is small, and it is a derived name because it is made up by the combination of *lekḥaal* and *lebyaaḍ* together, and there is nothing laid down for it either in Classical Arabic or Ḥassānīya poetry, and its *šawr* in the *tidīnīt* and *ardīn* is called *rrbaabi*.[4] However, the bulk of what I have heard them sing is: 'Death is a door wherein each person enters, would that I knew what abode will be mine after death', and also:

1. In the night of Ṣūl, breadth and length came to an end. It was as though its night was only joined to the very night itself.
2. If the morning ever be in my power, may it not depart from my hand, and if its first signs of whiteness appear as a blaze on the forehead and as a whiteness on the legs of a horse.
3. What a predestinator is God in that He should bring close to each other, at a distance, him whose abode is Ḥazn, and him whose abode is Ṣūl.[5]

[4] *rrbaabi* (*er-rbaabi*) in the 'white' way, seems to be the same as *zzraag* the 'black' and 'white' ways of *siññiima*.

[5] The author quotes three verses (nos. 1, 2, 7) of an eight verse poem by the poet Ḥunduj b. Ḥunduj al-Murrī. It is included in the Ḥamāsa of Abū Tammām, *Sharḥ dīwān al-ḥamāsa* by Abū ʿAlī al-Marzūqī, edited by Aḥmad Amīn and ʿAbd al-Salām Muḥammad Hārūn, Cairo, 1953, vol. iv, pp. 1829–31.

الفنّ من أهل السّاحل دون غيرهم من سائر أهله يسمّونها اَلْبَسِيطْ لا
يُحكى فيها الشّعر الحسّانيّ وفيها من العربيّ ما كقوله / ذاك المنار وقد
لاحت به دمن / مثل اليواقيت من آل السّعيدين // قوم سعيدون لا
يشقى جليسهم / مقالة رُويت عن ناصر الدّين // هم المشائخ هم هم
الولاة هم / هم المطاعم من زَيْن إلى زين // وبعد هذا لِبْيَاظ وإنّما
خُصّ بهذا الاسم كما قلنا فى لِكْحَالْ وفيه من الفروع لِحْجِبْ
والشَّوَّاشَاتْ إلى غير هذا ويدخلونه أهل التّدنيت وأردين بشيء يقال
له اِتّْبَيْبِ وفيه من لِغْنَ نوع يقال له لُبَيِّرْ هو صاحبه مثل قوله /
تِشْوَاشْ اِلْكِبْلَ هَوْنْ بَدّْ / اَعْلَ الْجَ امْعَاىَ مِنْ بْلَدْ // وَسْوَ يِشَّوَّشْ كِلّْ
حَدّْ / وَانَ بِي تَيَّارِتْ // مَانِ مِشَّوَّشْ غَيْرْ بَعْدْ / عِدتّْ اِعْلَ تَاشِنْيَّارِتْ //
وقوله / ظَلَّتْ لَرْيَاحْ اَلَّا اتْرَادْ / نَخْلْ اِزْضِنْڱَانْ اِلَيْنْ عَادْ // حَزْمِ ذَاتَّوْ
اَلِّ ابْعَادْ / اِزِيدُ هَزّْ اَجْرِيدُ // وُامْنَيْنْ اِنْظَلَّ الْيُومْ زَادْ / سَامع حِسّْ
اَتْوَدْوِيدُ // حَزْمِ ذَاتَّوْ اَلِّ اشْتَدّْ / اِزِيدُ هَزّْ اَجْرِيدُ // وِلَ مَزَادُ زَادْ بَعْدْ /

[1] The Sāḥel to a writer of the Trārza means the north-west, namely the coastal region extending into part of what is now the Spanish Sahara.

[2] Leriche, p. 741, notes that the intermediate 'spotted' form of the 'white' way of *siññiima* has a combination of this name.

[3] Verses from an ode by the Mauritanian poet Muḥammad wuld al-ʿĀqil al-Daymānī (d. 1280/1863/4).

[4] *lebyaaḍ* is a name used in the Trārza, corresponding to *meqaččuuga* in the Ḥawḍ. It is a subsidiary form of *siññiima* in the 'black' way, and is sometimes called *lebyaaḍ etbaybi*. Baroja, p. 416, refers to it specifically by name, and notes that in it are sung songs extolling the beauties of certain lands, the beauty and grace of certain women and states of the soul. He mentions *lubb*^{w}*ayr* in connexion with it.

Then comes another minor way which is peculiar to the musicians of the Sāḥel,[1] and which they call *al-basīṭ*.[2] No Ḥassānīya poetry is recited in it, but an example of Classical Arabic is:

1. That beacon, by which traces of deserted encampments have been lighted, is like the rubies from the family of Saʿīdayn,
2. a happy people whose companion is not wearied. A saying quoted by Nāṣir al-Dīn.
3. They are the elders, they are the saints, they are the hospitable ones from one gallant to another.[3]

After this is *lebyaaḍ*,[4] to which similar remarks as in the case of *lekḥaal* are applicable. Amongst its branches are *leḥjeb*,[5] *eš-šawwaašaat*,[6] and there are others. The players of the *tidīnīt* and the *ardīn* enter it through something called *ttbaybi*[7] and of the poetic metres used in it is a type known as *lubb*^{w}*ayr*. It is the predominant one in it, and an example is:

1. Longing for the south prevails here upon him who has come with me from a land,
2. and likewise everyone feels the same longing as I do for Tayyārit.
3. I am not one who yearns, but anyway I am one in the extremity of yearning.[8]

and:

1. Winds indeed continued buffeting the palms of Izḍingān,
2. until my longing arose at that time which was far distant. The shaking of the palm branches makes it greater,
3. and even today when I still hear the sound of their rustling,
4. my present passion is more vehement still and increases through the rustling of the branches.
5. Were it not to increase it, then the confused murmur of passion would increase it.[9]

[5] *leḥjeb*, 'the curtains', is a *šawr* of *čaynna* in the 'white' way of *siññiima*. It imitates the swaying of the saddles of the women of the Awlād Mubārak. According to Baroja, p. 415, this style of singing is the most popular in the Spanish Sahara.

[6] *eš-šawwaašaat*, expresses the emotional turmoil of a soul tormented by love. It is possibly a *šawr* in the 'white' way of *siññiima*, but little is known of it.

[7] *ttbaybi* (*etbaybi*) expresses verve, and pride, and high opinion, cf. p. 74.

[8] The poem is a *ṭalʿa* of three verses without a *gaaf*. The verses are attributed to a poet called Ibrāhīm wuld Mawlūd.

[9] The poem is a *ṭalʿa* of three verses followed by a *gaaf* of two verses.

لِكْرِيدْ اِلْحَزْمْ اِزِيدُ // وينشدون فيه من الشّعر على غير قياس ما قوله /
حرّم العالمون والحكماء / مع عيشان أن تزار نساء // هي فرض والنّساء
كنفل / يترك النّفل من عليه القضاء // وقوله / إنّ أمّ البنين وإنّ
نُعمى / لفتاتان حليتا الظّاعنينا // إنّ أمّ البنين تنسيك سلمى / ونعمى
تنسيك أمّ البنينا // وبعد هذا طريق يقال لها بَيْگِ وهي آخر الطّرق من F. 9
هذا الفنّ وفيها من جهة التّدنيت وأردين أَعَظَّالْ ولعْتيگْ ونوعه من
لِغْنَ لِبْتَيْتْ وهو أجناس متطاولات وأطوله اِبْتَيْتْ اَثْمَانْيَ كقوله / يَعَگْلٍ
رَاعِ تِيگِـگْلْتْ / اَخَيْرْ اِتُّوبْ اِگْبَلٍ مَا مِتّْ // وَامِلِّ ذَاكُ اَذْ كِدْيِتْ /
تُرَارِينْ أُذَاكْ اَلصَّابُونْ // حَاجِلَّكْ يَا لْعَگْلٍ اِتْفَگَّدْتْ / لَعَدْتْ اَلِّ مَانَكْ
مَجْنُونْ // تَعْرَفْ خِطْتْ اِمِّنْ هَوْنْ اُخِطْتْ / اِمِّنْ هَوْنْ اُخِطْتْ اِمِّنْ هَوْنْ //
ويليه اِبْتَيْتْ سِتّْ كقوله / هذَا الدَّهْرْ اَتْفُ بِيهْ / مَارِتْ عَنُّ غَدَّارْ // أُمَارتْ
عَنُّ مَا فِيهْ / حَلَاوَ مَا تِمْرَارْ // خِطْتْ اِعْلَ دَارْ اِلْيُومْ / اَهْلَ ايَّ يَا
لْقَيُّومْ // اُشِفْتْ اِگُومْ اَلتَّيْدُومْ / لِمْسَهْو كَانْ اَلدَّارْ // مَحْرُوگْ أُعَادْ
اِصْمُومْ / سُبْحَانَكْ يَا لْقَهَّارْ // مَعْودَ حَرَّاكْ اِگُومْ / مَاهُ فَاهِم لَخْبَارْ //

[1] A fairly recent Mauritanian poem by an unknown poet.

[2] The author is quoting a poem by the Mauritanian poet Mḥammad̲h̲ wuld Ṭalba al-Yaʿqūbī (d. 1240/1824/5). According to Muk̲h̲tār wuld Ḥāmidun the original text should read:

إنّ نعمى وإنّ أمّ البنينا x لفتاتان حلية الظاعنينا
إنّ أمّ البنينى تنسيك نعمى x إنّ نعمى تنسيك أمّ البنينا

[3] The poem is a *ṭalʿa* of four verses without a *gaaf*.

[4] The poem is a *ṭalʿa* of four verses, preceded by a *gaaf* of two verses.

They recite Classical Arabic poetry in it, after no special model; as for example:

1. The learned and the wise have forbidden that women, along with ʿAys͟hāna, should be visited.
2. She is a duty, and the women are like a work of supererogation. He who has a duty dispenses with the latter.[1]

Likewise:

1. Umm al-Banīna and Nuʿmā are two maidens who are the adornments of those who depart on camels.
2. Umm al-Banīna makes you forget Salmā, and Nuʿmā makes you forget Umm al-Banīna.[2]

Folio 9

After this is a way called *baygi*. It is the final way in this art. The *tidīnīt* and the *ardīn* play in it *aʿaḍḍaal* and *liʿtiig*. In Ḥassānīya poetry its special metre is *lebtayt*. The latter contains kinds which differ in length, and the longest of them is *btayt aṯmaaniya*, as, for example:

1. O mind of mine, see Tīgigilt. It is better for you to repent before you die.
2. Amillī is that mountain there, and this mountain is Turārīn, and that is al-Ṣābūn.
3. O mind, do you recall, if you are not mad,
4. you know you passed through here, you passed through here, you passed through here.[3]

Then comes *btayt setta*, and an example is:

1. This time, fie on it! A sign is that it is treacherous
2. and a sign is that there is no sweetness in it without bitterness.
3. Today I passed by a (deserted) habitation, of the family of Ayya, oh Eternal one!
4. I saw a branch of a baobab to the north of the habitation.
5. It was burnt and had become charcoal. Glory to Thee, O Almighty one.
6. How typical is the burner of the branch, he has no understanding of events.[4]

ويليه اِبْتَيْتْ خَمْسَ وهو المعروف عندهم بِحَذْوْ اِجْرَادْ كقوله / مُلَانَ لَعْلَ / مَا قَدَّرْ مَسْلَ // فِيكْ اِنْتِ تَغْلَ / غَيْرْ اِنْتِ خِلْطَ // ذَ مِنّكْ لَعْلَ / مَمْسُوسْ ابْشَكْطَ // وُامْعَ ذَاكْ اِبْلَ / صِكَّانْ اِمَلْطَ // وُامْعَ ذَاكْ اِعْطَاكْ / زَادْ اِنّكْ خِلْطَ // مَفَكَّرْ لِذَاكْ / يَخْتِ مِن مَّعْطَ // مُلَانَ . . . // ونوع يقال له اِحْوَيْوِيصْ وهو اِبْتَيْتْ اِرْبَعْ كقوله / اِمْنَيْنْ اِكِلّْ / اَتَايْ اِلنَّاسْ // اِعُودُ كِلّْ / اِثْنَيْنْ اِفْكَاسْ // وأكثر ما يستعملون فيه من الشّعر للطّويل من غير تعوّد كقوله / تسربلت سربال القناعة والتّقى / صبيًّا وكانا في الكهولة ديدني // أعظم من قطع اليدين على الفتى / صنيعة برّ نالها من يدي دنيّ // وقوله / عميرة ودّع إن تجهّزت غاديا / كفى الشّيب والإسلام للمرء ناهيا // توسّدني كفًّا وتثني بمعصم / عليّ وتخد رجلُها من وراءيا // وهبّت شمال آخر الليل قرّة / ولا ثوب إلّا درعها ورداءيا // فما زال ثوبي طيّباً من نسيمها / إلى الحول حتّى أنهج الثّوب باليا // وقوله / ولمّا رأيت السّيف جندل جعفراً / ونادى منادٍ للخليفة في يحيى // بكيت على الدّنيا وزاد تأوّهي / عليهم وقلت الآن لا تنفع الدّنيا // خاتمة

[1] The poem is a *ṭalʿa* of four verses, followed by a *gaaf* of two verses. The poem is intended to 'bite its tail', so that the *ṭalʿa* preceding the *gaaf* may be repeated.

[2] *ḥwaywiiṣ* is now five syllables although many experts on *leġna* would still accept the author's definition and claim that *ḥaṯu jjraad* is the proper name for a poem of five syllables.

[3] The poem is a single *gaaf* of two verses.

[4] Part of a poem by an unknown Mauritanian poet.

Then comes *btayt k̲amsa* known among them (the *īggāwen*) as *had̲(t̲)w jjraad*, with an example:

1. God most high has not decreed a cherished quality in you.
2. But you are a marvel.
3. This upper part of you is touched by a blemish,
4. but still, you are without legs lean in the hips.
5. Yet God has also given you (the gift) to be a marvel.
6. How amazing that is to me, o my sister, as a gift from God.[1]

Then a kind (of metre) called *ḥwaywiiṣ*,[2] called also *btayt arbaʿ*, as, for example:

1. When the tea of people is scarce,
2. each two will share in a glass.[3]

Most of the Classical Arabic poetry they use in it is *al-ṭawīl*, without making a habit of it, as, for example:

1. As a youth, I donned the garment of contentment and of piety, and in my prime they were my habit.
2. More fearful than the cutting of the hands to a youth, is a bountiful act done to him by the hands of a base man (?).[4]

And also:

1. ʿUmayra, say farewell. If you are ready for an early departure old age and Islam suffice for a man.
2. You (She ?) would cushion me with the palm of a hand and hold me (?) with a wrist, and let her (a mount's ?) foot go at a quick pace behind (me ?)
3. And a cold north wind blew at the end of the night, and there was no garment save her shift and my loose cloak,
4. and my garment continued to be fragrant from her zephyr for a whole year, until it was completely worn out.[5]

And also:

1. And when I saw that the sword had felled Jaʿfar and a herald proclaimed Yaḥyā to be Caliph,
2. I wept for the world and my moaning for them grew yet greater, and I said, 'Now the world profiteth nothing.'[6]

[5] The verses given here are a misquotation of a poem of ʿAbd Banū ʾl Ḥasḥās. The full text is in *Ṭabaqāt fuḥūl al-s̲h̲uʿarāʾ* by Ibn Sallām edited by Maḥmūd S̲h̲ākir, Dār al-maʿārif, Cairo, 1952, pp. 156–7.

[6] According to the *Kitāb al-mustaṭraf of al-Ibs̲h̲īhī*, Cairo, 1933, vol. i, p. 202, where these verse are quoted, they were recited by an old poet mourning the Barmacides, and they were reported by a servant of the Caliph al-Maʾmūn.

فد تركت طَرْقاً من هذا النّوع غير شهيرات في التّدنيت وأردين وليس ذلك عن جهل ولكن لإختلاف النّاس فيهم وتقلّبهم بتقلّب الأزمان وما في هذه الطّرق من لِغْنَ حكاية بعضه فى محلّ بعض لحن عندهم بعكس الشّعر فما شئت أن تحكي منه فى كلّ طريق فبالخيار فيه وقد قال بعض المغنّين شيًّا وأظنّه عبد الله العتيق بن أعمر بن بُدّ لكنّه ربّما اختلّ وهو / اَلطَّوِيلْ اَمْكَّابِلْ لِبْتَيْتْ / وُامْرَيْمِيدَ صَطْحْ اَلْوَافِرْ // وُالْخْفَيِفْ F.10
اِعْلِيهْ بِتَيْتْ / اَمْكَّابِلْ لُبَّّرْ اَلْكَافِرْ // وهذا ربّما وقع وربّما اختلّ وأكثر إختلاله من وقوعه وإن قال أحد إنّ هذا ممّا لا يُمدح الإشتغال به فقد اشتغل به أبو الفرج الإصبهانيّ وهو من مشاهير علماء عصره عن إمر من أمراء المسلمين ممّن يقتدى به وألّف فيه محمّد محمود بن عبد الفتّاح للشّيخ سيد محمّد وفي هذا أسوة حسنة وطُوبَى لمن شغله عيب نفسه عن عيوب النّاس ولله درّ القائل / فلا تذكرن يا صاح سؤات صاحب / فعندك سؤات وللنّاس أعين // وعينك إن أبدت إليك مساوياً / فقُلْ يا عين للنّاس ألسن // وعاشر بمعروف وسامح من اعتدى / ودافع ولكن بالّتي هي أحسن // وأطلب ممّن رأى هذا وطالعه أن يصلح ما فاتني من إصلاحه ويجعل محلّ ذمّه في امتداحه فإنّي لا آمن نفسي من الزّلل والله يعصمنا في القول والعمل وكان الفراغ من تأليفه عشيّة

Conclusion. I have refrained from taking a quick look at the lesser-known kinds of musical forms played by the *tidīnīt* and the *ardīn.* This is not due to ignorance, but because the people do not agree among themselves, and because of their change of taste with the change in the times. The recitation of some of it in the place of others is considered a fault, contrary to that which is feasible in Classical Arabic poetry where you can recite whatever you please according to your choice. One of the singers has said something (about it), and I think he is ʿAbdallāh al-ʿAtīq b. Aʿmar b. Budd but perhaps it is not correct, namely:

Folio 10

1. *Al-ṭawīl* exactly corresponds to *lebtayt* and *mraymiida* to *al-wāfir*
2. On *al-khafīf* is measured the corresponding metre, *lubb*ʷ*ayr el-kaafer.*[1]

Sometimes this has taken place, and sometimes it has been disturbed, the latter being more common than the former.

If it should be said that this is an unpraiseworthy object of study, then (my reply would be) that Abū 'l-Faraj al-Iṣfahānī made it his occupation, and he was among the most distinguished scholars of his age, by command of the Muslim princes. His example has been followed by others, among whom is Muḥammad Maḥmūd b. ʿAbd al-Fattāḥ, who wrote on this subject for Shaykh Sīdī Muḥammad. There is a good precedent in this, and blessed be he whose own imperfection has preoccupied him from the faults of men. He spoke well who said:

1. O companion, do not mention the disgraceful actions of a friend. You yourself commit them, and men have eyes to see.
2. If your eye reveals them to you, likewise, then say—'O eye, men have tongues'.
3. In your relations with others behave with equity and forgive him who acts unjustly. Withstand, but through the aid of that which is better.

I ask him who sees and reads this, to correct slips of mine which have escaped my notice and to offer praise instead of reproof, because I cannot feel sure of myself that I have not erred. May God preserve us in word and deed. The writing of it was finished

[1] The poem is a *gaaf* of two verses in *lebtayt et-taamm* metre.

الجمعة لثلاث بقين من صفر عام سبعة وخمسين وثلاثمئة وألف لمؤلّفه
محمّد بن محمّد اليدال / هَذَا التَّاليف اِفْيَمّْ اَمْكَادْ / لَمْنَادِمْ مِنْ لَشْرَافْ
اِجْدِيدْ // وُالْمَاهُ كَابِلْ عَنُّ زَادْ / مُفِيدْ اَثْرُ مَاهُ مُفِيدْ // انتهى تأليف محمّد
محمود بن عبد الفتّاح وتأليف محمّد بن محمّد اليدال على يد كاتبهما
لنفسه ثمّ لمن شاء الله بعده إبراهيم بن مولود بن دادّاه يوم الخميس
الثّامن من جمادى الأخيرة سنّة ستّ وسبعين وثلاثمئة وألف هجرية في
قرية بتلميت .

in the evening of the Friday, three days before the end of Ṣafar, in the year A.H. 1357 (28 April 1938), by its author Muḥammad b. Muḥammad al-Yadālī.

1. This work is about that which guides afresh a man among those who are honourable,
2. and he who does not concede that it is also useful, the effect it will have will be valueless to him.[1]

The copying of the works of Muḥammad Maḥmūd b. ʿAbd al-Fattāḥ and Muḥammad b. Muḥammad al-Yadālī is by Ibrāhīm b. Mawlūd b. Dāddāh for himself, and for whom God wills after his death. It was completed on Thursday, the 8th of Jumādā II, A.H. 1376 (10 January 1957), in Būtīlimīt.

[1] The poem is a *gaaf* of two verses in *lebtayt et-taamm* metre.

APPENDIX

THE author of the *Kitāb al-Wasīṭ* gives three examples of regional pronunciation in Ḥassānīya. He mentions that the inhabitants of the Adrār, Tagānit, and the Ḥawḍ pronounce the *qāf* as *ghayn*, while those of Afṭūṭ and the south pronounce these letters quite the contrary. In the area of the Trārza many of the people pronounce *tā'* as *ṭā'*, in such a word as *traab*—'earth'—for example. The Nmādi hunters of the Ḥawḍ omit the final *mīm* from the plural pronominal suffix *kum*, and in greeting say *as-salaam 'alayku*, instead of *al-salām 'alaykum*. These are among the features which most struck the author. The first of them is one which Ḥassānīya shares with other Beduin dialects—a logical development from its characteristic *qāf ma'qūda* or the correspondence of *g* (ڨ / ڭ, as represented in manuscripts) with the classical *qāf*—namely a free interchange *gh* > *q*, which Dr. Cohen, in his recent study of Ḥassānīya, has indicated is only conditioned in cases where the former letter happens to be doubled.

The second feature, namely the pronunciation of an emphatic *ṭā'*, peculiar to the Trārza, is clearly brought about under the influence of a following *r*. The third feature, that of elision of articulate sound, in that they have labialized variants, frequently occurs in the case of *m* and *b* at the end of a word. These last two phonemes have other features which are prominent in Ḥassānīya. One of these is the introduction of a labiovelar ^{w} between a labial and a vowel. This occurs, for example, in the name of a poetry metre, *lubb^{w}ayr*, 'the little well'. The mutation of *b* > *m* before an *n*, by nasalization, is common: *bint*, for example, is invariably pronounced *mint*. Assimilation takes place in *ld* > *ll*, where the former is a final grouping, for example *wuld*, 'son', is pronounced *wull*. The phoneme *f* is always pronounced as *v*, unless followed by an unvoiced letter, or doubled, or in final position in a word. The phoneme *č* is particularly common in words of Berber origin, amongst which are to be found the names of former Znāga-speaking tribes.

In Ḥassānīya a short vowel can occur in an open syllable, but Dr. Cohen has shown that the incidence of this is limited to specific phonetic contexts, and in general in Ḥassānīya, as in the other Maghribī dialects, a short vowel does not occur in an open (non-final) syllable.[1] Thus, for example, *ket-bu* contrasts with *k-teb*, and *rak-bu* with *r-kab*. In accordance with this and other factors determining syllable structure

[1] For a full description cf. Cohen, *Le Dialecte arabe ḥassānīya de Mauritanie*, pp. 81–84 and 89–91.

a word, or even a phrase, may alter in syllable structure, depending upon the total phonetic context. Thus *kbiir* with the definite article *el-* is *lekbiir* (viz. vC+CCv̄C > CvCCv̄C), and *fi+el+ḥwaaš*, *ef-leḥwaaš*. This is a striking feature of which the Moors themselves are fully aware, and which has prompted certain scholars among them to maintain that one of the chief differences between Arabic and Ḥassānīya is the extent to which 'vocalized letters' in the former are 'unvocalized' in the latter. The syllable structure is regular and predictable.

Ḥassānīya prosody takes advantage of a situation of this kind in order to vary metre patterns which are otherwise circumscribed by a series of variations of the more common forms of closed syllable. On the basis of the earliest authentic poetry which survives, syllabic forms show no appreciable change within the last two centuries or more.

In the conjugation of the verb Ḥassānīya with its eight-person system occupies an intermediate position between the ten-person system characteristic of certain dialects in the Near East, and the seven-person system found in other Maghribī dialects. There are two basic tenses, a perfect indicating that an action is completed, and an imperfect indicating that the action is still in progress. Beside the regular verb there are irregular verbs, which correspond to the doubled, assimilated, hollow, and defective verbs of Classical Arabic. Each of these has its peculiarities of conjugation in Ḥassānīya. In order to vary these tenses and in order to give them temporal significance, certain particles and auxiliaries are employed. *Laahi* preceding the imperfect tense indicates the near future, while *kaan*, in addition to being a verb in its own right, signifying existence, is employed with the imperfect to indicate a continuous action which took place in the past, and with the perfect to form a pluperfect. *'Aad* is another particle, also employed independently, indicating probability, change of state, or the continuity of an action. A number of extended themes may be derived from the simple verb, thus from *mša*, 'to go', *mašša*, 'to make to go'. The genius of the dialect has invented a theme of its own, which is connected with colours, points of the compass, and tribal or ethnic affiliation, as, for example, *sagbal*, 'to go south', from *gebla* 'south'. The simple verb has no passive forms except a participle, but a remarkable feature of the dialect is that derived verbal forms do have passive forms.

The verb has corresponding personal pronouns. Ḥassānīya here has links with both Maghribī and Near Eastern dialects. It approximates to the latter in having a feminine form in the second and third persons plural, and it has done so by the unusual suffixing of *aati* to the corresponding masculine forms.

Ḥassānīya is rich in the variety of its noun patterns. This has partly come about from the coexistence of Znāga, Azayr, and other Sudānic languages over long periods in the same terrain. Certain nouns have entered the dialect from remoter sources, from Turkish, German, Spanish, Latin, and English, and numerous French terms and expressions have been borrowed.

Unlike most Maghribī dialects, Ḥassānīya makes far greater use of the dual. Certain nouns which go in pairs, such as 'eyes' and 'feet', have lost their plural forms, and the dual is employed to express the plural in general. The plural proper, as in all forms of Arabic, is either of the 'sound plural' or the 'broken plural' type. The latter is of many kinds. In all, Dr. Cohen has tabulated twenty-four forms, and Ḥassānīya is certainly one of the dialects where forms of the 'broken plural' are the most diverse. A certain number of these in Ḥassānīya seem to combine both an internal change and the addition of a suffix. Berber words, which otherwise have their own Berber plural, are either of this double form or are turned into 'broken plurals' according to one or other of the Ḥassānīya patterns. In matters of gender Ḥassānīya is similar to Classical Arabic. Nouns which are feminine in pattern have a suffixed *a*, and this becomes *at* in the construct state, namely where it is in genitival association with a following noun or pronominal suffix.

Ḥassānīya makes great use of diminutives, and there is even a diminutive form of the verb, indicated by the occurrence of the diphthong *ay* between the first two radicals. This is a characteristic feature of the Beduin dialects. The series of prepositions, conjunctions, and adverbs in these dialects are likewise in common usage in Ḥassānīya, though some have a slightly different sense. Many words, however, are peculiar to the dialect. Professor Colin has indicated a few terms, common to the Beduin dialects of North Africa—*ḍark*, 'now', *yaames*, 'yesterday', *šawr*, 'towards', for example. Other words which have special meanings in Ḥassānīya are *wraa*, 'after', which is used specifically of time, *gaaʿ*, 'indeed', 'for sure', 'so', and *ḥatta*, 'very much'.

BIBLIOGRAPHY

JULIO CARO BAROJA: *Estudios Saharianos*, Instituto de Estudios Africanos, Madrid, 1955.

DAVID COHEN: *Le Dialecte arabe ḥassānīya de Mauritanie*, Études Arabes et Islamiques, Paris, 1963.

PAUL DUBIÉ: 'La Vie matérielle des Maures', Mélanges Ethnologiques. *Mem. I.F.A.N., no. 33*, Dakar, 1953.

—— 'L'ilôt berberophone de Mauritanie', *Bull. I.F.A.N.*, tome ii, 1940, pp. 316–24.

D. JACQUES-MEUNIÉ: *Cités anciennes de Mauritanie*, Librairie C. Klincksieck, Paris, 1961.

LA CHAPELLE (F. DE): 'Esquisse d'une histoire du Sahara Occidental', *Hespéris*, tome xi, 1930.

MOKHTAR OULD HAMIDOUN: *Précis sur la Mauritanie*. Études mauritaniennes, no. 4, Centre I.F.A.N., Saint Louis, Senegal, 1952.

THÉODORE MONOD: *Méharées*. Éditions 'Je sers', Paris, 1941.

R. MONTAGNE: *La Civilisation du désert*, Hachette, Paris, 1947, pp. 227–67.

CHARLES MONTEIL: *La Langue azer*, Contributions à l'étude du Sahara Occidental, Paris, 1939.

VINCENT MONTEIL: *Notes sur les Tekna* (Institut des Hautes Études Marocaines, no. iii), Paris, 1948.

—— 'Notes sur le toponymie, l'astronomie et l'orientation chez les Maures', *Hespéris*, 1949, pp. 189–219.

UNESCO. *Nomades et nomadisme au Sahara*, Recherches sur la zone aride, tome xix, 1963, pp. 51–58, 67–77.

INDEX